Lean Healthcare

Lean Healthcare

A Practical Guide for Executing Lean Improvements with Real-World Case Studies

Second Edition

Dennis R. Delisle

ASQ Quality Press
Milwaukee, Wisconsin

American Society for Quality, Quality Press, Milwaukee 53203
© 2020 by Dennis R. Delisle
All rights reserved
Printed in the United States of America

25 24 23 LS 5 4 3 2

Publisher's Cataloging-in-Publication data
Names: Delisle, Dennis R., 1984-, author.
Title: Lean healthcare, second edition: a practical guide for executing lean improvements with real-world case studies / Dennis R. Delisle.
Description: Includes bibliographical references and index. | Milwaukee, WI: Quality Press, 2020.
Identifiers: LCCN: 2020948264 | ISBN: 978-1-951058-44-9 (pbk.) | 978-1-951058-45-6 (epub) | 978-1-951058-46-3 (pdf)
Subjects: LCSH Health services administration. | Health services administration—Case studies. | Health care management. | Industrial management. | Industrial efficiency. | Business logistics. | Organization. | BISAC BUSINESS & ECONOMICS / Industries / Healthcare
Classification: LCC R728 .D45 2020 | DDC 362.1068—dc23

No part of this book may be reproduced in any form or by any means, electronic, mechanical, photocopying, recording, or otherwise, without the prior written permission of the publisher.

ASQ advances individual, organizational, and community excellence worldwide through learning, quality improvement, and knowledge exchange.

Bookstores, wholesalers, schools, libraries, businesses, and organizations: Quality Press books are available at quantity discounts for bulk purchases for business, trade, or educational uses. For more information, please contact Quality Press at 800-248-1946 or books@asq.org.

To place orders or browse the selection of all Quality Press titles, visit our website at: http://www.asq.org/quality-press

Quality Press
600 N. Plankinton Ave.
Milwaukee, WI 53203-2914
Email: books@asq.org

ASQ Excellence Through Quality™

To my girls: Rachel, Ophelia, and Josephine.

Table of Contents

List of Figures and Tables .... *xi*
List of Case Studies. .... *xvii*
Foreword .... *xix*
Introduction. .... *xxiii*

Chapter 1   Lean Thinking. **1**
　Performance Improvement Methodologies 1
　Lean Thinking. 3
　Roadmap for Creating a Lean Process. 7

Chapter 2   Principle #1: Define Value. **11**
　Determine Scope. 11
　Define Value through Customer's Eyes 14
　　Case Study: Presurgery Patient Flow 18
　Identifying Waste 19
　　Case Study: Clinical Lab Workflow 27

Chapter 3   Principle #2: Value Stream Mapping **33**
　Map the Current State 34
　Value Stream Maps. 39
　Collect and Analyze Data for VSM 51
　　Case Study: Patient Flow in the Patient Testing Center 55
　Putting the Pieces Together. 58
　　Case Study: OR/SPCC VSM Event 59

Chapter 4   Establishing the Lean Fundamentals **63**
　5S 64
　Layout. 69
　Visual Management 72
　　Case Study: Patient Flow in the Patient Testing Center 75

Chapter 5   Principle #3: Flow. **85**
　Determining Customer Demand 88
　Balancing the Process. 89
　　Case Study: Evaluating Gastroenterology Physician Office Visit 90
　　Case Study: Rapid Changeover in the Operating Room 96
　Importance of Standard Work. 98

vii

viii Table of Contents

Chapter 6   Principle #4: Pull **103**
   Create a Pull System 104
      Case Study: Patient Transportation 109
   Batching vs. Single Piece Flow 110
      Case Study: Pharmacy Batching 112
   Manage Inventory 112
      Case Study: Pharmacy Inventory 114

Chapter 7   Principle #5: Perfection **119**
   Root Causes 119
      Case Study: Inpatient Admission from Emergency Department 124
   Error-Proof Processes 125
   Sustaining Improvements 129
      Case Study: Operating Room Performance Dashboards 134

Chapter 8   Executing a Project through Lean DMAIC **137**
   Kaizen 137
   Lean DMAIC Model 140
      Case Study: Patient Flow through the Short-Procedure Unit (SPU) 156

Chapter 9   Facilitating Rapid Improvements **161**
   Facilitation Guidelines 162
   The Kaizen Problem-Solving Process 163
   Facilitator's Role in Group Dynamics 178

Chapter 10   Leading Change **183**
   Lean Management 184
   Leading Change 188
   Lessons from Jefferson Lean Leaders 197

Chapter 11   Pandemic Preparedness: A COVID-19 Case Study **203**
   Pandemic Preparedness DMAIC Checklist 204

Appendices **227**

   Appendix A   Rapid Improvement Event Portfolio 229
      High-Level Project Plan 229
      Define 229
      Measure 238
      Analyze 242
      Improve 245
      Control 250

   Appendix B   Define Folder 253
      DOWNTIME Matrix 253
      Lean Engagement Communication Plan 253
      Lean Opportunity Guide 258
      VOC Waste Questionnaire 259

Appendix C   Measure Folder **261**
    Process Value Analysis 261
    Workflow Value Analysis 262

Appendix D   Analyze Folder **263**
    5S Audit Tool 263
    Swimlane Template 264

Appendix E   Improve Folder **265**
    RIE Presentation 265
    RIE Facilitator Evaluation Form 265

Appendix F   Control Folder **267**
    Kaizen A3 Report 267
    Control Phase Action Plan 267
    Control Phase Action Plan—Gantt Template 270

References *273*
Index *281*
About the Author *287*

List of Figures and Tables

Figure I.1	Roadmap for creating a lean process (based on the Lean Roadmap from BMGI)	xxv
Table 1.1	Performance improvement methodologies	2
Figure 1.1	Purpose, process, people, and the leadership system	5
Figure 1.2	Lean thinking flowing horizontally	5
Figure 1.3	Strategy deployment (hoshin kanri)	7
Table 1.2	Lean project opportunity guide	8
Figure 2.1	Roadmap: Define value	12
Figure 2.2	Roadmap: Determine scope	12
Figure 2.3	Process map structure	12
Figure 2.4	Process scoping	13
Figure 2.5	SIPOC diagram	14
Figure 2.6	Lab receiving process SIPOC	14
Figure 2.7	Sterile processing SIPOC	14
Figure 2.8	Roadmap: Define value through customer's eyes	15
Table 2.1	Examples of VA, NVA, and NVA-R activities	16
Table 2.2	Physician's office visit example	17
Figure 2.9	VA versus NVA time for the physician's office visit	18
Figure 2.10	Before/after assessment of VA and NVA activities	18
Figure 2.11	Roadmap: Identify waste	19
Table 2.3	DOWNTIME waste matrix	20
Figure 2.12	Preliminary waste diagnostic tool	24
Figure 2.13	Lean thinking process	25
Figure 2.14	Operating room turnover (wheels out to wheels in) value analysis	26
Figure 2.15	Surgical equipment sterilization value analysis	26
Figure 2.16	Oncology infusion center patient flow value analysis	26
Figure 2.17	Clinical lab workflow process	27
Figure 2.18	Clinical lab receiving process for specimen throughput value analysis	28
Figure 2.19	Workflow value analysis for a lab technician	28

xii List of Figures and Tables

Figure 2.20	Rapid improvement event pictures of the clinical lab project	29
Figure 2.21	Results of the clinical lab project	30
Figure 3.1	Roadmap: Map the value stream	33
Figure 3.2	Roadmap: Map the current state	34
Figure 3.3	High- and midlevel process maps	35
Figure 3.4	Process map of physician's office visit	36
Figure 3.5	High-level process steps for physician's office visit	35
Figure 3.6	High- and midlevel process steps for physician's office visit	36
Figure 3.7	Cycle times for physician's office visit	37
Figure 3.8	First-pass yield	38
Figure 3.9	Value stream map for physician's office visit	41
Figure 3.10	First-pass yield for physician's office visit	42
Figure 3.11	VA and NVA categorization for physician's office visit	44
Figure 3.12	Identified opportunities for improvement for physician's office visit	45
Figure 3.13	Example of VSM with improvement (kaizen) prioritization	46
Figure 3.14	Example of VSM created by improvement team	47
Figure 3.15	Swimlane map template	48
Figure 3.16	Swimlane map example with position	49
Figure 3.17	Swimlane map example with patient flow process	49
Figure 3.18	Swimlane map example with process steps by position	50
Figure 3.19	Example of swimlane map created by improvement team	51
Figure 3.20	Roadmap: Collect and analyze data for VSM	52
Figure 3.21	Process value analysis screenshot	54
Figure 3.22	Process value analysis output example	55
Figure 3.23	Process value analysis output for PTC patient flow	56
Figure 3.24	Workflow value analysis screenshot	57
Figure 3.25	Workflow value analysis output example	58
Figure 3.26	Sterile processing SIPOC	59
Figure 3.27	Sterile processing VSM	60
Figure 3.28	Sterile processing process value analysis output	61
Figure 4.1	Roadmap: Establish lean fundamentals	63
Table 4.1	Lean fundamentals	64
Table 4.2	5S approach for organizing physical space and systems/processes	65
Figure 4.2	Example of process 5S	66
Figure 4.3	5S audit tool for physical space and layout assessment	67
Figure 4.4	5S audit tools for physical space and layout assessment	68
Figure 4.5	Layout example	69
Figure 4.6	Example of current state layout	70
Figure 4.7	Example of current state layout with labeled processing areas	70
Figure 4.8	Example of spaghetti diagram of current state	70

Figure 4.9	Example of spaghetti diagram of improved state	70
Figure 4.10	Comparison of spaghetti diagrams before and after improvement	70
Figure 4.11	Layout improvement 1 of 3	71
Figure 4.12	Layout improvement 2 of 3	72
Figure 4.13	Layout improvement 3 of 3	73
Figure 4.14	Example of visual management in the Clinical Lab	74
Figure 4.15	PTC current state swimlane map	76
Figure 4.16	PTC current state process value analysis	77
Table 4.3	Pre-/post-intervention process	78
Figure 4.17	Redesigned process swimlane map	79
Figure 4.18	Length of stay results	80
Figure 4.19	Length of stay results by hour	81
Figure 4.20	PTC visual management example	81
Figure 4.21	Process from value analysis to solution development	82
Figure 5.1	Roadmap: Establish flow	85
Figure 5.2	Roadmap: Determine customer demand	88
Figure 5.3	Takt time equation	89
Figure 5.4	Roadmap: Balance the process	90
Figure 5.5	Process value analysis example	91
Figure 5.6	Workload balance example: Before intervention	92
Figure 5.7	Workload balance example: After intervention	92
Figure 5.8	Workload balance example: Before/after comparison	93
Figure 5.9	How to analyze a workload balance chart	94
Figure 5.10	Process value analysis of OR turnover	96
Figure 5.11	Improvement team creating a swimlane map of OR turnover	97
Figure 5.12	Next case checklist	97
Figure 5.13	Roadmap: Standardize the work	98
Table 5.1	Standard work template	100
Figure 5.14	Standard work and continuous improvement	101
Figure 6.1	Roadmap: Implement pull	103
Figure 6.2	Roadmap: Create a pull system	104
Figure 6.3	Push process	105
Figure 6.4	Push process example	105
Figure 6.5	Push process example: WIP	106
Figure 6.6	Push versus pull	106
Figure 6.7	Pull process	107
Figure 6.8	Pull process example	108
Table 6.1	Transportation pilot results	109
Figure 6.9	Roadmap: Reduce batching	110
Figure 6.10	Batching versus single-piece flow	111

Figure 6.11	Roadmap: Manage inventory	113
Figure 6.12	Kanban template	114
Figure 6.13	Kanban example	114
Figure 6.14	Pharmacy storeroom before improvements	115
Figure 6.15	Pharmacy storeroom after improvements	115
Figure 6.16	Pharmacy storeroom shelves after improvements	116
Figure 6.17	Pharmacy decentralized storerooms before and after improvements	116
Figure 7.1	Roadmap: Strive for perfection	120
Figure 7.2	Roadmap: Identify root causes	121
Figure 7.3	Example of 5 Whys	122
Figure 7.4	Fishbone problem	123
Figure 7.5	Fishbone body structure	123
Figure 7.6	Fishbone categories	123
Figure 7.7	Fishbone with potential causes	124
Figure 7.8	Example of fishbone with potential causes	125
Figure 7.9	Roadmap: Error-proof process	126
Figure 7.10	Progression of error reduction	128
Figure 7.11	Roadmap: Sustain improvements	129
Table 7.1	Threats to sustainability	130
Table 7.2	Performance update table	131
Figure 7.12	Run chart examples	132
Figure 7.13	Bar chart example	133
Figure 7.14	Pie graph example	133
Table 7.3	Performance dashboard example	133
Figure 7.15	Performance dashboard example in the OR	134
Figure 8.1	PDCA cycle	138
Figure 8.2	Improvement kata model	139
Figure 8.3	Types of kaizen	140
Figure 8.4	Roadmap with DMAIC overlay	141
Figure 8.5	DMAIC checklist	142
Figure 8.6	Define phase checklist	143
Figure 8.7	Change readiness profile tool	145
Figure 8.8	Systems and process profile tool	146
Figure 8.9	Measure phase checklist	147
Figure 8.10	Analyze phase checklist	149
Figure 8.11	Improve phase checklist	151
Figure 8.12	Control phase checklist	153
Figure 8.13	Example of run chart, post-improvement	154
Figure 8.14	Example of a kaizen A3 report	155
Figure 8.15	Current state process map for OR patient flow	157

Figure 8.16	Value analysis breakdown for OR patient flow	157
Figure 8.17	Post-intervention process for OR patient flow	158
Figure 8.18	Improvement team piloting changes	158
Figure 8.19	Monthly average of SPU processing time	159
Figure 8.20	Process value analysis before and after intervention	159
Figure 9.1	Five-step kaizen problem-solving process	164
Figure 9.2	Step 1: Brainstorm issues and barriers	165
Figure 9.3	Examples of improvement teams brainstorming	165
Figure 9.4	Example of a fishbone diagram	166
Figure 9.5	Step 2: Filter and prioritize issues and barriers	167
Figure 9.6	In-control/out-of-control template	168
Figure 9.7	Example of categorizing issues and barriers	168
Figure 9.8	Examples of improvement teams voting	169
Figure 9.9	Step 3: Brainstorm solutions	171
Figure 9.10	Example of direct issue-to-solution brainstorming	172
Figure 9.11	Example of reverse engineering	172
Figure 9.12	Step 4: Filter and prioritize solutions	173
Figure 9.13	Payoff matrix	174
Figure 9.14	Example of Lamina tree of low-hanging fruit	175
Figure 9.15	Inventor of the Lamina tree	175
Figure 9.16	Step 5: Develop and implement an action plan	176
Table 9.1	Action plan template	177
Table 9.2	Recommendation template	177
Figure 9.17	Control phase action plan screenshot	177
Table 9.3	Stages of group dynamics	179
Figure 10.1	Change model	183
Table 10.1	States of change at the macro and micro levels	184
Figure 10.2	Segmenting roles and responsibilities	187
Figure 10.3	Change model with leadership responsibilities	188
Figure 10.4	Threat versus opportunity matrix	190
Figure 10.5	More of/less of chart	193
Table 10.2	Short-term wins plan	196
Figure 10.6	Lean thinking summarized as 5-8-4	200
Figure 11.1	Pandemic preparedness DMAIC checklist	205
Figure 11.2	Define phase checklist	206
Figure 11.3	Measure phase checklist	210
Table 11.1	Pandemic dashboard	211
Table 11.2	Surge plan	216
Figure 11.4	Analyze phase checklist	218

Figure 11.5	FMEA tool	221
Figure 11.6	Improve phase checklist	222
Figure 11.7	Control phase checklist	223
Figure A.1	Organization of tool/template documents	227
Table A.1	High-level project plan	230
Figure A.2	Project charter	232
Table A.2	Communication plan	234
Table A.3	Waste observations	235
Figure A.3	Waste diagnostic	235
Figure A.4	High-level process map	236
Table A.4	High-level SIPOC	236
Figure A.5	Change readiness profile	237
Figure A.6	System and process profile	238
Figure A.7	Process value analysis results example	239
Figure A.8	Workflow value analysis results example	239
Figure A.9	Current state VSM template	241
Table A.5	Voice of customer summary	241
Table A.6	Voice of customer more of/less of	242
Table A.7	Stakeholder analysis	243
Table A.8	RACI chart	244
Figure A.10	Fishbone diagram template	245
Table A.9	RIE agenda template	246
Figure A.11	Payoff matrix template	247
Table A.10	Action plan example	248
Table A.11	Recommendation example	249
Figure A.12	Future state VSM example	249
Figure A.13	Kaizen A3 report example	251
Table A.12	DOWNTIME matrix	254
Table A.13	Lean engagement communication plan	256
Table A.14	Lean opportunity guide	258
Figure A.14	VOC waste questionnaire example	259
Figure A.15	Process value analysis Excel screenshot example	261
Figure A.16	Workflow value analysis Excel screenshot example	262
Figure A.17	5S audit tool Excel screenshot example	263
Figure A.18	Swimlane Excel screenshot example	264
Figure A.19	RIE facilitator evaluation form	266
Figure A.20	Kaizen A3 report example: Phlebotomy 5S event	268
Figure A.21	Kaizen A3 report example: Rapid responses	269
Figure A.22	Control phase action plan screenshot	270
Figure A.23	Control phase action plan screenshot example	270
Figure A.24	Gantt chart screenshot example	271

List of Case Studies

Presurgery Patient Flow	18
Clinical Lab Workflow	27
Patient Flow in the Patient Testing Center	55
OR/SPCC VSM Event	59
Patient Flow in the Patient Testing Center	75
Evaluating Gastroenterology Physician's Office Visit	90
Rapid Changeover in the Operating Room	96
Patient Transportation	109
Pharmacy Batching	112
Pharmacy Inventory	114
Inpatient Admission from the Emergency Department	124
Operating Room Performance Dashboards	134
Patient Flow through the Short-Procedure Unit (SPU)	156

Foreword

by David B. Nash, MD, MBA

Dennis Delisle and our College of Population Health have essentially grown up together on the campus of Thomas Jefferson University in Philadelphia. Let me explain. The nation's first College of Population Health is now in its early adolescence, celebrating its 12th birthday. There are many new schools and colleges of population health across the nation, including at least 40 departments of population health spread across America's 150 allopathic medical colleges. Dennis, when I first met him, was a management fellow completing his health administration fellowship at our institution. A few short years later he became the senior administrative leader and vice president of operations for our south Philadelphia division. Jefferson Health itself is now nearly 20 hospitals and more than a $6 billion operation. Today Dennis is the executive administrator for The Ohio State University Wexner Medical Center's flagship hospital. What has not changed is the burning passion Dennis has for improving the outcomes of medical care, even as a non-clinician.

As I look back on my tenure as the founding dean emeritus, and the celebration of my three decades of service as a faculty member at our university, Dennis continues to stand out as a wonderful colleague. As I wrote in the first Foreword, I was so impressed with Dennis (when I met him) by his fund of knowledge and enthusiasm that it was indeed a great decision to ask him to join our affiliated faculty and charge him with creating some of our most successful online training in lean thinking.

Dennis has evolved into one of our most highly sought-after and most lauded faculty, and the portfolio of courses that he teaches are typically oversubscribed. Therefore, as I wrote in the first Foreword, it does not come as much of a surprise to me that the publisher of the first edition of his successful book has asked him to complete this thoroughly updated second edition. Much has happened in the interim period.

Lean thinking is solidly entrenched in our college curriculum with both a graduate certificate and a master's degree in operational excellence. Essentially, we believe that clinicians have two jobs to do each and every day: Job #1, which is the clinical job for which they were well trained, and Job #2, which is to improve Job #1. Few clinicians, including doctors, nurses, pharmacists, and others, have the requisite skillset to operationalize Job #2. Dennis Delisle to the rescue!

As I wrote in the first Foreword, from my perch, "lean" means eliminate waste, and after 30 years in academic medicine, I'm convinced that a third of all the procedures my clinical colleagues order, and the money we collectively spend as a society, is probably wasteful. A good portion of what we do is not based on solid scientific evidence but rather on a collection of the opinions of experts and the guild-like nature of our hierarchical training process. In a word, it still seems to me to be a world filled with "see one, do one, and teach one," with little regard for "Is that the right one in the first place?"

Along comes the second edition of *Lean Healthcare*, and it is not a clinical guide; rather, it is a new mindset, a paradigm shift, a sea change, a new lens, a disruption. Whichever adjective you choose to use, Dennis has given us a unique view of lean. This book clearly sorts out the differences in our jargon from lean to Six Sigma to business process redesign to continuous quality improvement. At the end of the day, it's all about improving what we do each day in order to reduce waste, reallocate resources, reduce error, improve outcomes, and, in a word, deliver value in the nation's largest industry.

With the concomitant expansion of the Jefferson College of Population Health master's degree in healthcare quality and safety, and the on-campus leadership training programs in high reliability, this book will serve as a cornerstone for our ever-expanding curriculum. It leads me to think about what the future of a truly clinically integrated delivery system—now numbering more than 20 hospitals—might look like. Let me share aspects of that vision.

As I wrote in the first Foreword, "imagine the clinically integrated delivery system of the future." The chief medical officer makes regular "gemba" walks to see for herself where inefficiencies in the complex process of a hospital might be lurking. Imagine, too, the daily huddle where clinicians, administrators, and others self-reflect about what went on the day before and how they could have made the process safer and more efficient for all our patients. Admittedly, there are some organizations that embrace the gemba walk and the daily huddle for safety, but they remain, 20 years after the publication of *To Err is Human*, frightfully few and far between. This second edition will go a long way in educating a large number of people who will, in turn, help their organizations to catapult us into such a future vision described herein.

I appreciate how well organized this book is with its ample figures and tables, all of which are clean and easy to grasp. The prose is crisp. The chapter organization makes sense. The definitions of lean principles and kaizen problem-solving are compelling.

It's now been more than a decade since the passage of the Affordable Care Act, and the nation is struggling with issues including access, disparity in care, inequities in income distribution, and frightful reversal of epidemiologic markers, including a decrease in life expectancy coupled with the diseases of despair (alcoholism, depression, drug abuse, and suicide). The nation seems to have lost its way. As a result, we need lean thinking now more than ever. As I wrote in the first Foreword, lean thinking is not just a destination, it is a new way to view the world. As emeritus dean, I sent faculty members for training in lean and actively promoted enrollment in Dennis' graduate-level course. Subsequent leaders in our college continue to support Dennis unabashedly, and, as a result, I remain supremely confident that lean thinking will continue to be one of the key tools we need to implement the vision of the Affordable Care Act, now a decade ago. I am equally confident that such implementation will put us on the road to redemption —the road paved with an increased attention to measurement, accountability, transparency, and, of course, closure of the feedback loop.

My 30-year career as a member of the faculty of this great university has taught me many important life lessons. Chief among them is the need for leadership training for the emerging class of new leaders forged during a time when our industry has consumed 20 percent of our GDP, and, yet, we continue to be wasteful in our spending and continue to harm patients. As a result, I believe everyone in a leadership role in our increasingly complex delivery system would benefit greatly from at least a rudimentary understanding of lean and, at best, a deep dive into each chapter in this second edition. Once again, kudos to Dennis Delisle for his many accomplishments, most especially the second edition of this important book. The only questions I have are: "Are we courageous enough as practitioners to embrace lean and actually change our thinking to reduce the waste that surrounds so many of our processes? Do we have the political will to confront harm in our system and publicly acknowledge our shortcomings? Will we commit to education to improve Job #2?"

As our college enters the next phase of growth and development under new leaders, I remain confident that we will expand our course offerings in lean thinking and move to a world characterized by operational excellence. I am more convinced than ever that Dennis Delisle will help lead us in this perilous but critical journey into the future.

David B. Nash, MD MBA
Founding Dean Emeritus
Jefferson College of Population Health

Introduction

1 + 1 or ((97 − 88)*65/(1 + 4) − 17)^(1/2) − (64^(1/2) + 73 − 12*3 + 6*8 − 85)
You decide . . . both equal 2.

—Dennis R. Delisle

Continuous improvement promotes the relentless refinement of systems and processes. Today's challenge in the healthcare environment lies in an organization's ability to rapidly improve at a greater rate than its surrounding competitors. The goal is not simply to get better but rather to become the best at getting better. To achieve this, the traditional problem-solving paradigm needs to shift.

This book focuses on the model, strategy, and lessons learned in implementing lean thinking in a healthcare organization. Using Jefferson's real-world case studies, the book provides approaches and tools to facilitate rapid improvements. The goal is to create an accessible and useable guide for beginner, amateur, and advanced lean and process improvement practitioners.

Through the Thomas Jefferson University College of Population Health, I developed a lean thinking course, which gained significant traction over the years and evolved into the master of science degree in operational excellence (OPX). The OPX program leverages lean thinking as a core model for waste elimination and continuous improvement. The university's commitment to build robust academic and professional OPX training programs speaks to the importance of developing these core competencies in our current and future healthcare leaders. As the program evolved, so too did my career. As a hospital executive, I integrate lean strategies and tools with our clinical and operational teams to drive higher levels of performance. This book bears the scars, sweat, and triumphs of the very real and very challenging work required to lead transformations.

> *If you like the way you think now and do not want to change, do not read this book. Once you get started, you will see the world from a different lens. You will see waste and opportunities for improvement everywhere. There's no turning back. The good thing is, you will learn how to do something about it.*

There are so many books about lean on the market. There are entire books dedicated to specific tools (e.g., value stream mapping, A3 problem solving) as well as the philosophy and influences that led to the development of lean thinking. This book is different. From years of experience with hundreds of projects and dozens of educational courses, I have refined the content to simplify the concepts and tools, boiling it down to practical application. There are many ways to skin a cat. I prefer to highlight a small number of concepts and tools that are proven effective rather than present every possible or known way. This is not a book about theory. It is about action. The book provides readers the knowledge and ability to develop and implement meaningful change in the most simple and straightforward manner. It is a big challenge!

To meet this challenge, the book requires an organized and logical model for improvement. The roadmap for creating a lean process serves as the book's framework (Figure I.1). The model is an adaptation of the Lean Roadmap from Breakthrough Management Group International (BMGI). This framework provides the backdrop for systematic process evaluation and improvement within the five principles of lean:

1. Define value
2. Map the value stream
3. Establish flow
4. Implement pull
5. Strive for perfection

In this book you will find the following:

- A structured approach to executing lean improvements
- Relevant real-world case studies
- Examples of tools and accompanying templates
- Hints, tips, and lessons learned
- Chapter challenges and questions prompting you to apply key concepts and tools in the work setting

WHO THIS BOOK IS FOR

This book's primary audience is individuals responsible for clinical and operational improvement in healthcare settings. The book appeals to a wide variety of healthcare professionals including, but not limited to: Lean Six Sigma practitioners, quality and process improvement specialists, and project managers, clinical and operational leaders, physicians, nurses, front-line managers and supervisors, improvement teams, professors teaching quality improvement and/or operations management, healthcare professionals responsible for performance improvement, and students in all related health professions (clinical and administrative).

Figure I.1 Roadmap for creating a lean process (based on the Lean Roadmap from BMGI).

The book promotes practical application. Readers are equipped with the skills to implement lean concepts and tools within their work setting. Additionally, the book provides insight and strategies for avoiding failure and developing buy-in. Remember, every organization is unique. You know your organization's history and culture. Use that knowledge to adopt and adapt certain tools and techniques that fit your environment.

HOW THIS BOOK IS ORGANIZED

Chapter 1 provides an overview of lean thinking. The chapter introduces readers to the roadmap for creating a lean process. The roadmap provides the framework for systematically implementing lean improvements and serves as the foundation of the book. Chapters 2–7 dive into the five principles of lean thinking by constructing the roadmap one block at a time. Readers will gain a comprehensive understanding of each element within the model. Readers explore each specific principle along with the associated concepts and tools. Case studies support tools, highlighting their use, as well as hints and tips to consider when using the tools. This comprehensive section of the book serves as the core to practical implementation.

The final section of the book, Chapters 8–10, ties execution and lessons learned to the tools and approach provided within Chapters 2–7. Chapter 8 defines the lean DMAIC (define, measure, analyze, improve, control) model. Readers learn the standardized approach for rapid improvements, which includes a checklist as a reference guide for project execution. Chapter 9 reviews the five-step kaizen problem-solving process. This structured model includes effective brainstorming and prioritization tools along with instructions for facilitating them. This chapter includes practical tips and techniques to lead multidisciplinary teams through problem-solving and action-plan development. Chapter 10, expanded in depth as part of the second edition, discusses strategies and challenges in leading change, as well as offers lessons learned from Jefferson's improvement journey. The chapter integrates practical application with the management and leadership skills required to implement and sustain improvements. The final chapter, Chapter 11, is a bonus section on pandemic preparedness. This chapter establishes a DMAIC framework for outbreak preparation and response using the COVID-19 pandemic as a case study. Integrating concepts and tools presented throughout the book, the final section provides a comprehensive model to position your organization for continuous readiness.

Once you learn how to see things through the lean thinking lens, you will not be able to "turn it off." Waste is everywhere and, at times, it will frustrate you. However, my goal is to show you how to not only to see it but also do something about it. The Appendix and accompanying templates provide the necessary resources to get started. Keep this book close by your side as you start or continue executing lean improvements.

Chapter 1
Lean Thinking

Seek first to understand, then to be understood.

– Stephen Covey

Changes in the healthcare landscape have led to innovative and adaptive efforts of organizations to stay afloat (Martin et al. 2009). Healthcare reform, with its focus on value-based reimbursement, serves as a catalyst for institutional and industry-wide change. Healthcare organizations are now starting to leverage improvement methodologies that have been proven effective in other industries such as manufacturing (de Souza 2009; McConnell et al. 2013). This effort is akin to evidence-based medicine, where organizations develop a systematic structure and process to produce high-quality results (Bradley et al. 2012; Bradley et al. 2006; Curry et al. 2011; Shojania and Grimshaw 2005; Shortell, Rundall, and Hsu 2007; Shortell and Singer 2008).

Though improvements in quality have been slower than desired (Brennan et al. 2005; Classen et al. 2011; Dentzer 2011; Leape and Berwick 2005; Wachter 2004), lean has shown to be effective in improving various healthcare processes, including operating rooms, emergency departments, and clinical labs (Aronson and Gelatt 2006; Farrokhi et al. 2013; Martin et al. 2009; Vermeulen et al. 2014). Having a structured approach is essential since most problems relate to management and system/process design (Chalice 2007). A silver bullet does not exist. The only way to be successful in this ever-changing environment is to be deliberate and agile in strategy and execution (Zidel 2012). Limited resources require a thoughtful, methodical way to evaluate opportunity areas and develop high-impact solutions.

PERFORMANCE IMPROVEMENT METHODOLOGIES

There are many performance improvement methodologies. Each methodology provides some degree of structure and guidelines for using tools to improve processes. The focus of this book is lean thinking. However, various tools and concepts influenced by methods like Six Sigma, quality assurance, and total quality management also appear (Pande and Holpp 2002). Table 1.1 depicts the more common approaches to performance improvement. The point is not to elaborate on each; dozens of texts are available for that. There is not a singular best approach. Ideally, the most effective method is a combination of many (Smith 2003).

Table 1.1 Performance improvement methodologies.

Method	Problem	Goal	Implementing improvements	Approach	One-line description
Lean	Process inefficiencies, space/layout issues, poor quality	Reduce/eliminate waste	Frontline-based improvements or 2-hour to 3-day rapid improvement with solutions implemented during and within 30 days	Frontline improvement through PDCA, project execution through DMAIC model	Identify and eliminate non-value-adding activity (waste)
Six Sigma	Variation in outcomes, complex processes	Reduce variation	Complex problem resolution, may take 3–9 months	Project execution through DMAIC model	Comprehensive statistical process improvement approach to reduce variation
Business process redesign	Not achieving desired outcomes with current process, want dramatic results	Fundamental rethinking and radical process redesign	Teams redesign process, no defined timeline	Identify processes, review/update/analyze, design future state, test and implement	Complete process redesign
Quality assurance	Not meeting standards, errors	Fit for purpose and right the first time	Systematic measurement and monitoring	Feedback loop, no defined approach	Error prevention, ensuring quality requirements are met
Total quality management	Poor quality	Quality of products and processes	All employees participate daily in improving processes, services, etc.	Management approach—everyone's responsibility	Quality is everyone's responsibility

A great analogy is the mixed martial arts. There are many techniques and styles of martial arts. Some emphasize using hands or legs, while others focus on grappling and ground control. The most effective martial artist is one who has competencies in all areas (i.e., skilled on his or her feet and adept on the ground). Depending on the situation, he or she will utilize certain tactics and techniques from the appropriate method/style to gain advantage over an opponent.

The perspective is similar for performance improvement methodologies. The approach varies depending on the organizational needs and current state of operations. This book takes concepts from other practices and incorporates them into the lean thinking framework. Fundamentally, though, there are elements that need to be present to ensure successful adoption and utilization. These elements include a clear purpose and direction, leadership support and staff empowerment, and a commitment to continuous improvement (Niemeijer et al. 2012).

Project and change management are two approaches that have the greatest impact on executing lean improvements. Project management provides the structure to implement improvement projects. Defined phases compose the project management approach to initiate, plan, execute, and then close. The DMAIC (define, measure, analyze, improve, control) framework comprises specific tasks and deliverables. Chapter 8 describes executing lean improvements through DMAIC in detail.

Change management is the underlying model for driving transformation. Sustainable change does not happen through happenstance or luck. There are defined and proven strategies to facilitate the assessment and subsequent management of interventions. Chapter 10 reviews such strategies as well as lessons learned along the way.

LEAN THINKING

This book will challenge you to see the world differently. It provides the tools and knowledge to lead positive change. Derived from Toyota, lean is an underlying management philosophy and way of thinking that permeates both professional and personal interactions (Womack and Jones 1996). Defining value through the eyes of the customer (i.e., patient, specimen, or department) exemplifies lean thinking (Graban 2012). The primary goal of lean is the identification and elimination of waste or those activities that do not add value to the process.

Empowering frontline employees to solve problems at the source and improve their workflow and quality is at the core of lean thinking (Graban and Swartz 2012; Tapping et al. 2009). The focus of lean in the healthcare arena is not money and time. It is safety, quality, and service delivery (Graban 2012). Focusing on quality as the highest priority leads to cost reductions (e.g., reduces rework and inefficiencies and improves productivity and throughput) (Imai 1997; Langley et al. 2009; Liker 2004). A continuous improvement framework and respect for people establish the foundation (Toussaint and Gerard 2010). To this end, lean tools identify and eliminate the interruptions, errors, and other tasks that take away from the main goal at hand. These concepts and tools apply anywhere, from work to personal activities (Jones and Mitchell 2006). We do not just want to do more with less; we want to do better with the right resources.

Lean thinking requires a different approach toward management. The emphasis in a lean management environment is to ask the right questions rather than provide answers (Bicheno and Holweg 2004; Womack 2011). The systematic nature of implementing lean thinking leads to effective problem assessment and resolution through this method (Joint Commission on the Accreditation of Healthcare Organizations 2006). Incremental improvements help make the current situation better while striving for perfection.

The ability to execute strategy and continuously improve enables an organization to achieve its vision (Hrebiniak 2013). Essential to this is leveraging human resources and optimizing their potential through education and hands-on problem solving. Lean thinking promotes the method of establishing purpose, process, and then people (Womack 2011):

- *Purpose:* Where are we going? The purpose serves as the destination (future state). Customers are central to the purpose (in healthcare this is usually the patient).

- *Process:* How will we get there? A process is the stream of value from start to finish, envisioning how to move from the current state to the future state.

- *People:* Who do we need to get us there, and what skills should they have? Educate and empower employees to solve problems. Effective management systems position employees in systems and processes that enable quality, not produce errors and inefficiencies.

> "Purpose comes first, then the processes to achieve the purpose, then engaged people to conduct the processes needed to achieve the purpose."
> – James Womack

Organizations can develop a leadership system that leverages the purpose, process, people framework (Figure 1.1) (Meyer 2010). The mission and vision define the purpose of an organization and articulate the customer-centric description of why the organization exists and what it aspires to become. Without purpose there is no direction. If employees do not understand how their contributions and roles fit into an overall strategy, their work feels directionless (Kotter 1995). The lean philosophy is top-down driven, bottom-up executed. Leaders communicate where the organization is going and what needs to get done, but staff define how the organization will get there. To this end, without commitment from leadership, teams may not have the required resources, priorities, and focus needed to move an initiative forward. From a leadership perspective, the challenge is to clearly define and communicate the purpose (vision) and align and integrate the work systems and processes to achieve it.

The mission and vision are realized through the process of strategic planning and execution of key initiatives aligned with the organization's short- and longer-term objectives. Processes flow horizontally across functions, departments, and/or teams (Figure 1.2). Process design and execution contribute to the overall impact and consistency of outcomes. Lean thinking targets the purpose and identifies the best, most efficient way to achieve it (process). When issues arise, lean thinkers systematically evaluate and identify ways to limit or reduce the likelihood of future occurrences (Wysocki 2004).

Figure 1.1 Purpose, process, people, and the leadership system.

Figure 1.2 Lean thinking flowing horizontally.

> Without a clearly articulated vision, your next step is arbitrary.
> "Alice: Would you tell me, please, which way I ought to go from here?
> The Cheshire Cat: That depends a good deal on where you want to get to.
> Alice: I don't much care where.
> The Cheshire Cat: Then it doesn't much matter which way you go.
> Alice: ...So long as I get somewhere.
> The Cheshire Cat: Oh, you're sure to do that, if only you walk long enough."
> – Alice in Wonderland

The people component aligns and cascades organizational goals down to the individual employee. This enables strategic management of human resources to optimize quality, productivity, and efficiency (Swensen et al. 2012). Employees can link their value to and impact on the organization through alignment of their tasks and responsibilities to overarching organizational goals.

The performance excellence framework activates the leadership system. The organization's improvement philosophy directs the systematic approach to align and integrate purpose, process, and people. Hoshin Kanri is a lean concept that drives the purpose, process, people approach. It represents the strategic deployment of projects to drive the organization's vision. Originally derived from Dr. Yoji Akao (Bicheno and Holweg 2004), the approach aligns all three elements into tangible tactics. Strategic objectives articulate the vision. High-level performance metrics (also known as key performance indicators, or KPIs) translate strategic objectives into measurable variables. KPIs are typically lagging metrics in nature, meaning they are the outcomes or end results of processes. Examples include revenue, market share, and customer satisfaction (McChesney, Covey, and Huling 2012). Operational and strategic projects focus on impacting the KPIs. Each project has its own defined metrics.

Unlike lagging metrics, project metrics are leading in nature. This means that leading metric performance should indicate the direction of the lagging outcome. For example, if your goal is to lose weight (lagging metric), you have to decrease your calorie consumption or increase calories burned (both leading metrics). Leading metrics tend to be within our operational control and, as a consequence, should be the focus of improvement efforts. They should be high-impact processes or behaviors that improvement teams can affect. The pivotal characteristics of good leading metrics are predictability of achieving the goal and being within the team's influence (McChesney, Covey, and Huling 2012). In other words, if you improve the leading metric, the lagging metric should likewise improve.

The Hoshin Kanri cascade from strategic objectives to project KPIs portrays the flow of the organizational vision down through improvement projects. Figure 1.3 is a simplified model that demonstrates the necessity to align and integrate activities to achieve results. Identifying the appropriate leading metric(s) is an essential skill that ultimately results in meeting, exceeding, or falling short of the strategic objectives or overall performance metrics (Hrebiniak 2013).

Evidence-based leadership, a concept popularized by Quint Studer, utilizes the framework alignment, action, and accountability. Similar to the Hoshin Kanri cascade, this leadership model is based on the premise that without alignment, you are not going to leverage the power and scale of the workforce, which means you will not achieve your results (Studer 2009):

- *Alignment:* What are the key priorities and objectives? How do you align systems, processes, people, and resources to achieve them?

- *Action:* What are the workflows that need to change? What projects and tasks are required to achieve these objectives?

- *Accountability:* How do you reward and recognize high performance, develop talent, and manage low performers?

Figure 1.3 Strategy deployment (Hoshin Kanri).

ROADMAP FOR CREATING A LEAN PROCESS

The roadmap for creating a lean process functions as the model for the performance excellence framework (Figure I.1). The model, when implemented, can contribute to strong performance, wise resource utilization, and, ultimately, a competitive advantage. Atop the model are the five principles of lean: (1) define value, (2) map the value stream, (3) establish flow, (4) implement pull, and (5) strive for perfection (Womack and Jones 1996). Each principle has three components. Each component represents a particular deliverable or concept with a corresponding tool (indicated in the white box below the component). The components are sequential, beginning with scope definition and ending with sustainability strategies. Chapters 2–7 construct the roadmap one block at a time. It is essential to have a comprehensive understanding of both the sequence and the significance of the model's elements.

The lean project opportunity guide (Table 1.2) provides a reference for healthcare processes that are appropriate for applying the roadmap. Remember, improvements are not only formal projects but also any activities that reduce inefficiencies and waste, resulting in better processes and outcomes (Graban and Swartz 2012). The scope of identified opportunities varies; however, the improvement approaches described throughout the book are consistent.

Table 1.2 Lean project opportunity guide.

	General improvement opportunities
Staffing	Workflow Workflow balancing	Time management Productivity
Physical organization/ inventory management	Ordering processes/par levels Space allocation	Visual management Physical layout/organization
	Examples of lean project metrics
Turnaround time Cycle/processing time	Throughput time (lead time) Customer, patient, employee satisfaction	Quality output Cost savings/avoidance
	Examples of department/function-specific improvement opportunities
Business services	Timeliness and accuracy of results/reports Transactional throughput	Request turnaround time
Emergency department	Length of stay Door to triage Door to physician	Door to disposition Door to discharge Admission order to transfer from ED
Diagnostic and ancillary departments	Patient transportation Patient registration Order to result	Request to completion Exam/procedure/testing scheduling Work assignments
Nursing and clinical units	Bed availability Bed empty to fill turnaround time	Patient flow Workload balance
Physician practice	Exam room utilization Access/scheduling	Patient flow Workload balance
Supply chain	Par levels Product standardization Space allocation/organization	Inventory locations Distribution process
Surgical services	Decontamination and sterilization processes Instrument availability Case assembly Operating room utilization	First case on-time start Scheduling process Operating room turnover Patient flow

⚠️ CHAPTER CHALLENGE

Think of a work-related problem you would like to improve (refer to Table 1.2 for ideas). Identify an area within your scope of control that could benefit from lean thinking. Where is it? What improvement opportunities exist? What are the expected benefits?

QUESTIONS

1. What performance improvement methodologies would fit your organization/department/area of responsibility?
2. Have you seen projects or decisions that were based on people, process, then purpose (rather than the other way around)?
3. Why is establishing the purpose an integral first step?
4. What aspect of managing/implementing change is most critical in your workplace or chosen scenario?
5. What are your strategic objectives?
6. Are employee goals aligned with organizational objectives?
7. What leading metrics can you address to drive key lagging indicators?

Chapter 2
Principle #1: Define Value

It is not the employer who pays the wages. Employers only handle the money. It is the customer who pays the wages.

– Henry Ford, Sr.

Chapter 1 discussed the framework of lean thinking—the roadmap for creating a lean process. The five principles provide the structure for initiating, executing, and sustaining process improvements. This section is the beginning of lean thinking. Defining value is the foundation of the principles. Central to the lean philosophy are our customers and how they define value (Womack and Jones 1996).

The focus of this chapter is on shifting your thinking from worker-centric to customer-centric process evaluation. Defining customer value is an essential step toward identifying and eliminating those activities that do not add value (synonymous with waste) (Graban 2012; Womack and Jones 1996). Three components are core to defining value (Figure 2.1):

1. Determine scope
2. Define value through the customer's eyes
3. Identify waste

These components, completed in sequence, provide an initial assessment of the current state, how the process is currently performing. In order to effect change, we must first understand the problems we are facing. To do this, we must go to the gemba, where the work takes place, to observe processes, ask questions, and engage staff in developing solutions (Womack 2011).

DETERMINE SCOPE

Every project needs to have a scope (Figure 2.2). The scope is a well-defined description or depiction of the project boundaries (Project Management Institute 2008). For process improvement projects, the best way to display the scope is through process maps. Process maps show what is happening as a visual breakdown of steps or activities (Figure 2.3). The map helps define the steps to evaluate and target for improvement.

12 Chapter Two

Figure 2.1 Roadmap: Define value.

Figure 2.2 Roadmap: Determine scope.

Figure 2.3 Process map structure.

Determining the scope begins with identifying the first and last steps of the process (Figure 2.4). Everything upstream (before the first step) and downstream (after the last step) is out of scope. This is a crucial concept. Many projects fail due to a poorly defined scope or an ever-expanding scope, also known as scope creep.

Figure 2.4 Process scoping.

> *"Don't boil the ocean."* Always remember this expression. This will make you an effective leader and problem solver. If you can scope a problem appropriately, your outcomes and objectives will be achieved. Too small and the impact is barely noticeable. Too big and nothing gets accomplished. The goal is to find the scope that is just right.

A common tool used to create a high-level process map is the SIPOC diagram (pronounced sy-pock). SIPOC stands for supplier, input, process, output, and customer:

- *Supplier*—Provides inputs to initiate the process (e.g., person, department, organization)
- *Input*—Materials, resources, and/or information required to execute the process (e.g., order, equipment, form)
- *Process*—Series of steps or activities to convert inputs to outputs
- *Output*—Product, service, or outcome resulting from the process
- *Customer*—Receives the outputs of the process

Building the SIPOC is a straightforward activity. It is important to remember to keep the initial map high-level. Depict the process from a 30,000-foot view, and do not get lost in the details early in the assessment phase. The SIPOC diagram provides a process overview and is the foundation for improvement.

Building a SIPOC (Figure 2.5)

1. Determine the start and end process steps
2. Identify the inputs and outputs
3. Identify the supplier and the customer
4. Indicate high-level steps in between (process) (30,000-foot view)

Figure 2.6 is an example of a SIPOC for the clinical lab. The process scope is the time from when a specimen arrives at the lab to the time the results are completed. The supplier and the customer are the test-ordering physicians. The physicians are sending the specimen (input) and receiving the test results (output).

Figure 2.7 is another example of a SIPOC for the sterile processing department. This department is responsible for decontaminating, cleaning, sterilizing, packing, and distributing surgical equipment and supplies to the operating rooms. This process highlights the steps from the time the operating room case is complete to the time the subsequent case using the surgical equipment begins.

Figure 2.5 SIPOC diagram.

Figure 2.6 Lab receiving process SIPOC.

Figure 2.7 Sterile processing SIPOC.

DEFINE VALUE THROUGH CUSTOMER'S EYES

After the scope has been determined, value is defined through the customer's eyes (Figure 2.8). For lean thinkers, the focus is identification and reduction of waste. Costs are viewed as an end result once quality issues are addressed and improved (Berwick, Nolan, and Whittington 2008). The ultimate goal of a process is to provide the customer value—what the customer wants, when the customer wants it, and in the correct amount (Chalice 2007).

The lean thinking philosophy targets and eliminates the "firefighting" mentality. Often staff think the value they contribute to a company is their ability to chase down problems and fight fires (Graban 2012). For example, if information on a form is missing, an employee might make several phone calls and send multiple emails to gather everything. All this effort, though well intentioned, is waste. Fighting fires is not a systematic approach to preventing and anticipating problems; it is reactive and inefficient. The reality is that firefighting is not a core competency or desired skill but rather an unnecessary workaround to poor system and process design.

The Five Principles of Lean

- Define value
  - Determine scope
  - SIPOC
  - Define value through customer's eyes
  - VA/NVA activity

Value-adding (VA) activity:
1. Something the customer is willing to pay for
2. Physically changes the product, good, or service
3. Done correctly the first time (no rework)

Non-value-adding (NVA) activity = waste

Non-value-adding but a regulatory requirement (NVA-R)

Figure 2.8 Roadmap: Define value through customer's eyes.

Employees want to do their best, but sometimes the system or process does not position them to be successful. At times, it can be difficult for employees to see the forest for the trees. Sometimes they cannot see past the mounds of work at hand. This is why lean thinking shifts the viewpoint from a worker-centric vantage to the eyes of the customer. The customer's perspective enables us to understand not only where we might be standing in the forest but also how to navigate through it.

Using the firefighting analogy, it is important to develop a systematic approach toward risk assessment, prevention, and anticipation of issues. Sprinkler systems demonstrate a higher level of problem solving. To truly innovate, the focus should be on eliminating the likelihood of fires starting in the first place, a concept discussed more in Chapter 7 ("Strive for Perfection").

Who Defines Value?

At the forefront of lean thinking is asking, "Who are your customers?" All concepts, tools, and strategies rely on the identification of customers and their value definition. There is an ultimate customer in a process (e.g., patient, clinician, another department), but there are also many internal customers along the way, from process step to process step. Without understanding the internal customer needs, employees could be passing along defects or unnecessary work and information without even knowing it. Differentiation between internal and external customers is important. The ultimate customer of the process is the main focus and the starting point for defining value (Womack and Jones 1996). Three criteria define value-adding (VA) activity (Graban 2012):

1. It is something the customer is willing to pay for.
2. It physically changes the product, good, or service.
3. It is done correctly the first time (no rework).

> *Some activities are non-value-adding (NVA) but unavoidable (e.g., excessive transportation due to geography or layout constraints). It is important to identify and acknowledge these NVA activities. They might be disruptive and frustrating, but if they cannot be addressed, work around them.*

The activity under review is waste or non-value-adding (NVA) if all three VA criteria are not met. Activities required by regulatory agencies such as the Department of Health or Joint Commission are considered NVA but are a regulatory requirement (NVA-R). These activities must be done, whether or not they meet the three VA criteria. Verifying a patient's identity using his or her name and date of birth before administering any medication is an example of NVA-R. NVA-R steps are infrequent and should be left alone since they cannot be removed. The focus is on differentiating VA and NVA steps and removing the waste. Table 2.1 lists examples of each type of activity category.

It is not always clear whether an activity is VA or NVA. In these scenarios, ask if the step can be eliminated or if there is a better way of doing the step. The point is not to have complete agreement on the classification but rather to look for the removable waste within the process. Identifying waste leads to improvement.

Table 2.1 Examples of VA, NVA, and NVA-R activities.

Value-adding examples	Non-value-adding examples	Non-value-adding but regulatory requirement examples
Processing lab specimens	Searching for e-mails, documents, or other information	Asking patient to verify name and date of birth
Performing surgery on a patient	Patient walking from registration to waiting area to exam room	Documenting information in multiple areas of medical chart
Doing diagnostic scans (e.g., MRI, X-ray)	Employee waiting for information to perform a task	Double-checking medications prior to administration
Interviewing an individual for a potential job	Calling physician's office to collect missing information	Storing medical charts in a records warehouse for years
Preparing/mixing medications in pharmacy	Nurse toggling between computer systems to document	Performing internal process audits (e.g., financial)

Example: Physician's Office Visit

You have been tasked with improving the patient flow process for a typical outpatient physician's office visit. After scoping the project from "Enter the office" to "Check out," you document all the steps that occur in between (Table 2.2). The customer in this example is the patient. From the patient's perspective, you determine VA and NVA steps. Using the three criteria, you define the following:

- VA steps: 1, 5, 7, 9, 11
- NVA steps: 3, 4, 6, 8, 10, 12, 13

Table 2.2 Physician's office visit example.

List of process steps: Before	List of process steps: After
1. Enter the office	1. Enter the office
2. Sign in	2. Sign in
3. Sit down in waiting area	3. Sit down in waiting area
4. Called back, walk into clinical space	4. Called back, walk into clinical space
5. Get vitals taken	5. Get vitals taken
6. Walk to exam room	6. Walk to exam room
7. Nurse interview	7. Nurse interview
8. Wait for physician	8. Wait for physician
9. Physician exam	9. Physician exam
10. Wait for prescription script	10. Wait for prescription script
11. Receive script	11. Receive script
12. Walk to checkout area	12. Walk to checkout area
13. Check out	13. Check out

The initial process evaluation shows that the patient's office visit was 82 minutes (Figure 2.9). Of that time, 62 minutes (77.5 percent) was attributed to NVA activities (steps 3, 4, 6, 8, 10, 12, and 13) and only 20 minutes (24.4 percent) was VA time (steps 1, 5, 7, 9, and 11). Through identification and elimination of NVA activities, the "after" office-visit process is 57 minutes. Now, only 37 minutes (64.9 percent) is NVA time, while the VA time remains the same at 20 minutes (35.1 percent). However, you can see that the VA percentage increased from 24 percent to 35 percent as a result of reducing the NVA time.

Remember, the goal with lean is to identify and reduce/eliminate the NVA activities (Bicheno and Holweg 2004; Chalice 2007). Some NVA activity in this example is unavoidable (e.g., walk to exam room), while other steps are pure waste (e.g., wait for physician). Differentiating process steps into VA and NVA steps enables identification of opportunities for improvement. Chapter 3 ("Value Stream Mapping") will dive into more detail on ways to analyze and prioritize opportunities based on quality and time-related issues.

Figure 2.9 VA versus NVA time for the physician's office visit.

Case Study: Presurgery Patient Flow

Patient flow in the operating room was inefficient. The patient traveled to multiple areas: from the registration office to check-in, to the short procedure unit for surgical preparation, to the holding area for IV insertion, and ultimately to the operating room. Delays and coordination issues made the front-end process disorganized. An analysis of the current state revealed that the process from patient check-in at admissions until being ready for transport to the holding area took 70 minutes. More than half of this time was NVA. The lean team assigned to this project targeted reducing the NVA activities, which yielded a 17-minute reduction in throughput (Figure 2.10). Notice how the team did not affect the VA time for surgical prep. This reinforces the approach to identify and reduce NVA activities.

Before improvements

Check in at admissions	Arrive at short-procedure unit	Prep for surgery	Wait for transportation
7 mins	8 mins	25 mins	30 mins

Total time: 70 minutes
54% NVA
36% VA

After improvements

Check in at admissions	Arrive	Prep for surgery	Wait for transportation	Efficiencies gained
6 mins	2 mins	25 mins	20 mins	17 mins

Total time: 53 minutes
42% NVA
47% VA

Figure 2.10 Before/after assessment of VA and NVA activities.

Before the improvement, the NVA activity accounted for 54% of the total processing time, whereas VA time made up only 36%. With the reduced NVA time, the patient experienced a shift in proportion of time between VA and NVA. Though the VA time remained at 25 minutes, the reduction in NVA yielded an increase in proportion of VA time within the process from 36% to 47%. From the patient's perspective, more of the processing time was VA and the overall process took less time.

Caution about NVA: *NVA activity is not to be mistaken for a value judgment of individuals or specific roles. Waste tends to be driven by the system and the design (or lack thereof) of processes. The presence of waste does not indicate that an employee is bad or is not working hard (Graban 2012).*

IDENTIFYING WASTE

Waste is synonymous with NVA activity (Figure 2.11). Waste exists in all work processes. Identification and elimination of waste is the central focus of a lean system and leads to solution development (Womack 2011). Effective lean practitioners are able to differentiate between VA and NVA activities within any process (Womack and Jones 1996).

The DOWNTIME acronym (defects, overproduction, waiting, nonutilized skill or intellect, transportation, inventory, motion, extra processing) categorizes waste. Table 2.3 details each waste based on its definition, examples, potential causes, questions to ask to help identify it, and countermeasures for reduction/elimination.

Figure 2.11 Roadmap: Identify waste.

Table 2.3 DOWNTIME waste matrix.

Waste	Definition	Examples	Potential causes	Questions to ask	Countermeasures
Defects	Rework, errors, incomplete or incorrect information	• Medication errors • Process step not performed correctly • Missing information	• Lack of understanding of what "defect-free" means • Insufficient training	• Are tasks clearly defined (who, what, when, how)? • Are errors dealt with directly and promptly or passed along?	• 5S • Visual management • Standard work • Error-proofing
Overproduction	Producing more than what is currently needed (too much or too soon)	• Medications administered early to accommodate start schedule • Printing extra copies of information just in case	• No clear understanding of what is needed, when, in what quantity • Poor communication • Inconsistent process	• Are there more supplies prepared than needed? • Is the demand known?	• Workload balancing • Standard work • Checklists • Pull systems
Waiting	Delays, waiting for anything (people, paper, equipment, information)	• Delays in bed assignments • Delays in receiving information or communication • Waiting for next process steps to begin	• Poor understanding of time required to complete a task • No visual cues to indicate next step in the process • Delays compounding one another	• Are there bottlenecks/delays in the process due to obtaining information, supplies, etc.? • Are there clear expectations for how long process steps should take?	• VSM • Swimlane map • 5S • Workload balancing • Cross-train staff
Nonutilized skill/intellect	Nonutilizing staff skills or knowledge, poor workload balance	• No cross-training • Nurses transporting patients • Physician drawing labs	• Lack of well-defined process • Unclear or undefined roles and responsibilities	• Are employees cross-trained? • Are employees encouraged to suggest/implement improvements?	• Swimlane map • Workload balancing • Standard work

PRINCIPLE #1: DEFINE VALUE   21

Transportation	Unnecessary movement of something being processed (e.g., forms, patient, specimen, equipment)	• Placing stretcher in hall and constantly having to move it • Transporting forms from building to building or electronically to several areas	• Poor physical layout • Poor system/process design	• Are forms, patients, or materials moved to temporary locations? • Is technology being leveraged to limit physical handoffs?	• 5S • Physical layout • Visual management • Standard work
Inventory	Excessive supplies, batch processing, work-in-process	• Extra/outdated manuals • Obsolete equipment	• Supply/demand not well understood • Outdated supplies/equipment not discarded • Disorganized area, unclear what is necessary/unnecessary	• Is there extra equipment/supplies lying around? • Do forms, supplies, or patients wait in groups/batches?	• 5S • Visual management • Standard work • Pull systems
Motion	Any excess movement of the employee	• Searching for anything (e.g., information, supplies, equipment, patients) • Hand-carrying paperwork to another area	• Poor physical layout • Poor system/process design	• How does the current layout impede the process flow? • Can walking be reduced by repositioning equipment, people, and/or supplies?	• 5S • Physical layout • Visual management • Standard work
Extra processing	Extra or unnecessary steps performed that do not add value to the process	• Ordering more tests than the diagnosis warrants • Entering repetitive/duplicative information	• Complex or multiple forms • Ineffective policies and procedures	• Is there more information available than what needs to be processed?	• VSM • Visual management • Workload balancing • Standard work

Defects

Rework is the result of doing something incorrectly the first time, a core element of defining value. The effort that goes into gathering missing information or correcting errors is waste. The consequence of defects could be significant (e.g., medication error). One of the major causes of defects is that the employee may not know what it means to be defect-free. In other words, the employee does not know that what he or she is doing is not correct. It is leadership's responsibility to provide this valuable feedback for good performance as well as opportunities for improvement and coach or train staff appropriately.

Overproduction

Both overproduction and excess inventory are byproducts of ineffective forecasting or not knowing actual demand. Overproduction means producing things in excess, too soon, or faster than the customer, employee, or process requires. Presence of this waste tends to indicate poor cross-functional communication and inconsistent processes between the supplier and the customer. Overproduction is a misuse of resources that does not meet the customer's needs.

Waiting

Waiting is usually the most pervasive waste in any system (Zidel 2012). In between each process step there is usually a period of waiting. Sometimes it is brief (seconds), but it can span hours or even days. Waiting results from many process inefficiencies, including lack of standardized tasks, poor communication between steps, and no visual management or cues to indicate work that needs to be accomplished. To make matters worse, waiting can have a compounding effect on the process and system, leading to massive bottlenecks. Waiting inhibits flow and the ability to deliver what the customer wants when they want it.

Nonutilized skill/intellect

Nonutilized skill or intellect addresses employee engagement and human resource management. Unengaged employees are working below their level of knowledge/ certification or feel unchallenged. Likewise, an imbalance in workload, too much or too little, can lead to suboptimization of staff. There are budgetary implications with nonutilized skill/intellect. Organizations that underutilize highly paid staff are not cost effective. Cross-training is an effective approach to address nonutilized skill or intellect as well as workload balancing. Additionally, cross-training challenges staff to do different tasks, which can promote buy-in and engagement.

Transportation

Transportation represents movement of an item in a process. In healthcare, examples include patients, lab specimens, equipment, medication, and forms, among others. Any movement is NVA activity if it does not transform the good, product, or service. Though traveling from one location to another might be unavoidable due to geographic constraints, it does not make it VA. The presence of transportation indicates a worker-centric process design rather than a customer-centric one. Many processes within the delivery system (probably most) are not designed as patient-centric models and thus patients have to do most of the work (i.e., travel, navigate documentation) (Teich and Faddoul 2013).

Inventory

Inventory includes physical items and supplies in stock as well as electronic information and work-in-process (WIP). Supplies can take up valuable physical space and tie up cash. Additionally, there is a risk for expiration with certain perishable supplies like medications. WIP describes the backlog of items in between process steps. WIP develops when processes are not evenly balanced and standardized. Patients sitting in a waiting room are a form of WIP.

Motion

Motion represents the movement of the worker. It is different from transportation (movement of item being processed). Just because an employee looks busy and constantly moves around does not mean he or she is doing VA tasks. Do not confuse movement and activity with productivity and efficiency. Motion is an NVA activity if it takes up unnecessary time and energy in between VA steps. When it comes to process design, it is better to observe more motion than transportation. This is indicative of a process that brings the work to the customer, not the other way around.

Extra processing

Extra processing defines any extraneous processes or tasks that do not add value. These tasks are not necessary to produce the end product or service. In other words, they are tasks or outputs that the customer does not require or want. Extra processing is the result of poor process knowledge and understanding of customer needs, similar to overproduction. The end product is variable, leading to other wastes like inventory and rework.

The moral of the story is that VA, NVA, and NVA-R are not black and white, which is why we use red, green, and yellow. There are a lot of cases in which steps fit both categories. In those instances, it is best to ask:

- How long does the step take? If it is not long, do not worry about it. If it is significant, break it into smaller components to differentiate between VA and NVA activities.

- Can we live without doing the step? If yes, then eliminate it.

Understanding waste includes acknowledgment of the elements and factors of the surrounding environment. No process or system operates in isolation. Changes in one process or step can affect the efficiency of another elsewhere. Understanding the interplay of processes and drivers of waste will lead to effective problem-solving. All employees should learn and develop the ability to differentiate VA and NVA activities. Waste recognition is an integral skill set for effective lean thinkers. Figure 2.12 shows a preliminary waste diagnostic tool that provides another way to depict the presence and impact of waste on process flow. Evaluate wastes along a continuum from low to high impact. The example shows waiting and defects as high drivers of inefficiency along with transportation and motion. Use this simple diagnostic tool during gemba walks.

24 Chapter Two

Waste	
Defects	●(high)
Overproduction	●(low-mid)
Waiting	●(high)
Nonutilized skill/intellect	●(mid)
Transportation	●(mid-high)
Inventory	●(low)
Motion	●(mid-high)
Extra processing	●(low)

Low — Impact of waste on process flow — High

Figure 2.12 Preliminary waste diagnostic tool.

Figure 2.13 shows the logical progression that leads to solution development. The lean thinking process asks four basic questions:

1. Who is the customer?
2. How does the customer define value?
   - It is something the customer is willing to pay for.
   - It physically changes the product, good, or service.
   - It must be done correctly the first time (no rework).
3. If a step is determined to be NVA, what kind of waste is it?
   - DOWNTIME
4. Based on the type of waste, what is the best countermeasure to implement?
   - Refer to the DOWNTIME matrix for countermeasures.

The following are examples of process analyses from various Jefferson lean projects. Each of the pie charts shows distributions of VA and NVA activities. The NVA is broken down into the DOWNTIME wastes. This categorization enables lean teams to target improvement strategies. The process value analysis, a Microsoft Excel tool, produces this analysis (detailed tool review in Chapter 3).

Figure 2.14, the operating room (OR) turnover process, is over 80 percent NVA activities. The largest portion of waste is waiting (45 percent). Patients wait to be transported out of the OR while staff break down surgical equipment, wipe surfaces, and complete documentation. Transportation (movement of the patient) and motion (movement of the OR staff) make up the remaining 37 percent of NVA activities.

The surgical equipment sterilization process (Figure 2.15) shows a process that is predominantly VA (66 percent). A large portion of VA time is equipment sterilization. Again, waiting is the most prominent waste at 19 percent.

PRINCIPLE #1: DEFINE VALUE   25

Figure 2.13 Lean thinking process.

Patient flow is a common process evaluated through a lean thinking lens. In the oncology infusion center, patients were experiencing delays in receiving care due to several administrative steps and logistical barriers. Patients had a cumbersome check-in process that resulted in a significant amount of waiting (48 percent) (Figure 2.16). Employee workflow was suboptimal, leading to communication challenges, workarounds, and delays in receiving and disseminating information. As a result, two-thirds of the process was NVA through the eyes of the patients.

26 *Chapter Two*

Value analysis—DOWNTIME breakdown

- VA: 18%
- Waiting: 45%
- Transportation: 23%
- Motion: 14%

Legend: VA, NVA-R, Defects/rework, Overproduction, Waiting, Nonutilized skill, Transportation, Inventory, Motion, Extra processing

Figure 2.14 Operating room turnover (wheels out to wheels in) value analysis.

Value analysis—DOWNTIME breakdown

- VA: 66%
- Waiting: 19%
- Transportation: 3%
- Inventory: 4%
- Motion: 8%

Legend: VA, NVA-R, Defects/rework, Overproduction, Waiting, Nonutilized skill, Transportation, Inventory, Motion, Extra processing

Figure 2.15 Surgical equipment sterilization value analysis.

Value analysis—DOWNTIME breakdown

- VA: 37%
- Defects/rework: 5%
- Waiting: 48%
- Transportation: 6%
- Motion: 4%

Legend: VA, NVA-R, Defects/rework, Overproduction, Waiting, Nonutilized skill, Transportation, Inventory, Motion, Extra processing

Figure 2.16 Oncology infusion center patient flow value analysis.

Case Study: Clinical Lab Workflow

The clinical lab was experiencing delays in processing lab requests. A lean team helped the lab analyze workflows and facilitate an improvement effort to ensure optimal turnaround times of lab specimen results. Delays in results reporting can inhibit the clinical team's ability to make timely decisions regarding a patient's plan of care. Such delays impact quality indicators as well as operational capabilities. This lean project focused on improving the efficiency of lab processes from order entry to result reporting.

The lean team conducted several process value analysis time studies to evaluate the specimen flow from receipt within the clinical lab to the results. The lean leaders walked through the process from the perspective of the specimen and documented all related tasks and wastes (Figure 2.17). Employees from the lab described their responsibilities, discussed common barriers and issues, and offered suggestions for process improvement.

1. Specimens arrive via a tube system
2. Technician takes specimens and lab test orders out of the tube
3. Specimens and tests are time-stamped
4. Specimens are registered in information system
5. Technician distributes specimens for processing
6. Specimens are loaded onto processing rack
7. Technician loads specimens onto analyzer

Figure 2.17 Clinical lab workflow process.

Through observations and data collection, the lean leaders identified opportunities for improvement within the front end of the process. The pie chart (Figure 2.18) displays the proportion of NVA activity that leads to delays in timely resulting. The process consisted of only 25 percent VA activities but 75 percent NVA activities. Upon further evaluation, the team identified transportation as the main waste (49 percent).

Figure 2.18 Clinical lab receiving process for specimen throughput value analysis.

Workflow and layout issues resulted in unnecessary movement of the lab technician. The technician bounced from bench to bench like a pinball, without a sense of organization or flow. After following the lab technician through her work, the lean leaders calculated 74 percent of the technician's time as motion. Chapter 3 presents the workflow value analysis tool used for this analysis. The technician had to move throughout the receiving and processing area to move specimens from station to station. The lab processing area is very small; therefore, it was a lot of movement in a tight space, which created a sense of chaos. Figure 2.19 shows the results of the analysis.

Figure 2.19 Workflow value analysis for a lab technician.

In order to effect change, the lean team conducted a rapid improvement event with process experts within the lab. The lean leaders shared their analysis and observations with the improvement team. It was clear that the layout needed to be improved to promote efficiency. Bench assignments, where other technicians processed the specimens and prepared them for analysis, were organized in a single-piece flow to establish smoother production. The specimens could move down the line without requiring an individual to transport them by foot. A floater position helped handle add-ons, problem specimens, triage, specimen tracking, and processor loading. This new role enabled the process to run smoothly and address problems as they occurred.

Changes were developed through gemba walks and brainstorming activities. The improvement team reviewed proposed solutions with staff prior to piloting (Figure 2.20).

Improvement team participants (lab personnel) explain the new pilot process to their colleagues.

Lean leaders facilitate action plan development with the improvement team.

Figure 2.20 Rapid improvement event pictures of the clinical lab project.

As a result of the change, the lab saw meaningful improvements in turnaround times (Figure 2.21). The lab KPIs included overall tests as well as tests from the emergency department (ED). Every test has a defined goal for the turnaround time based on best practices. The percentage of time that STAT tests achieved their targeted turnaround time for all tests rose from a pre-intervention mean of 73 percent to a post-intervention mean of 82 percent (95 percent confidence interval of 79.76 percent–84.52 percent, standard deviation of 0.0413, $p = 0.008$). ED STAT processing improved from a pre-intervention mean of 76 percent to a post-intervention mean of 86 percent (95 percent confidence interval of 83.875 percent–87.985 percent, standard deviation of 0.0356, $p = 0.004$).

Figure 2.21 Results of the clinical lab project.

Remember, NVA activity is not to be mistaken for a value judgment of individuals or specific roles. Waste tends to be driven by the system and the design (or lack thereof) of processes. The lab technician in this example spent three-fourths of her time doing NVA activities as a result of the poor layout. The technician worked tirelessly to keep the process running despite the inefficient layout. Lean thinking helps objectively identify the wastes and systematically pilot and sustain appropriate countermeasures.

⚠ CHAPTER CHALLENGE

Identify a problem you can investigate by going to the place of action (gemba). Perform a waste walk and document examples of each DOWNTIME waste. Conduct informal staff interviews to learn about their barriers and concerns.

QUESTIONS

1. What happens when the scope is too broad or too narrow?
2. What is the significance behind the statement "Don't boil the ocean"?
3. What is the difference between internal and external customers? Why does the differentiation matter?
4. Why are some NVA activities unavoidable? How do you address them?
5. What is the impact of a process step not performed correctly the first time?
6. What are examples of VA, NVA, and NVA-R activities in your work area?
7. What waste is the most prevalent in your own workflow?
8. What percentage of your time (daily or weekly) is spent on activities that do not add value and/or are not aligned to departmental/organizational goals and priorities? What would it take to free more time up for the things that matter?

Chapter 3
Principle #2: Value Stream Mapping

The best way to predict your future is to create it.

– Thomas Jefferson

The previous chapter stressed the importance of asking "Who are our customers?" in order to define value. In addition, the eight DOWNTIME wastes provide the basis for categorizing all NVA activity. This chapter guides further process analysis utilizing a core lean tool known as the value stream map (Figure 3.1). To improve, we must first understand where we are (current

Figure 3.1 Roadmap: Map the value stream.

state) and then determine where we should be (future state). This becomes our path of incremental improvement.

MAP THE CURRENT STATE

The current state is how the work actually happens, not how it should or could be done (Jimmerson 2010). The current process baseline provides the foundation for improvement. The future state, defined as what could or should be done, becomes the goal. Lean thinking promotes working backward from the future state (Bicheno and Holweg 2004). There are many forms of process maps (Figure 3.2). An important consideration is the level of detail to document. Process maps can be segmented and refined, showing layers of detail.

The starting point, as described in "Determine Scope" in the previous chapter, is the high-level map. The high-level map documents the major steps (30,000-foot view of a process). The midlevel map includes more detailed steps in between the high-level steps (Figure 3.3). The most effective way to build a process map is to walk the process. Follow the flow of the patient, specimen, form, and so forth, from start to finish, and evaluate the work from the customer's eyes (Womack 2011).

Figure 3.2 Roadmap: Map the current state.

PRINCIPLE #2: MAP THE VALUE STREAM   35

High-level process map

Step A → Step D → Step G → Step J → Step L

Midlevel process map

Step A → Step b → Step c → Step D → Step e → Step f → Step G → Step h → Step i → Step J → Step k → Step L

Figure 3.3   High- and midlevel process maps.

The following is an example of process mapping using the physician's office visit from Chapter 2.

Example: Physician's Office

Step 1: Start by documenting all steps (it is OK to start granular here) (Figure 3.4 on page 36)

List of Process Steps

1. Enter the office
2. Sign in
3. Sit down in waiting area
4. Called back, walk into clinical space
5. Get vitals taken
6. Walk to exam room
7. Nurse interview
8. Wait for physician
9. Physician exam
10. Wait for prescription script
11. Receive script
12. Walk to checkout area
13. Check out

Step 2: Identify five to eight key high-level steps (30,000-foot view) (Figure 3.5)

Step 3: Fill in midlevel steps (Figure 3.6)

Step 4: Estimate/calculate processing times for each midlevel step (Figure 3.7)

Enter → Vitals → RN interview → Physician exam → Check out

Figure 3.5   High-level process steps for physician's office visit.

36 Chapter Three

Enter → Sign in → Wait → Called back → Vitals → Walk → RN interview → Wait → Physician exam → Wait → Rx → Walk → Check out

Figure 3.4 Process map of physician's office visit.

High-level process map

Enter → Vitals → RN interview → Physician exam → Check out

Midlevel process map

Enter → Sign in → Wait → Called back → Vitals → Walk → RN interview → Wait → Physician exam → Wait → Rx → Walk → Check out

Figure 3.6 High- and midlevel process steps for physician's office visit.

PRINCIPLE #2: MAP THE VALUE STREAM   **37**

High-level process map

Enter → Vitals → RN interview → Physician exam → Check out

Midlevel process map

Enter (1 minute) → Sign in (1 minute) → Wait (25 minutes) → Called back (1 minute) → Vitals (5 minutes) → Walk (1 minute) → RN interview (8 minutes) → Wait (28 minutes) → Physician exam (10 minutes) → Wait (20 minutes) → Rx (4 minutes) → Walk (1 minute) → Check out (5 minutes)

Figure 3.7 Cycle times for physician's office visit.

38　Chapter Three

A process can have a lot of complicated steps. The first-pass yield (FPY) estimates the percentage of time a process step is performed correctly the first time. Each subsequent step relies on the quality, validity, and reliability of the previous one. If a process step is not performed correctly, whether it takes someone 10 minutes or one hour, the end result is the same—rework. Rework often comes at a higher cost, too. As the saying goes, a dollar of prevention is worth $100 of intervention. Think about that saying: usually when a mistake occurs, it goes to the supervisor, who might have to take it to his or her boss. This could result in meetings/discussions held with other leaders, a work group could form, and so on. All this costs time, resources, and money, not to mention whatever consequence the error could have on the customer. This is why understanding FPY is so important. We want to design quality into the system, not just work faster.

Lean is about doing better with less, not just being faster and more efficient and producing more output. How do you become better? Fix quality-related issues. First, when evaluating the current state of a process, determine whether any underlying quality issues exist. There is no point in streamlining process steps without addressing quality issues first. Why? If you streamline a process that creates a lot of defects, you just made it faster to create more problems. Always look to improve the FPY before attempting anything else.

Figure 3.8 demonstrates the impact of addressing process quality. The current-state FPY for the four-step process is 67.92 percent. There are two main strategies: improve the process step quality or eliminate the step. Of the four steps within the process, step 2 is the clear issue. If you improve step 2 quality from 70 percent to 90 percent, the overall process FPY increases to 87.32 percent. However, if you eliminate step 2, the FPY jumps to 97.02 percent. This simple demonstration highlights the significant impact quality issues can have on a process.

Current state

Step 1 (99%) → Step 2 (70%) → Step 3 (99%) → Step 4 (99%)

First-pass yield = (0.99*0.7*0.99*0.99) = 67.92%

Improvement strategies

Improve the first-pass yield

Step 1 (99%) → Step 2 (90%) → Step 3 (99%) → Step 4 (99%)

First-pass yield = (0.99*0.9*0.99*0.99) = 87.32%

Eliminate the step

Step 1 (99%) → Step 3 (99%) → Step 4 (99%)

First-pass yield = (0.99*0.99*0.99) = 97.02%

Figure 3.8　First-pass yield.

> **First-pass yield (FPY):** *The percent of time a process is done correctly the first time. If data are not available, ask the people who do the work, the process experts, to estimate the FPY. Calculate the overall FPY by multiplying the FPY for every process step. The resulting number is the percent of time the process will work without an error occurring. The goal is to have every process step at or close to 100 percent.*

VALUE STREAM MAPS

A value stream map (VSM) is a process map that documents the sequence of steps from start to finish, using specific information like material, information, and workflow and associated processing and wait times (Jimmerson 2010; Tapping et al. 2009). Value flows horizontally (Womack 2011). VSMs are effective tools in breaking down silos by looking at processes from a customer-centric perspective (Graban 2012; Kenney 2011; Øvretveit 2005). Without an understanding of the stream of value, decisions and workflow are designed suboptimally, which inevitably leads to building workarounds.

> *In the clinical setting, the complexities and multidisciplinary approach amplify the importance of effective communication and coordination. This is why lean thinking is horizontal, not vertical. We need to ask these questions: How are we communicating key information across the value stream? What is our mechanism for feedback to ensure our internal and external customers' needs are being met?*

Healthcare processes are complex and multifaceted. Patient flow is impacted by many areas (ED admissions/volume, OR inpatient cases, intensive-care unit capacity/census, telemetry utilization/census, ability to discharge efficiently, off-unit diagnostics, transportation, etc.). We operate in vertical functional/department silos while work flows horizontally (Ballé and Régnier 2007; de Souza and Pidd 2011; Mazur, McCreery, and Rothenberg 2010). Care coordination across the entire continuum is a major issue in healthcare (Armstrong, Fox, and Chapman 2013; Neufeld et al. 2013). We are designed to function in silos, which affects the way decisions are made and what work gets done. As a result, the processes are fragmented. The lack of coordination and effectiveness is typically more obvious to customers of the process than to employees working within a silo.

Systems and processes with complex interrelationships between groups, departments, and so forth require a well-thought-out plan that targets incremental improvement over time. It is vital to narrow the focus to manageable bite-sized chunks. Clinical service lines attempt to use a matrix/hybrid infrastructure to manage "streams" of similar patients (i.e., by procedure, disease) from admissions through outpatient and home care (Kenney 2011). This is one strategy used to address horizontal flow.

The VSM serves as the primary tool for documenting the baseline (current state) from which to develop a roadmap to improvement (future state). Opportunities or gaps between current and future states mark the jumping-off point for improvement activities.

> **VSM Key Terms**
>
> - **Cycle time:** Time needed to complete a specific process step. *Example: Patient registered*
> - **Lead time:** Total process time from start to finish (order to completion). *Example: From patient arrival to discharge*
> - **Current state:** Process as it currently stands, what actually takes place, not what should
> - **Future state:** How the process could or should be
> - **First-pass yield:** Percent of time process step is performed correctly the first time
> - **Value-adding ratio:** Percent of VA time divided by lead time (total time)

The process of building a VSM is similar to that for the process maps shown earlier. The first four steps are the same. Using the same example, we will continue to build out the map (Figure 3.9). For the VSM, you can add the supplier/input and customer/output at the high level. This is the SIPOC, as reviewed in Chapter 2.

Process mapping steps:

1. Document all steps (it is OK to start granular)
2. Identify five to eight key high-level steps (30,000-foot view)
3. Fill in midlevel steps
4. Estimate/calculate processing times for each step. Include time spent waiting in between steps

Building a VSM

Many different approaches, tools, and pieces of information are used in value stream mapping. The following four steps provide simple, straightforward instructions rather than offering a confusing or complicated approach. Remember that the current-state VSM enables you to target potential areas for improvement through waste identification. Once you analyze and determine where the opportunities lie, you can then dive into the details of the tasks and inefficiencies. The next section within this chapter describes process analysis tools.

Steps for Building a VSM (continuing from steps 1–4 of process mapping)

5. Estimate/calculate FPY for each step and identify communication flow where applicable (Figure 3.10).

Figure 3.9 Value stream map for physician's office visit.

42 Chapter Three

Figure 3.10 First-pass yield for physician's office visit.

6. Evaluate VA versus NVA activity. Evaluate each midlevel step's contribution to customer value (Figure 3.11). Indicate which steps are VA, NVA, or NVA-R using their associated colors.

7. Identify opportunities for improvement based on FPY and NVA activities (Figure 3.12).

    – Look for sections of the VSM with consecutive NVA steps and target long-duration NVA steps. For example, the third midlevel step "wait" accounts for 25 minutes. The first section identified for improvement is the "sign in" to "vitals" component. The first four steps of the process total 28 minutes, of which only one minute is VA. The second opportunity identified is waiting from "RN interview" until "Rx." Within this section of the process, waiting accounts for 48 minutes of the total process.

8. Prioritize improvement opportunities and reduce/eliminate NVA activities.

    – In this example, two targeted areas for improvement narrow the focus within the 13-step midlevel physician's office visit. Given the large portion of NVA activity at the front end, it makes the most sense to begin problem-solving here. Waiting from "RN interview" until "Rx" is the subsequent opportunity. Front-end efficiencies will not necessarily help downstream flow.

> **VSM calculations**
> - **Cycle time:** Duration of process step (VA plus NVA activity)
> - **Wait time:** Duration between process steps
> - **Lead time:** Cycle times plus wait times (total time start to finish)
> - **Value-adding ratio:** (Value adding time)/(Lead time)
> - **First-pass yield:** Multiply every process step FPY

Focus on the future state once the current state VSM is constructed. The future-state map depicts what the process should or could be (Jimmerson 2010). It provides the path toward progress, how to get from the current state to the future state through continuous incremental improvement. Figure 3.13 details the process within the sterile processing department. Using the current state assessment, a lean team identified upstream and downstream opportunities. They prioritized the focus based on the longest time delays and the lowest FPY. Kaizen 1 and kaizen 2 indicate the prioritized improvement approach. Kaizen (pronounced ky-zen) is a Japanese word representing change for the good. In this example, kaizen 1 and kaizen 2 describe the focus of rapid improvements with lean facilitators and process experts. Figure 3.14 depicts the VSM made by the team before converting it to an electronic document.

44 Chapter Three

Figure 3.11 VA and NVA categorization for physician's office visit.

PRINCIPLE #2: MAP THE VALUE STREAM   45

Figure 3.12 Identified opportunities for improvement for physician's office visit.

Figure 3.13 Example of VSM with improvement (kaizen) prioritization.

Figure 3.14 Example of VSM created by improvement team.

> **Tips for VSM**
> - Walk the process
> - Talk with staff
> - Listen and observe
> - Write down all wastes that you see

The VSM is not always the appropriate tool to use. Some processes require a different approach for documentation and evaluation. Swimlane maps are useful for processes that contain a lot of handoffs and responsibilities across several roles and/or departments. Swimlane maps help identify work process problems that arise from handoffs, suboptimal sequencing of steps, or other inefficiencies (Joint Commission on the Accreditation of Healthcare Organizations 2006). The swimlane map depicts process flow by position (Figure 3.15).

Figure 3.15 Swimlane map template.

How to Construct a Swimlane Map

Using the physician's office visit process, we will review the steps in creating a swimlane map:

Step 1: Document the positions involved in the process (Figure 3.16)

Step 2: Document the patient/chart/specimen flow (Figure 3.17)

Step 3: Document the process steps by position (Figure 3.18)

The swimlane map shows the sequence of steps by position along the patient flow process. Every arrow that crosses a swimlane indicates a handoff. Handoffs pose potential risks for miscommunication, lack of standardization, and delays in queuing next steps (Jimmerson, Weber, and Sobek 2005). This mapping tool creates a strong visualization of the process and identifies each position's contribution to value (Figure 3.19).

For a more advanced application of the swimlane map, apply steps 5–8 from the VSM. By adding cycle and wait times and FPY, and by categorizing activities as VA or NVA, you can easily identify the opportunities for improvement.

> **Questions to Ask**
> - Are there steps/activities that do not add value?
> - Can steps run in parallel?
> - Are there redundant steps?
> - Are there hand-offs that can be eliminated?
> - Are steps appropriately allocated based on roles/responsibilities?
> - Is the workload evenly distributed?

PRINCIPLE #2: MAP THE VALUE STREAM   49

Figure 3.16 Swimlane map example with position.

Figure 3.17 Swimlane map example with patient flow process.

50 Chapter Three

Figure 3.18 Swimlane map example with process steps by position.

PRINCIPLE #2: MAP THE VALUE STREAM   51

Completed current state swimlane map before converting to an electronic document.

Electronic version of swimlane map for the OR turnover process.

Figure 3.19   Example of swimlane map created by improvement team.

COLLECT AND ANALYZE DATA FOR VSM

Once the VSM or other current state map has been drafted, the next step is to collect and analyze data (Figure 3.20). These tasks are gemba activities (Bicheno and Holweg 2004). The gemba is where the work takes place (Womack 2011). Going to the gemba ensures verification of observations. Evaluate the process through the eyes of the customer as well as the employee workflow (Graban 2012).

Dr. W. Edwards Deming popularized the phrase "In God we trust, all others bring data." Measuring the impact of a problem or the potential of a project can help create a real sense of urgency. This is especially important for projects that

52 Chapter Three

require resources such as people, money, and equipment. The executives/decision-makers look for hard data to quantify the return on investment since there are always many competing priorities for the same limited resources. When assessing the need for change, you need quantitative and qualitative information to provide adequate context. Data are important but not sufficient. Without understanding the impact on staff and customers, you cannot fully grasp the urgency of the situation.

The process value analysis tool assesses the activity of the product or patient (Lighter 2013). It is one of the most important and effective lean tools for streamlining processes. The tool output consists of pie and bar graphs that display the proportion of VA to NVA activity. This visual tool makes areas of opportunity for improvement obvious.

> *Taking five to ten cycle-time measurements will give you a good sense of the process effectiveness (not sufficient to infer statistical significance). Try to observe during different times of the day and days of the week to understand how the process and volume may vary.*

Figure 3.20 Roadmap: Collect and analyze data for VSM.

Conducting a Process Value Analysis

1. Go to the gemba with a stopwatch in hand.
2. Shadow a customer/patient, recording every step you observe from his or her perspective (include waiting times).
   - Identify high-level and midlevel process steps
   - Record waste observed and other general comments
   - Input observation times into the process value analysis tool in Microsoft Excel
3. Assess the results and identify opportunities for improvement. (Hint: Look for large portions of NVA activity.)

The process value analysis tool is a Microsoft Excel-based document (Figure 3.21). The following steps explain how to use the tool:

1. Write the high-level steps in column B.
   a. There should be five to eight high-level steps.
2. Add midlevel steps in column C.
   a. Repeat the high-level step as the first task in column C. For example, high-level step, row 7, column B "Enter" and midlevel step, row 8, column C "Enter."
   b. There should be no more than six midlevel steps. If you have more than that, it might be too granular and detailed for this analysis. Condense process step descriptions.
3. Add observation times for each midlevel step.
   a. Average observed cycle times. Typically five to ten observations will give you a good, general idea of the capability of the process. The more observations you have during different hours of operation, the more reflective the results will be to the actual current state.
   b. All rows in gray will auto-sum the results. Do not overwrite the formulas.
4. Determine whether midlevel steps are VA, NVA, or NVA-R.
   a. Indicate the category by placing a "1" in column E, F, or G.
   b. Do not place "1" in more than one column. If you do, the template will double count the time and skew the results.
5. If NVA, categorize the activity by type of waste.
   a. Indicate category by placing a "1" in column H through O.
   b. As above, do not place "1" in more than one column.

54 Chapter Three

6. Evaluate process value analysis output. The output of the table is three graphs.

   a. Value analysis: Pie chart that depicts proportion of VA, NVA, and NVA-R at a high level.

   b. Value analysis: DOWNTIME breakdown—pie chart segmenting NVA activities by specific DOWNTIME wastes. This chart enables you to effectively diagnose the major process issues.

   c. Process value analysis: bar graph showing proportion of VA, NVA, and NVA-R times per high-level process step. This output is one of the most important components of effective problem identification. The bar graph provides an assessment of opportunity per step and enables targeted lean improvements.

Figure 3.21 Process value analysis screenshot.

We can use the physician's office visit example to see how the tool works. List the high-level and midlevel process steps. Then add observed cycle times and categorize VA, NVA, and NVA-R with further refinement of DOWNTIME wastes for all NVA steps

The output of the physician's office visit shows 74 percent of the process as NVA (Figure 3.22). The DOWNTIME breakdown highlights waiting (66 percent) as the predominant waste. Extra processing is the second highest at 5 percent. The process value analysis bar graph shows the distribution of NVA across the patient's visit. Large portions of NVA activity sit atop the VA steps. This graph suggests the best opportunities for improvement lie within the first two steps, "Enter" and "Vitals," with subsequent opportunity between steps 3 and 4.

Figure 3.22 Process value analysis output example.

Case Study: Patient Flow in the Patient Testing Center

The patient testing center (PTC) is responsible for pre-surgical history and physicals, screening, and other tasks. Figure 3.23 shows 56 percent of the process is NVA. The NVA is broken into the eight DOWNTIME wastes, of which waiting accounts for 39 percent. Similarly, the bar graph shows the distribution of VA and NVA steps. There is a significant opportunity for improvement within the first three steps since no VA activities take place until step 4 (clinician 1 assessment). This would be the first area of focus for waste elimination.

Figure 3.23 Process value analysis output for PTC patient flow.

Workflow Value Analysis

In addition to process value analysis, another way to evaluate processes is through assessing employee workflow. Workflow inefficiencies lead to NVA activities and customer dissatisfaction. A tool called the workflow value analysis evaluates employee workflow.

Conducting a Workflow Value Analysis

1. Go to the gemba with a stopwatch in hand.
2. Shadow the employee, recording every step you observe (include waiting).
   – Record observed wastes and make notes for other general comments
   – Input observation times into the workflow value analysis tool in Microsoft Excel (Figure 3.24)
3. Assess the results and identify opportunities for improvement. (Hint: Look for large portions of NVA activity.)

PRINCIPLE #2: MAP THE VALUE STREAM   57

Figure 3.24 Workflow value analysis screenshot.

The workflow value analysis tool is a Microsoft Excel–based document. The following steps explain how to use the tool:

1. Write all observed tasks in column C.

   a. When observing employee workflow, it is important to document all tasks, including walking and waiting.

2. Add observation times for each task.

3. Determine whether midlevel steps are VA, NVA, or NVA-R.

   a. Indicate a category by placing a "1" in column E, F, or G.

   b. Do not place "1" in more than one column.

4. If NVA, categorize the activity by type of waste.

   a. Indicate the category by placing a "1" in column H through O.

   b. As above, do not place "1" in more than one column.

5. Evaluate workflow value analysis output. The output of the table is two pie charts.

   a. Workflow value analysis: pie chart that depicts proportion of VA, NVA, and NVA-R at a high level.

   b. Workflow: DOWNTIME breakdown—pie chart segmenting NVA activities by specific wastes. This chart enables you to effectively diagnose the major process issues.

Figure 3.25 displays 64 percent of the employee's time as NVA activity. The DOWNTIME waste breakdown indicates waiting (25 percent), motion (18 percent), and defects (12 percent) as the primary contributors of NVA. In the subsequent chapters, we will uncover strategies to address these results.

Figure 3.25 Workflow value analysis output example.

> **Hints for Identifying Opportunities**
>
> *Remember to always address quality issues first! Fix the FPY in order to design quality into the process. If process steps are not performed correctly the first time, the downstream result is rework, extra processing, delays, increased resources/costs, and frustrated staff and customers.*

PUTTING THE PIECES TOGETHER

Once you reach this point, it is time to put all of the pieces together. The diagnostic tools, from VSM to process analysis, tell a story about the process under review. Each tool helps assess and isolate areas of opportunity. This process evaluation phase enables you to pinpoint the main barriers and challenges leading to quality and operational issues. The following chapters will explore strategies and tools for developing and implementing high-impact solutions.

Case Study: OR/SPCC VSM Event

As part of the perioperative department's strategic plan, a team of lean leaders was assigned to analyze and improve the sterile processing and case cart (SPCC) workflow process (Delisle 2013). Through data analysis and voice of the customer, it was determined that surgical equipment was not turning over efficiently, causing delays throughout the system. The lean leaders facilitated a value stream mapping event. The event focused on identifying and prioritizing key improvement initiatives within the value stream. Delays in SPCC cause bottlenecks and workflow inefficiencies and negatively impact both patient and staff satisfaction (Farrokhi et al. 2013).

The objective of the value stream mapping event was to identify the first and subsequent improvement areas of focus. The SIPOC starts with the operating room (OR) sending the dirty equipment to sterile processing (SP) (Figure 3.26). The last step is the subsequent OR case starting with sterile surgical equipment.

Figure 3.26 Sterile processing SIPOC.

The lean team worked with process experts to conduct observations and document midlevel steps. The VSM includes wait times between processing steps (Figure 3.27).

The process value analysis indicated that 73 percent of the process was NVA (Figure 3.28). The DOWNTIME waste breakdown revealed that waiting (59 percent) was the largest component, while extra processing was the second largest (10 percent). The bar graph shows the distribution of VA and NVA activities. Waiting was pervasive due to missing items and poor communication between the SP department and the OR. The majority of issues began upstream and caused subsequent bottlenecks and inefficiencies. As a result, the lean team recommended that the first improvement project scope address the time from when the OR case is completed to the time the equipment is cleaned. The objective of this initial effort was to ensure that all the surgical equipment was sent down on the appropriate trays, sorted correctly, and cleaned in a timely manner. Following the standard guidelines would limit the likelihood of missing equipment and delays caused by waiting on parts or rework.

60 Chapter Three

Figure 3.27 Sterile processing VSM.

Figure 3.28 Sterile processing process value analysis output.

⚠ CHAPTER CHALLENGE

Identify a process that has quality-related issues. Go to the gemba and talk with staff. Discuss the problem/issue and ask what percentage of time the process step is done correctly the first time. What is the reaction you got? Was it expected? Why or why not?

QUESTIONS

1. Why is it easier to start by documenting all the steps first when building a process map?
2. What is the difference between high-level and midlevel steps? What is the purpose of drilling down to lower-level steps?

3. How can the FPY affect a process?
4. What are the best strategies to improve the FPY?
5. How do VSMs differ from process maps?
6. Why do you need to prioritize improvement opportunities on the VSM?
7. What information does a swimlane map provide? When is it most effective to use?
8. Why do the process analyses tools need to be performed at the gemba? What information do these tools produce?
9. Why is the process value analysis considered one of the most effective lean diagnostic tools?
10. What are the main considerations for conducting the workflow value analysis?

Chapter 4
Establishing the Lean Fundamentals

Nothing worth doing stays done forever without diligence, discipline, and hard work.

– David Mann

The lean fundamentals are central to creating lean processes (Figure 4.1). Lean improvements do not just happen; they require ready and willing individuals as well as an efficient and organized work setting. The lean fundamentals focus on the preparation and facilitation of efficient processes.

Figure 4.1 Roadmap: Establish lean fundamentals.

The fundamentals serve as the starting block for lean improvements. If the fundamentals are not in place, a process will not achieve optimal results. Each fundamental is effective on its own, but when combined, they serve as a powerful tool set (Table 4.1).

Table 4.1 Lean fundamentals.

Fundamental	Description
5S	Prepare the workplace to enable improvements to be effective and implemented efficiently
Layout	Arrange the physical space to enable flow and provide improved communication and quality
Visual management	Provide an immediate understanding of a situation or condition

5S[1]

5S was first introduced in the late 1980s and early 1990s (Nakajima 1988; Takahashi and Osada 1990). The 5S framework (Table 4.2) supplies a logical, user-friendly approach toward the assessment, design, and implementation of improvements to systems and processes, as well as developing standardized tasks to improve quality and patient safety (Graban 2012). Traditionally, 5S organizes physical space and items (i.e., workspace, desk, charts, department) (Tapping et al. 2009). The 5S approach eliminates waste, provides visual control, and prepares the workplace to enable improvements to be effective and implemented efficiently. 5S does this in distinct phases: (1) sort; (2) store; (3) shine; (4) standardize; and (5) sustain (Graban 2012). This framework is not unfamiliar. Professional organizers take the same steps to help people de-clutter their homes (e.g., TV shows *Hoarders* and *Hoarding: Buried Alive*). As stated in the law of entropy, over time organized systems move toward increasing states of disorganization (Mann 2010). Hard work, discipline, and structure are required to fight against this natural tendency (Zidel 2012).

The potential of 5S remains largely untapped due to its narrow application typically only on physical space and organization. 5S has tremendous opportunity to also enhance system/process design and improvement. Figure 4.2 illustrates a hypothetical example of applying 5S to a process. The first row is a current state process map. The current state is a display of how the process actually functions prior to any improvements, with an overall processing time of 95 minutes. The first task in 5S is to sort and evaluate items/steps based on need. Though seemingly simple, this is profound. Most processes have NVA steps that delay throughput and consume resources. During the sort phase (rows 2 and 3), steps 2 and 6 were determined to be NVA and removed from the process.

---

[1] Content from "Everything Is 5S: A Simple Yet Powerful Lean Improvement Approach Applied in a Preadmission Testing Center" (Delisle and Freiberg 2014).

Table 4.2 5S approach for organizing physical space and systems/processes.

Phase	Description for organizing physical space	Description for organizing systems/processes
Sort	Sort the necessary from the unnecessary. Remove items and supplies that do not belong in that area.	Sort the necessary steps/components from the unnecessary. Remove activities that do not add value.
Store	Store the needed items in the appropriate location based on frequency of use, keeping the things used most often in easily accessible areas.	Store the necessary steps/components in the appropriate order based on sequence and timing.
Shine	Shine the space. Keeping areas clean and clear of clutter enables easy location of items and aids in the identification of missing or misplaced things.	Shine or streamline the step. Refine processes (e.g., cycle times) to further reduce the impact of NVA activities.
Standardize	Standardize the organizing approach to all applicable areas. Label drawers and shelves with the same nomenclature. Stock storage areas the same way. Consistent, standard approaches reduce wasted time searching.	Standardize the system/process to all applicable areas (e.g., standard operating procedures) to ensure every step is done the same way, every time, by everyone.
Sustain	Sustain the improvement through discipline and follow-up. Monitor storage to assure everything is in its proper place.	Sustain the improvement through discipline and follow-up. Monitor key performance indicators to track outcomes and employ audits to ensure compliance.

Process sequence evaluation occurs during the store phase (row 4). Step 4 shifts ahead of step 3 in an effort to increase efficiency and productivity. Row 5, streamlining steps 3, 4, and 5, shaves off additional processing time. The overall time is now 57 minutes. Standard work for steps 4, 5, and 7 ensures consistent productivity (row 6). The new process will undergo sustainability measures to maintain processing times around 48 minutes. Core to sustainability is hardwiring a performance assessment and feedback loop to staff. Effective approaches include regularly posting process outcomes on run charts, daily huddles to discuss barriers and issues, and periodic brainstorming sessions to determine further refinements. Row 7 demonstrates sustainability of results achieved through rows 1–6.

> *Sorting is critical in just about everything you do. In process improvement or life in general, the ability to sort the necessary from the unnecessary is an essential skill.*

Figure 4.2 Example of process 5S.
Source: Delisle and Freiberg 2014.

5S Audit Tool

To assess the physical organization of a workspace, you can apply the Excel-based 5S audit tool (Figure 4.3). The tool enables workspace evaluation through each "S" based on defined questions. For each item that applies, enter "1" to indicate "Yes." The radar map provides an output that highlights the strengths and opportunities within an area. The tool is an objective assessment of the work area.

After improving an area, the post-5S audit illustrates progress in each of the five components, a representation of which is shown in Figure 4.4. The radar chart indicates if the work area aligns to promote efficiency.

	Area: _____ Date: _____	
	Criteria	**1 if "yes"**
Sort	Is the floor/workspace clutter-free?	0
	Are unnecessary equipment and supplies removed?	0
	Are items stored in appropriate locations?	0
	Is there an appropriate amount of equipment and supplies as needed?	0
Store	Do all equipment, supplies, and personnel have a dedicated location?	0
	Do storage areas and floor indicate where to or not to place things?	0
	Are workstations organized?	0
	Are there designated storage areas for temporary items?	0
Shine	Is the work environment conducive to productivity (well lit, clean)?	0
	Are the floors clean?	0
	Is equipment clean and well maintained?	0
	Are workstations free of clutter?	0
Standardize	Are staff trained on the 5S approach?	0
	Is visual management appropriately used?	0
	Are workstations set up similarly?	0
	Are issues/problems made readily apparent?	0
Sustain	Are checklists used to detail tasks and expectations?	0
	Is the area periodically audited for 5S elements?	0
	Are visual cues or pictures used to highlight expectations?	0
	Are staff maintaining progress and identifying other areas for 5S?	0

Pre-5S audit

Figure 4.3 5S audit tool for physical space and layout assessment.

> *The power of 5S exceeds application in the workspace. 5S can be applied to your personal life and home, as well as your emails!*

Pre/post-5S audits

Figure 4.4 5S audit tool for physical space and layout assessment.

5S Applied to Emails and Electronic Information

The balance with storing things electronically is the ability to do so in an organized way. The challenge with physical space is that it is limited. There is only so much room for "stuff." In the electronic environment, storage is almost limitless. Space is not the issue. The issue becomes finding what you have saved. This is the reason why 5S is a fundamental of lean. Without an effective and sustainable 5S approach to process design and physical space, you will perpetuate waste (especially motion, nonutilized skill, transportation, and inventory).

Electronic storage, especially for emails, can make you more productive. Use folders to sort and store emails accordingly. It becomes very easy to sustain once you get through the initial phases. Try using an email triaging system (folder categories below) with a goal of having an inbox with zero emails. Take the approach that if you open it, do something with it: respond, file, or delete.

1. *To read:* Any interesting email/attachment/article that is not time sensitive

2. *Needs response:* Any email that requires a response from you

3. *To do:* Anything that requires you to do something/follow up on an action/request

4. *Awaiting response:* A personal favorite, emails from you to other people go directly into this folder when asking someone to do something (i.e., project follow-up, response). By the end of the week, you can review this folder and see what is still outstanding. When the appropriate time passes, forward that email back to the person as a friendly reminder. This is highly effective and makes your life easier, so you do not have to try and remember who owes you what, by when.

Searching for information is a major issue that pervades most areas. Remember with the lean fundamentals, the goal is to organize things in a way that promotes efficiency and quality. This is not limited to the physical organization of "stuff." It includes the virtual/electronic organization of documentation, files, etc., as well as the design/redesign of systems and processes. The most valuable step in 5S is the first one, sort. Remove the necessary from the unnecessary; declutter. Sorting, like in the email example, is an ongoing process that does not end. Sorting closely links to standardization and sustainability.

LAYOUT

Layout, the second lean fundamental, focuses on work area design. The goal of layout is to enable flow of the things processed (e.g., patient, specimen) (Liker 2004). Efficient layouts make it easier to accomplish work by reducing the wastes of motion, transportation, and waiting. Figure 4.5 depicts a process in which the layout redesign reduces the amount of required travel from one step to the next. Additionally, due to the improved layout, there is more free space in the "after" scenario. Layout is an intuitive improvement solution.

Figure 4.5 Layout example.

Assessing Layout with the Spaghetti Diagram

The best way to assess layout is to create a visual representation of the actual flow. The spaghetti diagram illustrates the wastes of transportation (item) and motion (worker). The tool is simple to use.

STEP 1: Draw a scaled diagram of the layout (Figure 4.6).

STEP 2: Mark processing areas and indicate who does which tasks at each location (Figure 4.7).

STEP 3: Walk the process. Use different colors for different parts/staff if applicable or necessary (Figure 4.8).

STEP 4: Document travel time/distance. Do a before and after to assess improvement (Figure 4.9).

The before and after layouts depict improvements in workflow and reductions in motion and transportation (Figure 4.10). The new layout releases previously used floor space for other purposes.

70 *Chapter Four*

Figure 4.6 Example of current state layout.

Figure 4.7 Example of current state layout with labeled processing areas.

Figure 4.8 Example of spaghetti diagram of current state.

Figure 4.9 Example of spaghetti diagram of improved state.

Figure 4.10 Comparison of spaghetti diagrams before and after improvement.

There are several ways in which layout can improve flow. Figures 4.11–4.13 compare traditional configurations with improved layouts. Figure 4.11 shows how to achieve workload balancing by sharing the workspace and increasing access to each employee rather than working in isolated silos. Similarly, Figure 4.12 depicts employees working independently versus collaboratively. Finally, Figure 4.13 compares straight-line flow with the U-shaped orientation. U-shaped orientations allow employees to evenly distribute workflow and reallocate effort to ensure flow.

Configuration 1: Bad layout—employees are working in isolation and cannot share work between them.

Configuration 2: Improved layout—employees can share workload.

Figure 4.11 Layout improvement 1 of 3.
Source: Adapted from Jacobs and Chase, 2008.

Configuration 1: Bad layout—employees are working in isolation.

Material flow

Configuration 2: Improved layout—employees can help each other.

Material flow

Figure 4.12   Layout improvement 2 of 3.
Source: Adapted from Jacobs and Chase, 2008.

VISUAL MANAGEMENT

Visual management, the final component of the lean fundamentals, is a set of strategies that creates a productive work environment that reduces the likelihood of errors and delays in information (Bicheno and Holweg 2004). Visual management focuses on the ability to communicate important information to anyone without requiring a verbal exchange between two parties. In areas with strong visual management you should be able to scan the workspace in a brief amount of time and understand the current state, including issues to address.

Visual management aims to provide an immediate understanding of a situation or condition and make waste, problems, and abnormal conditions readily apparent (Graban 2012). There are many benefits, including to:

- Reduce confusion in completing a task
- Reduce opportunities for error and defects
- Assist in adhering to a process standard
- Improve productivity
- Improve staff/customer satisfaction

Configuration 1: Bad layout—employees are working in a straight line, which makes it difficult to balance the workload.

Configuration 2: Improved layout—employees are organized in a U shape, which enables them to share work and enhances flow.

Figure 4.13 Layout improvement 3 of 3.
Source: Adapted from Jacobs and Chase, 2008.

In order to create effective visual management cues, complete the following (Breakthrough Management Group International n.d.):

1. Define information that needs to be available
2. Select the appropriate mechanism to communicate the information (e.g., picture, checklist, sound)
3. Determine the prompt that creates a "call to action"
4. Create the visual signal that produces the "call to action" alert

Be cautious of overutilization of visual cues. For example, alerts are a form of visual management used to communicate information without requiring a verbal exchange between individuals. The alert might mean something is wrong, a warning, or approval for something is needed. Too many alerts creates alert fatigue, and people start ignoring them. This also happens with posters, flyers, signs, or other mechanisms. Too many visual cues leads to "noise" that ultimately blends into the work setting.

In workspaces without visual management, staff members tend to ask a lot of questions. Some of the questions repeated throughout the course of the workday suggest required information is consistently unavailable. Examples of such questions include the following (Graban 2012):

- Does the patient have any more tests or can he or she go home?
- Have these medications been double-checked?
- Which patient should be brought back next?
- Who is the physician for this patient?
- Is this room available?

The Clinical Lab utilized visual management to communicate the status of lab specimens (Figure 4.14). Tubes placed in the red section are STAT or urgent, tubes in the green section are normal/no rush, and tubes in the yellow row require more information before processing. This simple approach taken by the lab enables the employees to prioritize work as it arrives and reduces the need to look up every tube specimen to determine its status as either STAT, normal, or requires additional information.

Figure 4.14 Example of visual management in the Clinical Lab.

Case Study: Patient Flow in the Patient Testing Center

Content from *"Everything Is 5S: A Simple Yet Powerful Lean Improvement Approach Applied in a Preadmission Testing Center"* (Delisle and Freiberg 2014)

The application of 5S for process improvement was tested as a case study. A team of lean leaders was assigned a project to analyze and improve the pre-admission testing (PAT) processes. PAT is a vital part in perioperative flow, responsible for screening scheduled patients prior to surgery. Patient evaluation includes registration, chart preparation, evaluation by a nurse practitioner and anesthesiologist, blood draws, electrocardiogram, and an occasional chest x-ray.

Delays in PAT patient processing cause bottlenecks and workflow inefficiencies. Streamlining patient throughput enables the PAT to effectively manage variation in its daily schedule while delivering efficient, patient-focused service. The wide degree of variation in patient flow was erratic, resulting in long delays for both patients and providers (i.e., nurse practitioners, anesthesiologists). The project objective was to improve the overall mean length of stay (LOS) by 39 minutes (from 141 minutes to 102 minutes).

On average, the PAT services nearly 60 patients every day from 7:00 a.m. to 4:00 p.m. The scope of the initiative was from patient arrival at PAT until checkout. The study design was a pre-/post-intervention assessment utilizing the 5S framework. The primary outcome measure was patient LOS.

Implementing 5S

Sort: Sort the necessary step components from the unnecessary. Remove those things that do not add value.

The lean team conducted several voice of customer (VOC) interviews from representatives of all roles (technicians, registrars, administration, nurse practitioners, anesthesiologists, etc.). Salient issues that came out of the VOC interviews included: (1) lack of patient and staff flow coordination; (2) insufficient cross-training; (3) duplication of effort; (4) scheduling—both how it is done and patient compliance to arriving at set time; and (5) low staff morale.

Next, the team analyzed the process utilizing multiple lean tools including the SIPOC. The process begins when a patient arrives at the PAT and ends when he or she leaves the department. The patient checks in at the front desk and then sits in a waiting room. The registration clerk calls for the patient, registers him or her, and then the patient returns back to the waiting room. When an exam room is available, an employee escorts the patient to the clinical area, and the patient waits for an available nurse practitioner (NP) to conduct the history and physical. Then, the patient waits for the anesthesiologist interview, laboratory technician blood draw, and EKG. Upon completion of testing, the patient awaits discharge. In the process map, clinician 1–4 indicates interactions with EKG/lab technicians, NPs, and anesthesiologists (which happen in no particular order).

A second tool used to evaluate the process in more detail is the current state swimlane map (Figure 4.15). Through swimlane map analysis, the team identified several steps that occurred prior to the patient seeing the first clinician. Data were gathered through time study observations, in addition to collection from the information system. Each process step was evaluated and categorized as VA or NVA. After review, the PAT patient flow process VA ratio (the total VA time divided by total time) was 36 percent. This means nearly two-thirds of the process was NVA time for the patient.

76 Chapter Four

Registrar reception	Greet patient	Sign in	Direct patient to waiting area	Make consent form	Notify reg. staff	Sign patient reg. start time
Registrar				Pick up paperwork	Registration	Walk patient to waiting area 2
PAT clerk						
Patient flow coord.						
EKG						
NP						
Anesth.						
PAT care coord.						
Phleb.						
Patient	Check in	Sit in waiting area		Registration	Sit in waiting area 2	
Chart				Labels, blue plate print		

Figure 4.15 PTC current state swimlane map.

To evaluate the distribution of NVA time, the team used the process value analysis. The result of the tool is a bar graph depicting the distribution of VA to NVA per step (Figure 4.16). The opportunity clearly lies within the first three process steps, as they are purely NVA activities (waiting accounted for nearly 50 percent of all NVA).

Data analysis shows patient volume peaking before 11:00 a.m., which leads to bottlenecks between noon and 2:00 p.m. Nearly 50 percent of all patients arrive by 10:00 a.m. (first three hours of the day). Initial delays lead to subsequent bottlenecks. Additional factors reducing PAT efficiency include poor visual management throughout the clinical area. The lack of visual information reduces the ability of staff and the PAT flow coordinator to appropriately assess the current situation and allocate resources as needed.

Store: Store the necessary steps/components in the appropriate order based on sequence and timing.

The intervention component (store/shine/standardize) of the project was a team-based, three-day rapid improvement event (RIE). The RIE focused on identifying critical issues and barriers and then developing and piloting high-impact solutions. The team reconstructed the current state swimlane map and identified opportunities to streamline duplicative efforts and remove NVA activities. Issues were prioritized based on impact on the primary metric of LOS. Solutions were prioritized based on impact with the aim to identify those actions that produce the highest payoff with relatively low degree of effort.

Figure 4.15 PTC current state swimlane map. *(Continued)*

Figure 4.16 PTC current state process value analysis.

The process was redesigned (store) using the swimlane mapping approach. The team conducted several observations of the process prior to redesigning the flow. Based on the prioritized issues and solutions, the team determined that there were opportunities to run tasks in parallel and eliminate NVA activities. As a result, the newly designed process was simulated with "mock" patients (members of the team) to assess efficacy and effectiveness.

Shine: Shine or streamline the step. Refine processes (for example, cycle times) to further reduce the impact of non-value-adding activities.

Evaluation of mock patients led to refinement of the new changes. The end process contains a reduced number of steps, bringing the patient back upon arrival, and better utilizing staff by cross-training and multitasking. Table 4.3 compares pre-/post-intervention processes.

Table 4.3 Pre-/post-intervention process.

Pre-intervention	Post-intervention
Patients would check in, wait in registration area, get registered, wait in PAT waiting area, and then get called to exam room.	Patient checks in, then PAT clerk escorts patient directly to exam room. This improvement eliminates two waiting rooms and brings the service to the patient, not the other way around.
Registration was completed "out front" right after check-in.	Registration takes place in the exam room. This change puts the patient in process immediately rather than waiting 10–20 minutes prior to entering the exam room. This reduces the waste of transportation as well as motion for staff.
NP only did patient history and physical, then patient waited for EKG tech and/or lab tech.	NPs do workup (including EKGs and labs). This change enables better flow of work, as patients are no longer waiting for techs to do EKG and/or lab. In addition, this better utilizes the NPs.
No visualization of PAT room/patient status.	Added whiteboard for status indicator of patient progress and staffing for PAT flow coordinator. This improvement idea alleviates the lack of visual management throughout the area. The PAT flow coordinator is better equipped to manage and coordinate resources throughout the day.
Patient checks out at front desk after examination.	Patient discharged in exam room. This further reduces waiting. In order to cue the work of staff, "registration" and "discharge" tags were added to exam room doors.

Standardize: Standardize the system/process to all applicable areas (for example, standard operating procedures) to ensure every step is done the same way, every time, by everyone.

After the RIE, final process changes were documented, along with a new swimlane map depicting new responsibilities (Figure 4.17). All employees were educated on the new process, and weekly follow-up meetings are held to evaluate progress, troubleshoot issues, and further refine improvements.

Figure 4.17 Redesigned process swimlane map.

Sustain: Sustain the improvement through discipline and follow-up. Monitor key performance indicators to track outcomes and employ audits to ensure compliance.

In order to assure sustainability, LOS data continue to be monitored and the PAT process will undergo re-evaluation and iterative improvements every few months.

Results

Reducing or eliminating steps that do not add value lessens the time patients spend in the process. Figure 4.18 depicts the weekly length of stay pre-/post-intervention. During the pre-intervention time period, the PAT achieved its daily target of a 90-minute average LOS 4.29 percent of the time. Post-intervention, the target was exceeded 35 percent of the time, marking a 715.9 percent improvement (p < 0.000).

Figure 4.18 Length of stay results.

LOS by hour shows a dramatic reduction at every time interval (Figure 4.19). The new process design reduces overall process variation (pre-intervention range of 36.5 minutes, standard deviation of 10.23; post-intervention range of 17.02 minutes, standard deviation of 4.7). A correlation analysis of volume to LOS confirms this assertion. The pre-intervention Pearson correlation of LOS and volume was 0.474 (p = 0.000), indicating a moderately positive relationship. Post-intervention, however, yields a Pearson correlation of 0.085 (p = 0.604). There is no statistically significant correlation of volume to LOS since the process is stable. Throughout the course of the day, changes in volume do not have the same impact on LOS midday in the post-intervention data. Since PAT can process patients more efficiently, the bottlenecks are limited.

Delays in PAT patient processing led to compounding workflow interruptions, creating inefficiencies and negatively impacting patient satisfaction. Through the use of lean thinking and the 5S framework, the team of lean leaders and PAT staff streamlined patient throughput (Figure 4.20). The result was the ability for PAT to effectively manage arrival and volume variation in its daily schedule.

Crucial to successful implementation of the 5S framework was the inclusion of process experts from PAT. The multidisciplinary team led the store phase of the project (solution development and subsequent pilots). Their active involvement enabled the entire team to garner support from PAT staff not directly participating in the RIE. Staff buy-in is an essential element to success. Consistent two-way communication by the lean team and PAT leadership before, during, and after the intervention increased employee engagement through solicitation of ideas and discussions regarding challenges.

The improvement ideas developed over the three-day effort were not earth-shattering innovations. The application of lean thinking in process assessment and use of 5S as a framework for improvement generally lead to straightforward solutions. Despite the relative simplicity of countermeasures, their impact is significant.

ESTABLISHING THE LEAN FUNDAMENTALS   81

Figure 4.19   Length of stay results by hour.

Example of visual clues implemented to notify physicians of exam room/patient status.

Figure 4.20   PTC visual management example.

Source: Modified from "Everything Is 5S: A Simple Yet Powerful Lean Improvement Approach Applied in a Preadmission Testing Center" (Delisle and Freiberg 2014).

82 Chapter Four

By following a systematic lean approach and applying it to healthcare processes, improvement teams can realize dramatic results in a relatively short period of time (Figure 4.21). The lean fundamentals serve as the foundation for improvement. The DOWNTIME waste matrix provides the corresponding countermeasures for the specific wastes. For many of the wastes, 5S, layout, and visual management are ways to remediate or eliminate them.

Value analysis

- VA
- NVA (74%)
- NVA-R (1%)

Large portion of NVA but not specific enough to act on

Value analysis—DOWNTIME breakdown

- VA (25%)
- NVA-R (1%)
- Defects/rework
- Overproduction
- Waiting (66%)
- Nonutilized skill
- Transportation (3%)
- Inventory (5%)
- Motion
- Extra processing

66% of waste is waiting—how should we address this?

Waste	Definition	Examples	Potential causes	Questions to ask	Countermeasures
Waiting	Delays, waiting for anything (people, paper, equipment, or information)	• Delays in bed assignments • Delays in receiving information or communication • Waiting for next process steps to begin	• Poor understanding of time required to complete a task • No visual cues to indicate next step in the process • Delays compounding one another	• Are there bottlenecks/delays in the process due to obtaining information, supplies, etc.? • Are there clear expectations for how long process steps should take?	• VSM • Swimlane map • 5S • Workload balancing • Cross-train staff

Figure 4.21 Process from value analysis to solution development.

CHAPTER CHALLENGE

Identify a process or physical area in which to apply the lean fundamentals. Work with staff through the 5S framework. What were the main barriers or reasons for the disorganization? What were the main improvements made? Is the change sustainable? Why or why not?

BONUS CHALLENGE:

5S your work email using the triage process provided.

QUESTIONS

1. Why are 5S, layout, and visual management considered fundamental?
2. Why is "Everything 5S"? What are examples of areas/processes where you can apply the 5S approach?
3. What is the potential impact of unorganized electronic information (e.g., email, computer hard drive)?
4. How does layout contribute to process flow?
5. What happens in an area with limited or no visual management?
6. What are common questions you hear or ask in your area on a daily basis? Would visual management address these questions?
7. What visual management tools exist in your work setting?

Chapter 5
Principle #3: Flow

There is no right way to do the wrong thing.

– Ken Blanchard

The third principle of lean is establishing flow (Figure 5.1). The goal is to reduce disruption of VA activity by identifying and eliminating waste and sources of unevenness. The three components of flow provide a stable, predictable process: (1) determine customer demand, (2) balance the process, and (3) standardize the work. Flow is a critical lean management approach, highlighting

Figure 5.1 Roadmap: Establish flow.

the significance of doing things correctly the first time. This concept is something most managers do not recognize or promote (Womack 2011). Unevenness and overburdening of processes create excessive waste throughout the system. Variation in processing times, customer demand, and work responsibilities leads to an unstable process filled with NVA activity.

Continuous flow results in more VA than NVA activity (Liker 2004). In continuous flow, the people, products, and information move along the process with limited waiting and interruptions. The concept of flow derived from the Ford River Rogue Plant, where the assembly line was famously started (Chalice 2007). In healthcare, there are many different types of flow, for example (Graban 2012):

- *Patients:* The patient's journey spans the care continuum from outpatient to acute to post-discharge care. Flow is internal within an organization (e.g., ED to ICU) or external between organizations (e.g., transfer from community hospital to academic medical center). Other examples include patient flow in the ED, OR, outpatient physician office, and oncology infusion center.

- *Staff:* Employees move within and across departments as part of their workflow.

- *Information:* Whether verbal, electronic, or hard copy, information flows among people, departments, and organizations. Other examples include human resources transactions, finance department processes, and information systems processes.

- *Supplies/equipment:* These are the components needed to perform the workflow throughout a department and organization. The flow of supplies and equipment can include medications, lab specimens, and wheelchairs and stretchers, as well as medical/surgical supplies. Other examples include clinical labs (specimen collection, lab receiving, result reporting) and surgical equipment (sterilized, used in OR case, decontaminated and cleaned).

Waiting is reduced by establishing flow. From the customer's perspective, waiting is nonproductive, NVA time. A 1985 Harvard Business School report defined the implications of processes that produce waiting. In the paper, "The Psychology of Waiting Lines," the author states (Maister 1985):

$$Satisfaction = Perception - Expectation$$

Waiting was subsequently broken down into core principles. For service delivery organizations, those principles help identify opportunities to manage customer expectations in order to influence their satisfaction with waiting. Using patients as the customer, four of the article's eight principles follow:

1. Unoccupied time feels longer than occupied time. Time passes more slowly when there is nothing for a person to do while waiting. This void in activity makes the perception of waiting longer.

    - Example: A patient sits in a waiting room that does not have reading material, music, or a television

    - Strategies to address this principle: Provide resources or distractions for patients while they wait. By providing magazines or even informational television shows, the time spent waiting could be seen as productive, especially if the patient is learning something related to his or her visit.

2. Pre-process waits feel longer than in-process waits. The time it takes before the process actually starts is unproductive. From the patient's viewpoint, nothing is happening or moving forward in the pre-process phase. The lack of forward-moving progress can create anxiety and dissatisfaction with service delivery.

    – Example: Consider two scenarios: (1) a patient signs in at the physician's office front desk and then sits down and waits, and (2) a patient waits in the exam room to see the physician. The first scenario describes a pre-process wait. The patient has not entered the clinical space and therefore the process, from the patient's perspective, has not yet begun. In the second scenario, the patient is in-process. By then, the patient has had his vitals taken, was interviewed by the medical assistant or nurse, and now awaits the physician. If the waiting time for each scenario was 10 minutes, the perception would be that the pre-process wait felt longer since nothing had started yet.

    – Strategies to address this principle: Apply various process changes to expedite patients getting into the process. For example, immediately take patients back to the exam room (rather than sign in and wait) and complete registration in the room.

3. Anxiety makes the wait seem longer. When a person is anxious, time can appear to slow down. Anxiety can arise from many sources, including fear of the unknown.

    – Example: A patient is going to the hospital for a major operation. She has to wake up early, drive to the hospital, navigate the building to find registration, and then go through the pre-surgical preparation. She is unsure of the procedure duration, the subsequent length of stay, and the expected clinical outcome.

    – Strategies to address this principle: Identify potential sources or reasons for patient (and family) anxiety. For components within your control (e.g., communicating expectations regarding the process, procedure, and expected outcomes), develop mechanisms/processes to anticipate and ease patient worrying.

4. Unexplained waits seem longer than explained waits. Waiting can seem infinite if the person does not know when to expect something to happen.

    – Example: After being triaged, a patient sits in the ER and waits to be called back by a clinician. The patient is not told how long that will take. To make matters worse, the patient is not updated as to when to expect service. Think about when you call a customer service representative and are put on hold. How do you feel when the representative clicks hold and all you get is an endless loop of songs without any idea how long that will go on? What if you were told the wait would be 10 minutes? Remember: Satisfaction = Perception − Expectation. If the representative returned in six minutes, you would be delighted with how quick it was. Alternatively, if you were not given a time and waited six minutes, it would seem much longer, and you would not be happy.

– Strategies to address this principle: Develop a communication approach (consider visual management) to notify patients of expected waits. In the example, when the customer service representative notifies you of the 10-minute wait, you can adjust your expectation. During the defined waiting time period, you might even multitask by performing a brief activity while waiting.

Achieving flow and addressing the principles of waiting are critical in delivering VA services to customers. There are three core components to meet this end:

1. *Determine customer demand.* Know the pace or rate of demand. Serve customers more readily and nimbly by understanding the rhythm of a process.

2. *Balance the process.* Balance the workload and sync process timing with demand. Process balance is essential in optimizing resource utilization.

3. *Standardize the work.* Follow the same steps and practices to ensure a consistent outcome every time.

DETERMINING CUSTOMER DEMAND

Demand will vary depending on the process (Figure 5.2). Understanding the process rhythm enables workload balancing to maximize flow and reduce waiting.

$$\text{Takt time} = \frac{\text{Available time (minutes per working day/shift)}}{\text{Volume (daily customer demand)}}$$

Figure 5.2 Roadmap: Determine customer demand.

To meet this goal and create smooth flow, we need to define the demand. The term used to calculate this is Takt time (Figure 5.3). The objective is to match the pace of the process to the pace of customer demand. Takt time is the rhythm of the process based on customer demand (Liker and Meier 2006).

$$\text{Takt time} = \frac{\text{Available time (minutes per working day/shift)}}{\text{Volume (daily customer demand)}}$$

Figure 5.3 Takt time equation.

> *Takt is German for the beat that an orchestra conductor uses to regulate the speed at which the musicians play* (Lean Enterprise Institute)

Example of Takt Time Calculation

- Physician's office operates from 7:00 a.m. to 5:00 p.m. (with an hour for lunch).
  - Available time = Total time excluding breaks and lunch
  - Total time = 10 hours
  - Breaks and lunch = 1 hour
  - Available time = 9 hours
- Patients go through an eight-step process (from arrival to checkout)
- Average patient volume = 30 per day

What is the Takt time?

- Takt time = (9 hours * 60 minutes)/30 = 540/30 = 18 minutes per patient

Interpretation of results: To keep pace with demand, complete each process step within 18 minutes.

> *Note on demand: Unevenness in demand occurs naturally. However, most imbalances result from our own scheduling approach, policies, and other decisions that drive variability. Patient arrival is challenging because it is an important component that is out of our control. The best way to address demand variation is to inform and prepare patients appropriately prior to arrival as well as design a process capable of managing variation.*

BALANCING THE PROCESS

Once customer demand is determined, process balancing follows (Figure 5.4). The goal is to balance and equalize the amount of time required to complete each process step. The duration should be in sync with the Takt time. A balanced process ensures the ability to meet customer demand based on the Takt time rate (Liker and Meier 2006). An unbalanced process can result from variation in demand (inputs), lack of standardization in tasks/process steps, and in healthcare, clinical challenges unique to the individual patient. Operational stability, just-in-time service, and high-quality processes are ways in which unevenness can be addressed.

Figure 5.4 Roadmap: Balance the process.

Case Study: Evaluating Gastroenterology Physician Office Visit

The best way to describe the importance and effectiveness of balancing a process is using a real-world example. Physicians' offices offer a good example of understanding demand and matching the process to meet customer needs. In the gastroenterology (GI) physician's office, patient flow was not smooth. Visits by new patients often took longer than scheduled, which had a compounding effect on subsequent delays. To improve the process, a team of lean leaders observed the physician and medical assistant workflow and matched the process times to demand. One of the key tools used was the workload balance.

How to Determine if the Process is Balanced:

1. Conduct process observations and complete the process value analysis (Figure 5.5).

PRINCIPLE #3: FLOW   91

Process value analysis

[Bar chart showing Time (minutes) on y-axis from 0 to 35, with five process steps on x-axis: Check in (~10 min, NVA), MA rooming (~6 min, mostly VA), Physician visits (~33 min, split between VA ~12 and NVA ~21), Phlebotomy draw (~4.5 min, VA), Check out (~4.5 min, NVA). Legend: VA (green), NVA (orange), NVA-R (yellow).]

Figure 5.5 Process value analysis example.

2. Calculate Takt time.
   – The physician's office operates from 8:00 a.m. to 5:00 p.m. (with an hour for lunch).
     • Available time = Total time excluding breaks and lunch
     • Total time = 9 hours
     • Breaks and lunch = 1 hour
     • Available time = 8 hours
   – Patients go through a five-step process (from check-in to checkout)
   – Average patient volume = 30 per day
   – Takt time = (8 hours * 60 minutes)/30 = 480/30 = 16 minutes per patient

3. Compare Takt and cycle times to create the workload balance chart (Figure 5.6).

4. Identify sources of unevenness.
   – Once the Takt time line is overlaid on the process value analysis graph, it's easy to see where the internal resources do not match up with customer demand and where the bottlenecks occur.

5. Develop countermeasures to reduce NVA activity and redistribute work in an even manner.
   – In the GI physician's office visit example, the primary issue was the third high-level step, "Physician visits." This step was associated with a large portion of waiting. To remediate, two countermeasures were implemented. First, patients change into a gown before the physician enters. This reduces the amount of time a physician waits for the patient to be ready for the exam. Previously, the physician would do a brief interview and then ask the patient to put on a gown. The physician would leave and come back after a period of time to do the full evaluation. The second countermeasure uses visual cues to alert the medical assistant and physician when the patient has changed into the gown. Exam room flags indicate when the patient is ready (similar to Figure 4.20).

92 Chapter Five

6. Repeat step 3 post-intervention and assess opportunities for improvement.
   - The post-intervention workload balance chart shows a level process that better aligns with the Takt time line (Figure 5.7). Two of the high-level steps still exceed the Takt time line; however, the impact diminishes compared with the pre-intervention process.

Figure 5.6 Workload balance example: Before intervention.

Figure 5.7 Workload balance example: After intervention.

PRINCIPLE #3: FLOW   93

A side-by-side comparison demonstrates the effectiveness of simple solutions leveraged by workload balancing (Figure 5.8). The end result of this effort reduced the length of new patient visits by 26.7 percent (from 62.5 minutes to 45.8 minutes). The physician visit portion of the process was reduced by 18.3 minutes (51 percent), with the proportion of VA time increasing from 34 percent to 69 percent.

Figure 5.8 Workload balance example: Before/after comparison.

Figure 5.9 describes how to analyze the workload balance chart. The Takt time depicts the expected process rhythm compared with the cycle times. When there is a mismatch between them, there are three outcomes: idle time, work-in-process (WIP), and overtime. For cycle times that are short (e.g., step 3), the person working that particular step completes his or her work at a faster rate than the subsequent step. As a result, there is an excess of WIP. In other words, the work will pile up for the person working step 4 because he or she cannot keep up with the pace of production. The person working step 3 will also have a lot of idle time because the task is quick, and he or she will not have any incoming WIP.

Employees working down the line will subsequently experience a high volume of WIP and incur overtime to complete the required work. This example demonstrates the significant negative consequence of an uneven process. The goal is to create a process in which the cycle times are slightly below the Takt time, creating a cushion. This results in decreased waiting, inventory, and non-utilized skill.

Redistribution or reallocation of work is an effective strategy to balance workflow (Jacobs and Chase 2008). Ways to reallocate include combining tasks, shifting the sequence of steps, and redistributing work assignments based on quantity, duration, and complexity. It is important to note that workload balancing is not about workforce reduction but rather appropriate utilization of available human resources. Other methods that are effective include cross-training and standard operating procedures.

Figure 5.9 How to analyze a workload balance chart.

Rapid Changeover

Rapid changeover is an effective method for creating continuous flow and directly reducing the interruptions between steps (Chalice 2007). The main emphasis is on reducing the amount of time between process steps. The best analogy for rapid changeover is a professional racing pit crew. The pit crew has one goal: service the race car effectively in as short a time as possible. Essential to this effort are preparation and a well-orchestrated plan.

> *Rapid changeover is a common tactic for ORs, inpatient beds, and exam rooms. The organization is not creating value when these rooms are not in use. Therefore, it is essential to get the room ready for the next patient as quickly as possible.*

Efficient changeovers reduce bottlenecks, decrease overall lead time, and improve process reliability. Changeovers, going from one process step to the next, are NVA activities because they interrupt VA steps. Implementing rapid changeover involves four steps:

1. Document all process steps. List all the tasks from start to finish.

2. Segment external and internal steps. External steps are those steps that can be completed before the current process starts or after it begins. Internal steps are required to be completed between the transition. For example, you must transport the patient out of the OR before you can clean the operating table and the floor (internal). However, you can pack up the surgical equipment and begin throwing out used supplies before the patient leaves the room (external).

3. Reorganize tasks. What NVA activity can be eliminated? What internal steps can be done externally? Make everything an external step unless it is absolutely necessary to keep it as an internal step. Through proper preparation and timing, most of the changeover can occur before the process step ends. This reduces the amount of work that needs to be completed between steps (time between steps is NVA—waiting). For example, airline flight attendants begin cleaning the cabin before the plane lands. Thus, the crew has a limited cleanup job once the plane has landed and the passengers exit. This gives them the ability to quickly prepare the plane for the next wave of passengers.

4. Improve processes by reducing NVA activity. Continuous improvement demands that all processes be consistently evaluated and refined to meet customer needs.

Case Study: Rapid Changeover in the Operating Room

Delays in the OR cause bottlenecks and workflow inefficiencies, and negatively impact both patient and staff satisfaction. A lean team was assigned to help facilitate the reduction of OR turnover time. Streamlining the room changeover process would enable the department to effectively manage the daily schedule while delivering efficient, customer-focused service. The time interval selected was "close to cut." This means the first process step begins when the physician starts closing the surgical site of patient #1 and ends upon initiation of the subsequent case (patient #2) by way of incision.

The lean team evaluated the process through gemba walks and time study observations (Figure 5.10). The team completed the first two steps of rapid changeover with the process experts (i.e., OR nurses, technicians, nursing assistants, and managers).

Figure 5.10 Process value analysis of OR turnover.

The process value analysis illustrates the distribution of VA and NVA activities throughout. The process was 60 percent NVA. The team used a swimlane map to break the process into manageable chunks (Figure 5.11).

The team identified primary issues that led to inefficient room turnovers. These issues included lack of clarity and structure (who is supposed to do what by when), limited staff availability due to scheduled breaks and staffing model, and lack of a standard process. To address these challenges, the team defined specific responsibilities for each role using the swimlane map as a method to communicate. The team also developed a "Next Case Checklist" to appropriately prepare for the upcoming patient (Figure 5.12).

The countermeasures implemented led to a statistically significant improvement in turnaround time (from 48 minutes to 44 minutes, $p = 0.003$). The post-implementation process also demonstrated less variation, as evidenced by the standard deviation (pre-improvement 6.7, post-improvement 3.7). By stabilizing and standardizing the process, future improvement efforts will have a higher impact.

Figure 5.11 Improvement team creating a swimlane map of OR turnover.

Next Case Checklist

Bed position
____ Gel arm rolls
____ Head at bottom
____ Lateral/arm board and vac pack
____ Lateral/arm board without vac pack
____ Lithotomy/stirrups—head at bottom
____ Prone/check rolls with 3 pillows
____ Sleds
____ Supine/head at top

Equipment needed
____ Argon
____ Bair hugger
____ C arm and monitor
____ CO_2 tank
____ D&E machine
____ Doctor's specialty cart
____ Double bovie
____ EGD tower
____ Fluid warmer
____ Harmonic generator
____ Headlight and box
____ Ligasure machine
____ Nitrogen tank
____ Pediatric warmer
____ Pediatric cart
____ Sharps/recyclables exchange
____ Slave monitor
____ Universal arm board
____ Video tower
____ X-ray shield

Other:
_____
_____

Equipment to remove from room:
_____
_____

Figure 5.12 Next case checklist.

IMPORTANCE OF STANDARD WORK

The last component of principle 3, establishing flow, is to standardize work (Figure 5.13). Standardized work is an approach that creates consistent processes that reduce variability (Lean Enterprise Institute n.d.). Standardized work (or standard work) is the current best way to do a process/step. It is the foundation for improvement. Lack of standard work leads to waste (primarily defects), which inhibits process capability and employee effectiveness. Without a standard in place, there is no base from which to improve (Jones and Mitchell 2006). Improvement advice usually follows as (Mann 2010):

1. *Stabilize:* Get the process in control. Call a time-out if necessary so you can wrap your head/arms around what is currently happening.

2. *Standardize:* Develop the current best approach and train everyone to do the same thing, everywhere, every time.

3. *Improve:* Using the standard as a baseline for improvement, refine and improve.

The process experts define standard work. To start, identify the process steps and determine the best method to perform each of them. These steps should define who does what, when. Everyone performs steps in the same way, every time

Figure 5.13 Roadmap: Standardize the work.

(Toussaint and Gerard 2010). Standard work frees your mind of the simple tasks and processes because they are hardwired and consistent. Therefore, you have more time and energy to address anything else that comes your way.

Processes should be mostly standard (80 percent to 95 percent) and only a small portion customizable (5 percent to 20 percent). There are tacit activities, or those things that require a more artful approach or interpretation, that cannot be written as instructions. Standardizing care through vehicles like clinical pathways has met significant resistance over the years (Martens et al. 2014; Shortell, Rundall, and Hsu 2007). The cooking analogy works best to explain the importance and impact of standardizing tasks.

Recipes serve as the basis for creating a consistent meal. The recipe describes the ingredients and method of cooking in detail. However, there are built-in components that require an "art" or sense that cannot be articulated in a list or directions. For example, every grill or oven cooks slightly different. It is therefore important to understand the performance of the grill or oven to interpret instructions that state "cook for 8 to 12 minutes." The message is powerful. When the kitchen concept is applied to clinical pathways, it does not promote cookie-cutter medicine but rather a standard and consistent way (as demonstrated by the best clinical evidence) to do the majority of work and make the majority of the decisions while still leaving room for interpretation and latitude to diverge if indicated (Rycroft-Malone et al. 2002; Shortell 1998).

There is some degree of stability and known variation throughout a normal workday. For the most part (perhaps 80 percent of the time), you get what you expect. You might encounter unique or challenging scenarios (maybe 20 percent of the time) in which you have to do something different. How you prepare and standardize the 80 percent greatly affects your capacity to effectively and efficiently address the 20 percent. If you do not have control around the "typical" tasks and processes (what we are calling the 80 percent), then everything will appear and feel chaotic.

> *There is a reason for recipes when you cook. You want to have limited variation in the outcome. You want your mother's chicken soup to taste like her chicken soup every time you make it. If you do not follow a recipe, it will taste different every time. It also is impossible to improve the dish if there is no baseline from which to refine. You can draw the same correlation to care delivery. For 65–75 percent of patients, there is a standard of care that does not need to be individualized patient to patient. These steps should be standardized based on best practice and refined as appropriate. The remaining 25–35 percent of the care delivery process relies on the clinical team's experience, knowledge, and so forth (the art and science of medicine). The overall goal is to reduce the unnecessary variation in outcomes by doing the same thing every time (as appropriate).*

Creating standard work requires the input of process experts. Developing standard work is straightforward.

1. Identify problems or sources of variation. Determine what you are trying to improve.

2. Document the process steps in the current state. The content experts are likely to develop the best method of completing tasks given their experience and technical expertise. Remember to look for external best practices as well.

3. Evaluate the current state and determine which steps to eliminate. Then, identify the steps to be standardized.

   - For standardizing steps, use the standard work template in Table 5.1. Document the step and key points for performing it correctly. Provide a rationale for the defined best method. Identify who is doing the task, when they are doing it, and how long it should take to complete.

   - Questions to consider when evaluating the process and building the standard include the following: What is the purpose? Where should the step be completed? How should the step be performed? Who should do it?

4. Train and cross-train staff.

5. Implement.

6. Monitor, refine, and continuously improve.

Table 5.1 Standard work template.

Steps	Key points	Rationale	Responsible person	When the step is performed	How long the task should take

Standard operating procedures (SOPs), a manual, training presentations, or other methods can document standard work. The method of documentation is not as important as the fact that the documentation serves as the standard. Developing standard work should coincide with the lean fundamentals. Workspace layout and organization have a major impact on process efficiency and the ability of staff to consistently perform tasks.

Standard work is a dynamic approach to streamline processes and reduce variation. The operative word is "current best" approach. Continuous improvement aims to make things better on an iterative basis. Standard work should live through the staff and be refined periodically to ensure compliance with the current best methods. Figure 5.14 shows how standard work acts as a wedge to reduce performance regression while the next iteration of improvements drives toward the future state

Figure 5.14 Standard work and continuous improvement.
Source: Adapted from Rother 2010.

> *Without standard work there is no basis from which to improve.*

Checklists

The "single-person" process is something encountered frequently. One could argue that a "single-person" process means there is no process. Relying on one person to do something is not systematic or sustainable. If that person wins the lottery tomorrow, does the process look entirely different for whoever takes over? If yes, no process exists. Processes that are people-dependent make sustainability essentially impossible. This also applies to employees who customize their approach to work in a way that reduces standardization and challenges sustainability. Leaders often fall victim to relying on individuals instead of designing and improving processes that maximize everyone's capabilities.

Aviation has driven the use of checklists in healthcare given the high reliability and safety within the industry (Gawande 2009). Though at times fatiguing, a checklist provides the required reminders that could be overlooked due to the nature of human beings and their tendency to make mistakes unknowingly or unintentionally (Gawande 2009). Checklists remove the need to remember everything that needs to be done. This frees up an individual's mind to think about the other things requiring attention.

At some point, checklists become hardwired into the tasks and are no longer necessary or are used as a reminder rather than a core checkpoint. There is a balance between the quantity of checklists and the frequency of their use, which is why reviewing their use and effectiveness periodically is critical. There is a significant difference between "checking the box" and actually doing the work. A useless checklist is a terrible waste of time.

⚠ CHAPTER CHALLENGE

Identify a process that needs to be standardized. Develop an SOP with staff in the area. What are the challenges in implementing standard work? Why do these issues/barriers exist? How can you overcome them?

QUESTIONS

1. What flows within your area (e.g., patient, specimens, paperwork)?
2. How does waiting affect the processes in your area? How are waiting expectations managed?
3. Why is it important to understand customer demand?
4. What types of waste can an uneven process produce?
5. What is the impact of an uneven process on employee productivity and morale?
6. Is there a process in your area where rapid changeover can be applied? If so, what internal tasks can be moved externally or eliminated?
7. Why do standards need to be in place before improvements can occur?
8. Are standards static or dynamic?
9. How does standard work promote creativity?
10. What are the benefits of checklists?
11. How can checklists be utilized in your area?

Chapter 6
Principle #4: Pull

Simplicity is the ultimate sophistication.

– Leonardo da Vinci

Establishing flow creates smooth processes. Interruptions of VA activity are reduced or eliminated. Once flow is established, the goal becomes just-in-time production. The two principles of flow and pull are closely related (Figure 6.1). Each emphasizes the balance of resources to improve throughput.

Figure 6.1 Roadmap: Implement pull.

Chapter Six

Without flow, it is difficult to implement a pull system. Without a pull system, it is difficult to ensure flow and just-in-time production.

Implementing pull, especially in the healthcare environment, is challenging. From batching to inventory management, the requirement for process reliability and responsiveness is mandatory. The fourth principle of lean comprises three components: (1) create a pull system, (2) reduce batching, and (3) manage inventory. Pull highlights the right product/service in the right amount at the right time. Sometimes it is surprising to learn what you need versus what you have.

We live and work in a world of excess. In the current healthcare environment, it is becoming clear that this mentality is not sustainable. Organizations cannot afford (literally) to manage supplies haphazardly as reimbursement rates continue to decline. Unfortunately, many organizations will need to employ drastic cost-saving measures in order to reduce the impact of operational expenses.

CREATE A PULL SYSTEM

A pull system is a method of controlling and balancing the flow of resources (Liker 2004; Tapping et al. 2009). Processes are designed to eliminate waste and unevenness while producing only what has been requested. This concept is just-in-time production (Liker and Meier 2006). Just-in-time production emphasizes a pull approach to demand rather than the traditional push mentality (Figure 6.2).

Figure 6.2 Roadmap: Create a pull system.

Push Systems

The push approach produces products/service regardless of demand (Figure 6.3) (Womack and Jones 1996). Processes are contingent on demand forecasting. If the predicted demand is not accurate, it will lead to excess inventory and wasted resources (i.e., time, equipment, materials). These types of systems push work to employees whether or not they are ready. As a result, a significant backlog of WIP accumulates.

Take the following scenario as an example. A department is predicting its customer demand tomorrow to be 10. Based on the forecast, the employees prepare 10 boxes of supplies (represented by the blue boxes in Figure 6.4). The "day before" diagram shows the 10 boxes ready for processing. If the customer demand for the

Figure 6.3 Push process.

Figure 6.4 Push process example.

"day of" service is only 3, there is an inventory of 7 excess boxes. These supplies can be reserved for the next day's operation; however, if the supplies are perishable, they will be waste.

Similarly, evaluating push systems at the process level demonstrates the impact of WIP on productivity. Using the same example, if the system pushes all 10 boxes through regardless of demand and the employees' ability to process them, an excess of WIP will build. Figure 6.5 demonstrates what happens when all 10 boxes are pushed to step 1. If step 2 takes a longer time for processing, the WIP will pile up here, thus creating a bottleneck. In this push system, the uneven workload interrupts flow.

Pull Systems

In contrast to the push system, a pull system balances resources and workflow (Lean Enterprise Institute n.d.). Demand or a request initiates the process. Demand is upstream rather than the downstream push effect (Figure 6.6). A pull system aims to improve flow through limiting interruptions caused by overloading and uneven distribution of work.

Figure 6.5 Push process example: WIP.

Figure 6.6 Push versus pull.

Principle #4: Pull

Pull system examples include inpatient nursing units pulling patients from the ED or departments utilizing par levels to manage supplies (Figure 6.7). Vending machines are another example of common pull systems.

Figure 6.8 illustrates how pull systems work. Diagram A shows an inventory of 10 boxes ready for processing. In the pull system, the inventory level is determined by historical demand, the time from order to replenishment, and a buffer to ensure required resource availability. Once the first product is requested (Diagram B), one box is processed through all five steps. Additionally, one box remains at each step, ready to be pulled through the process upon the second request.

Diagrams C and D show what happens once the second box is requested. At step 5, the box is finished and delivered to the customer. There is an empty slot now at step 5. In order to replenish, the employee in step 5 pulls the resource from step 4. The cascading effect continues as step 4 pulls the box from step 3, and so on. Step 1 will then pull a new, unprocessed box of supplies from the inventory. By each step having a box ready to pull from the subsequent step, the process is highly responsive to demand and reduces the throughput time. In this scenario, customer demand pulls the product through the process.

The example shows WIP throughout the process. For inventory management within a lean system, the goal is not zero inventory but rather a process that reduces disruption of flow caused by lack of available resources when needed. It is important to control WIP based on the signaling cue to pull as well as the initial supply for step 1. Flow will be smooth and consistent if inventory and processing are managed effectively. Processes that push demand through steps produce bottlenecks and delays. Similarly, processes that do not have steps ready for just-in-time production are not reaching their potential. Pull enables maximal throughput by positioning every step to perform what is requested, at that time, in the specified amount necessary. In other words, work entering a process step initiates once work exits that step. The approach is simple in explanation but difficult to implement. The next two sections discuss strategies and tools to enable flow and efficient use of resources.

Figure 6.7 Pull process.

108 *Chapter Six*

Diagram A

Diagram B

Diagram C

Diagram D

Figure 6.8 Pull process example.

Case Study: Patient Transportation

A team of lean leaders utilized the pull system approach to improve the patient transportation process. Transport request delays, cancellations, and rescheduling have a negative systemic effect on patient flow. The project focused on inpatient nursing unit transportation requests. Due to the high volume of transportation requests, the need for an efficient process is critical in ensuring high-quality and timely care, as well as promoting patient and employee satisfaction through reliable service. The overall project objective was to reduce the number of pickup delays, cancellations, and transportation rescheduling requests.

The team worked with key stakeholders (i.e., nurses, unit clerks, transportation aides, and management) to identify the root causes and develop targeted solutions. The main issue was a push approach to transportation. A unit would request a transportation aide (e.g., send patient to radiology for MRI). The transport aide was dispatched to the unit without any notification to the unit (a push). As a result, the patient and/or clinical staff were not ready for transportation, causing delays and cancellations. The team devised a pilot to test a transportation aide pull system to address these issues.

Upon transportation request confirmation, the requesting nursing unit would receive a call notifying when the transport aide would arrive on the floor. This provided unit staff time to prepare the patient or cancel the request prior to the transport aide arriving. If the patient or staff were not ready, the dispatcher notified the transport aide prior to his or her arrival on the unit, reducing the possibility of delaying subsequent assignments.

The pull system created improved communication between departments and ensured services provision when ready. As a result, the overall percentage of successful transfers increased from pre-pilot 54.8 percent to post-pilot 89.6 percent (Table 6.1). The two pilot units experienced a large uptick in successful transportation requests. The pilot debrief revealed lessons learned:

- Coordination and communication can significantly reduce waste, delays, cancellations, and reschedules.
- Inbound information provided

Table 6.1 Transportation pilot results.

	Successful request before	Successful request after
Pilot Unit 1	51.1%	95.1%
Pilot Unit 2	60.3%	83.3%
Combined	54.8%	89.6%

BATCHING VS. SINGLE-PIECE FLOW

Establishing flow is a challenge. The just-in-time mentality is not always embraced in healthcare, so shifting from batching to single-piece flow is difficult, but doable. There are two ways in which products or services are processed: batching or single-piece flow (Figure 6.9). Batching emphasizes processing large amounts/quantities of the same item at a time (e.g., elevators batch individuals, fill up before moving to next floor) (Liker 2004). Alternatively, single-piece flow focuses on processing items based on customer demand. Single-piece flow provides the customer what they want, when they want it, and in the right amount (Womack and Jones 2005). Escalators, unlike elevators, operate in a single-piece flow transporting individuals up and down floors continually rather than doing batch runs.

Batching interrupts VA steps. The result is elongated throughput times and delays. Batching processes also make it difficult to detect issues at the time of occurrence. In a batching process, a defect is not easily or quickly identifiable since there can be long times between the start and completion of the batch. Single-piece flow enables rapid identification of issues and problem solving, creating a more nimble and responsive system. Batching is not always a bad thing, though.

Figure 6.9 Roadmap: Reduce batching.

Batching is advantageous in the following scenarios (Breakthrough Management Group International n.d.):

- Time-consuming setups
- Steps that cannot be synchronized due to specific restraints/requirements
- Geography/physical distance between processing steps

Figure 6.10 demonstrates the impact of batching versus single-piece flow. There are four processing steps in the example. Each item (indicated by a circle) requires 2.5 minutes of processing per step. In the Batching A example, each step takes 10 minutes to complete (2.5 minutes per four items). The cycle continues through completion. The overall lead time for one individual item is the same as the entire batch, 40 minutes.

The single-piece flow process can move the item through independently (remember the escalator analogy). Each item must spend 2.5 minutes at processing steps before advancing. The lead time is 10 minutes. Batching B (Figure 6.10) shows the process through three steps. The batch cannot be completed until every item has been processed. In comparison, single-piece flow B shows how items can move along the process independent of one another. This approach enables continuous flow and reduces the delays and bottlenecks batching produces.

Figure 6.10 Batching versus single-piece flow.

> ### Case Study: Pharmacy Batching
>
> The pharmacy department was evaluating opportunities to improve workflow processes, reduce waste, and manage inventory. One of the areas of opportunity was the process for preparing and distributing small volume parenterals (SVPs). SVPs are solutions used to deliver medications in small quantities. Before the lean project, the SVP process was batched (one time per day). Pharmacy technicians would complete all SVP orders for the upcoming 24 hours.
>
> The batch process led to excess waste. Patient needs could change between order submission and batch production. As a result, the pharmacy technician could end up preparing an unneeded SVP. To meet customer demands (patients and ordering clinicians), the process needed to be redesigned and responsive to changes in needs.
>
> A team of lean leaders, all of whom served as clinical pharmacists in their full-time responsibilities, evaluated the process. There were several issues that contributed to wasted supplies and suboptimization of resources, including staff and physical space. The team facilitated a 5S rapid improvement event to redesign the workspace and develop a new workflow.
>
> The SVP batch process was broken down to three times per day, rather than once. Though still batching, the more frequent time intervals yield production closer to just-in-time. Given the other responsibilities of the pharmacy technicians and staff, true single-piece flow was not an option. A checklist accompanied the new process to ensure consistency and sustainability, along with a log for documenting production.
>
> The SVP process redesign led to a decrease in wasted supplies. Pharmacy staff indicated a noticeable drop in calls from nursing units regarding missing SVP doses. The team targeted medication usage of those most likely to be affected by the project based on volume/utilization. Based on four of the top five high-cost drugs monitored, annual cost savings are more than $140,000.

MANAGE INVENTORY

Inventory management aims to provide customers and staff what they need, when they need it, and in the right amount (Figure 6.11). To accomplish this, use the lowest level of required resources and inventory as needed. Inventory management is difficult to apply in the healthcare setting. Supplies tend to be overstocked since the risk or consequence of not having something can be catastrophic for patient outcomes. There are, however, ample opportunities to streamline and standardize supply management in order to optimize resources. Small changes make a huge impact due to the large volume of patients a hospital will see. The one-off supplies in rare cases make systematic storage/inventory management nearly impossible. Planning for such instances is not always practical and often it makes more sense to keep excess supply since the risk of not having it when needed is much greater than the cost and burden of storing it. This section focuses on the more common inventory-related issues.

Why is excess inventory a bad thing? As described in earlier chapters, excess inventory is NVA. Excess inventory is a symptom of underlying distribution and utilization issues. Take, for example, supplies on a nursing unit. If the nursing unit does not trust the replenishment system, employees are likely to hoard supplies. Issues include supplies replenished at a variable rate (e.g., order to replenish ranges from 1 to 10 days) and incomplete or inaccurate order fulfillment. Excessive inventory takes up valuable storage space, ties up available cash, and creates the

PRINCIPLE #4: PULL   113

Figure 6.11 Roadmap: Manage inventory.

risk of expiration (especially with medications). However, excessive inventory is appropriate in some scenarios. Unknown or uneven demand, long lead times from order to replenishment, and the consequence of stock-outs all justify higher inventory levels (Womack and Jones 2005).

Par Levels

Inventory management systems attempt to create a pull process from the user of the supplies to the supplier. The goal is to replenish items in the quantities in which they are used. Par levels offer a simple approach to identify the time and quantity needed to reorder. Par levels are based on average use of supplies as well as the delivery frequency and lead time. A buffer is included to remediate the risk of a stock-out. Inventory management requires oversight and control of supplies. If you cannot keep track of it, you cannot control and manage it.

The kanban card is the implementation tool of pull systems and par levels. Kanban is a Japanese word that means "sign" or "card" (Graban 2012). The tool provides a visual cue that indicates supply replenishment (e.g., red strip on receipt roll indicates paper is running low and a new roll will be needed soon). Kanbans reduce inventory by creating a reliable replenishment system. The kanban card identifies the part (description and number), quantity to order, and replenishment lead time, along with order and due dates (Figure 6.12).

114 *Chapter Six*

Part description				Part number	
Quantity		Lead time		Order date	
Supplier				Due date	
Orderer			Location		

Figure 6.12 Kanban template.

Diagram A

Step 1 → Step 2 → Step 3 → Step 4 → Step 5

Diagram B

Step 1 → Step 2 → Step 3 → Step 4 → Step 5

Figure 6.13 Kanban example.

Figure 6.13 explains kanbans using the prior example for creating a pull system. Diagram A shows the pull system taking a box from step 4 and transitioning it to step 5. Subsequently, the boxes are pulled until step 1 pulls from the inventory. Diagram B indicates use of a kanban card. The red box signals the employee at step 1 to order seven boxes to replenish the stock. The three remaining blue boxes are a buffer to reduce the likelihood of running out.

Case Study: Pharmacy Inventory

Due to shortages and stock-outs, the pharmacy is in a different arena when it comes to supplies. There are known and unanticipated shortages that promote the hoarding behavior as an organizational defense mechanism. Uninterrupted patient care is paramount, and at times hoarding-like behavior is acceptable due to the dynamic nature of pharmaceutical supply availability. The pharmacy storerooms provide inventory/stock to central and satellite locations. The pharmacy department wanted to improve workflow and inventory management by consolidating storerooms on the second, fourth, and fifth floors into a singular storeroom on the second floor.

The pharmacy storeroom was decentralized and did not have a systematic process for inventory management. It was difficult for staff to find requested supplies and led to wasted motion and nonutilized skill. Also, due to the inefficient practices, several non-storage locations held supplies. These practices affected ordering accuracy and appropriateness as well as distribution (Figure 6.14).

Storeroom shelves were overstocked with unneeded supplies and not organized.

Figure 6.14 Pharmacy storeroom before improvements.

A team of lean leaders led the pharmacy storeroom project. The goal was to create a systematic inventory management process that enabled staff to readily retrieve and distribute supplies on demand. The team also aimed to reduce inventory levels and put processes into place to control ordering, distribution, and use of supplies (Figures 6.15–6.17).

All supplies were sorted and stored based on frequency of use.

Figure 6.15 Pharmacy storeroom after improvements.

116 Chapter Six

Shelves were organized and properly labeled to help guide staff to appropriate locations.

Figure 6.16 Pharmacy storeroom shelves after improvements.

Before: Decentralized storage areas were unorganized. It was nearly impossible to manage inventory because no one knew what exactly was on hand.

After: Unneeded supplies were appropriately discarded or returned. Supplies that belonged in the main storeroom were relocated and the decentralized storerooms were organized.

Figure 6.17 Pharmacy decentralized storerooms before and after improvements.

The improvement effort served as a transition prior to a complete physical redesign of the pharmacy storeroom (pending one year from project date). The countermeasures developed modeled the future layout and processes. The team used the 5S approach to remove and restock all medications from the satellite storerooms to the main storeroom. As a result, storage space was reclaimed in the main storeroom, unused items were removed, and excess stock of medications was returned to the wholesaler.

⚠️ CHAPTER CHALLENGE

Streamline your inventory, either in the office or at home or both. How hard is this to do? Are there certain things/items in which the inventory can be more easily managed? What visual cues are in place to determine the appropriate amount as well as the reorder points?

QUESTIONS

1. How do flow and pull relate to each other?
2. Why is a pull system more favorable than the traditional push approach?
3. What processes in your area can apply the pull methodology? How difficult is it to do?
4. How does excess inventory hide system and process issues?
5. Why is single-piece flow ideal?
6. What are batching examples in your workflow? Can they be converted to single-piece flow? Why or why not?
7. Why are kanbans useful in managing inventory? How can they be applied to supplies in your area?

Chapter 7
Principle #5: Perfection

The art and science of asking questions is the source of all knowledge.

– Thomas Berger

Continuous improvement demands focusing on reducing errors and rework. Perfection underlies the previous four principles. As you have seen and read throughout the book, the philosophy of lean thinking is to identify and eliminate NVA activity, much of which derives from errors not eliminated or dealt with directly, in a timely manner. The fifth principle of lean, strive for perfection, consists of three core components: (1) identify root causes, (2) error-proof processes, and (3) sustain improvements (Figure 7.1).

ROOT CAUSES

Lean improvements emphasize a focus on improving systems and processes rather than working harder or faster (Graban 2012). Lean thinking is not about having solutions to all problems. Effective problem solvers focus time and observation on the current state process. Before any meaningful change can be developed and implemented, you must first truly understand the underlying root causes (Figure 7.2). A lean thinker leverages the knowledge and experience of process experts to help uncover problems and develop effective solutions. The measure of an effective lean thinker lies in his or her ability to discover such root causes through interviews, observations, and analysis.

Root causes are at the heart of problem-solving. Addressing symptoms rather than the root cause of the problem can lead to ineffective solutions and build customer and employee frustration. For clinicians, if a patient presents in the emergency department with a fever, do you simply say, "Take some ibuprofen, and if it persists, come back in a few days"? Or do you explore the issue by doing a physical exam, diagnostic tests, and so on, to find out what is causing the fever? If there is an underlying bloodstream infection, you need to address it. Dealing with symptoms does not solve the problem. The same applies to processes. Operational problems might show themselves as poor patient/customer satisfaction or slow turnaround times. However, the root cause might be limited visual management, poor communication, or lack of coordination of tasks. The key is to ask why!

Figure 7.1 Roadmap: Strive for perfection.

The root cause is the underlying issue that leads to the observed symptoms. Identifying root causes starts with going to the gemba. Go to the work area, talk with the staff, and use the tools and concepts you have learned throughout the book to ask probing questions. When errors are identified, the system/process issues are isolated and remediated with an end goal of eliminating the likelihood or chance for it to occur again in the same or a similar place. That is the mark of an effective root cause analysis and remediation. If it happened once, it is highly likely that it will happen again (Mann 2010).

Tools to Help Identify Root Causes

Two tools that are highly effective in identifying root causes are the 5 Whys and the fishbone diagram.

5 Whys

The 5 Whys method explores potential root causes by diving below the surface of a presenting symptom. Upon discovering the underlying root cause, applied countermeasures reduce or eliminate the likelihood of future occurrences.

PRINCIPLE #5: PERFECTION   **121**

Figure 7.2 Roadmap: Identify root causes.

> *Root cause analysis for process improvement mirrors that of clinical diagnostics.*
>
> **Symptoms versus Root Causes**
> - Illness
>   - **Symptoms:** headache, fever
>   - **Ask 5 Whys:** diagnostic tests, physical exam
>   - **Root cause:** bloodstream infection
> - Process
>   - **Symptoms:** slow turnaround times, long throughput, dissatisfied customers/patients
>   - **Ask 5 Whys:** observations, staff rounding, data analysis
>   - **Root cause:** lack of visual management and coordination of workflow

The 5 Whys approach is straightforward. Figure 7.3 is an example of how to employ it. The identified problem is that unit nurses are unhappy with their workflow. It is not clear what is causing the unhappiness, so it is too soon to jump to a conclusion or solution. As you ask why, the issue comes to light. After asking why four times, the root cause is unmasked: there is no systematic approach to inventory management. This root cause is the reason nurses are unhappy with the workflow. In this example, you had to ask why only four times. You may need to ask it 10 or more times, or sometimes, as in this example, there is a direct path to the root cause.

Another way to look at this flow diagram is to take it in reverse. Start with the root cause and work your way back up to the identified problem. The reverse, using therefore, tells the story of the consequences a root cause produces:

- There is no systematic approach to inventory management, therefore
- Everyone stores supplies in his or her own way, therefore
- Supplies are not uniformly stored, therefore
- Supplies are not readily available, therefore
- Unit nurses are unhappy with their workflow

Figure 7.3 Example of 5 Whys.

Fishbone Diagram

Dr. Kaoru Ishikawa developed the fishbone diagram. Other names for the tool include the Ishikawa diagram or cause and effect diagram. The tool guides systematic identification of issues and causes of the problem under review (Lighter 2013). This type of analysis is qualitative and effective in group brainstorming sessions.

Building a Fishbone

1. Select the problem (effect) (Figure 7.4)
2. Create the body (structure) (Figure 7.5)
3. Label categories (Figure 7.6)
4. Brainstorm potential causes (Figure 7.7)

Figure 7.4 Fishbone problem.

Figure 7.5 Fishbone body structure.

Figure 7.6 Fishbone categories.

Figure 7.7 Fishbone with potential causes.

> *Typical Fishbone Categories*
> - Personnel
> - Materials/supplies
> - Measurement
> - Method/processes
> - Machine/equipment

A completed fishbone analysis enables the team to narrow the focus toward the probable causes of the problem. This type of analysis leads to the issues that are directly within your control as opposed to those barriers and issues you cannot impact. Data can accompany the analysis to verify potential sources of the problem.

Case Study: Inpatient Admission from Emergency Department

The patient flow management center (PFMC) is a comprehensive, best-practice center overseeing patient flow within and across units/organizations at Jefferson. The PFMC integrates seven departments: bed management, transfer center, environmental services, external transportation (air and ground transport), nursing, patient transportation, and case management. The multidisciplinary PFMC utilizes a robust information system to assign inpatient beds, among other functions.

For patients awaiting admission from the emergency department (ED) to an inpatient floor, employees use the information system to submit the request. ED nursing staff enter the attribute data (i.e., patient demographics, isolation precautions) into the system. While the PFMC has dramatically improved patient flow, inaccurate and omitted attribute selections continue to delay bed assignments. Delays in inpatient bed assignments result

PRINCIPLE #5: PERFECTION   125

in longer ED boarding hours and wait times for new ED patient arrivals. Accordingly, these delays manifest in reduced patient satisfaction levels. Bed assignment delays may also indirectly contribute to a greater number of patients leaving the ED before having a physician evaluation.

In order to drill down to the main issues, the lean team utilized the fishbone diagram (Figure 7.8). The team compiled the fishbone through voice-of-customer interviews, data analysis, and gemba walk observations. The tool was vetted with process experts and refined to reflect the current state. The fishbone depicts the issues leading to "delays in ED admission process." The two root causes are "attributes not entered in timely fashion" and "incomplete or inaccurate attributes."

To address these root causes, the improvement team developed a standard checklist of required patient attributes along with a process for who completes the checklist, by when. The mandatory attributes require ED staff to supply the PFMC with the information it needs to assign the appropriate bed as quickly as possible. The improved process reduces rework by way of reassigning beds, phone calls between departments for status updates or troubleshooting, and delays in subsequent process steps.

Figure 7.8   Example of fishbone with potential causes.

ERROR-PROOF PROCESSES

> "Human error is inevitable. We can never eliminate it. We can eliminate problems in the system that make it more likely to happen."
>
> – Sir Liam Donaldson, World Health Organization

Errors are learning opportunities. The goal is to prevent the error from occurring again. Error-proofing is one lean strategy to achieve this (Figure 7.9). Using the error-proofing approach, the likelihood of an error occurring is designed out of the process (Grout 2007; Lean Enterprise Institute n.d.). The focus is prevention

Figure 7.9 Roadmap: Error-proof process.

and avoidance of errors by building quality directly into the system/process. This approach derives from the Toyota Production System (jidoka—preventing errors at the source) (Liker 2004). Lean thinking emphasizes doing things correctly the first time, every time (Toussaint and Gerard 2010). The term error-proofing may seem foreign, but its application is not. Many everyday items use error-proofing strategies. Examples include the following:

- New cars have keys that detect when they are inside or outside the vehicle, thereby making it impossible to lock your keys inside the car.
- Microwaves stop when you open the door.
- An alert pops up if you try to send an email without a subject line.
- Three-pronged plugs cannot fit into an ungrounded two-prong electrical outlet.

These are just a few examples that you might encounter throughout the day. In the healthcare setting, there are simple and sophisticated error-proofing mechanisms:

- Medical gas connection safeguards
- Medication labeling/identification

- Bed alarms
- Radio-frequency identification surgical sponges

> Mistake-proofing the Design of Health Care Processes, a publication of the Agency for Healthcare Research and Quality (AHRQ), provides a comprehensive overview with examples of error-proofing applied in the healthcare setting (Grout 2007). The literature uses "mistake-proofing" and "error-proofing" interchangeably. "Mistake" has a negative connotation, which is why in this book I use the term "error-proofing."

Error-proofing is an effective intervention when there are consistent defects within the process. The lean thinking philosophy supports this approach toward defects:

1. Do not accept a defect
2. Do not produce a defect
3. Do not pass along a defect

The price of prevention is insignificant compared with the cost of intervention once an error has occurred. Error-proofing leads to lower costs as a result of improved quality and decreased rework (Martin et al. 2009). Error-proofing occurs in a few simple steps (Silverstein, Samuel, and DeCarlo 2009):

1. Identify the defect/error and its location
2. Determine the root cause
3. Review the current process and standard work
4. Identify any deviation from the standard work
5. Develop intervention/countermeasure to correct for future occurrences
6. Implement improvement and evaluate for effectiveness

Identifying the source of the defect is paramount. Root causes are system and process based. Remember to ask why, not who. Employees will devise creative workarounds to deal with poor process design but remember that creativity and rework can sometimes be the same thing (Womack 2011). Error-proofing targets the design of processes that lead to errors. Learning from mistakes is the fastest way to improve (Bicheno and Holweg 2004). There are a variety of methods to apply to drive defects out of the system. These include flags, inspection, alerts/warnings, and standard operating procedures.

Error-proofing should progress from mitigation to elimination/prevention (Figure 7.10). Over time, a more sophisticated approach detects issues as they arise. Subsequently, an improvement approach is taken to clean up the process and reduce variation of outcomes. Where possible, higher-performing and reliable processes replace less efficient ones. The ultimate goal is to design errors out of the system.

Figure 7.10 Progression of error reduction.
Source: Adapted model based on Lean and Six Sigma International Board 2011.

Preventing Human Error

Humans are the main processors in the healthcare environment. As described in *To Err Is Human*, people are fallible; thus, process designs should reduce and eliminate the potential for human error (Kohn, Donaldson, and Committee on Quality of Health Care in America, Institute of Medicine 2000). Shigeo Shingo, a key influence in the Toyota Production System, identified common reasons humans make errors (Breakthrough Management Group International n.d.):

- *Lack of experience:* Employees with little experience or knowledge of the process.

- *Misunderstanding:* Not understanding the situation and subsequently choosing an inappropriate course of action.

- *Forgetfulness:* Despite repetition and familiarity, an employee might still forget to do a particular step or task.

- *Lack of standards or supervision:* Employees are more likely to create errors if they do not know what is expected or do not receive training on how to properly perform tasks.

- *Willful errors:* Intentional mistakes made without bad intentions. An example is someone doing a process "her own way" because she believes it is more efficient.

- *Inadvertent errors:* Caused by lack of attentiveness, discipline, or a standard operating procedure.

- *Intentional errors:* Malicious errors made to the process without the goal of providing a better result (unlike willful errors).

Understanding these sources of deviation enables proper identification of error-proofing tactics. Lean thinking encourages empowering individuals to solve

SUSTAINING IMPROVEMENTS

Sustaining gains is the biggest challenge in an improvement effort (Figure 7.11). A multifaceted approach supports sustainability. The main goal for sustainability is to monitor performance against expected outcomes and course-correct as indicated. There are many ways to monitor progress (e.g., dashboards, run charts, balanced scorecards). What you employ is largely dependent on your environment and available tools and data.

As mentioned earlier, errors will occur. The response to these errors makes the difference in quality outcomes and sustainable progress. Early identification of problems will enable rapid remediation and elimination. Employees should be positioned to produce high-quality outputs. To that end, evaluate several factors:

- *Priority of tasks:* Employees understand the priority and nature of urgency for tasks.

- *Distractions:* Distractions should be removed or reduced to encourage focus.

Figure 7.11 Roadmap: Sustain improvements.

- *Workload balance:* Workloads should be appropriate and evenly balanced to support flow.

- *Direction/guidance:* Instructions and expectations should be clear.

Many factors threaten sustainability. Table 7.1 describes the various factors and potential countermeasures to address each.

Table 7.1 Threats to sustainability.

Issue	Description	Potential countermeasure
Process variation	Uneven flow (too much, too little)	• Standard work • Pull system • Performance dashboards
Unanticipated events	Equipment malfunction/failure, accidents, external events (e.g., weather)	• Error-proofing • Visual management (alerts)
Cultural resistance	Individuals stuck in the "old way" of doing things	• Standard work • Training
Lack of standards	No consistent approach to perform work	• Standard work • Visual management
Poor training	Employees not trained on how to do the job correctly	• Standard work • Training
No visual management	No readily accessible information to support work	• Visual management
No performance dashboards	No feedback mechanism to depict progress versus goals	• Visual management • Performance dashboards
Poor quality	Lack of understanding of customer needs, lack of standard process, variation in outcomes	• Voice of customer • Standard work • Error-proofing

Performance Dashboards

Performance dashboards are visual management tools that monitor and communicate actual versus expected outcomes. Dashboards can be created by using a variety of chart types. The dashboard design displays current performance compared with set goals/targets. Variance from targets indicates an opportunity for improvement. There could be quality issues, bottlenecks, or system and process problems that are creating underperforming outcomes. Consistent visual assessment of performance is critical to sustainability.

In Chapter 4 we discussed visual management, one of the lean fundamentals. Visual management aims to create an immediate snapshot of the current state and communicate key information to appropriate stakeholders. Visual cues like dashboards provide status updates and make performance gaps or problems readily obvious. Performance dashboards can provide feedback on process adherence, productivity, and customer satisfaction. Feedback is an essential component to foster employee buy-in in both the short term and the long term.

Dashboards can be created through information systems (if available) or by using simple charts in tools like Microsoft Excel (Bass 2007). There are two common types of metrics:

- Operational metrics (e.g., length of stay, throughput, turnaround, wait times)
- Satisfaction metrics (e.g., patient/customer satisfaction, employee satisfaction)

Table 7.2 is a simple tool that can serve as a performance dashboard. The table compares a metric's target with the actual performance as of the date indicated. Variance is either favorable or unfavorable (positive or negative depending on the desired direction for change). If there is an unfavorable variance, a reason should accompany it, followed by a corresponding corrective action plan. Continuous monitoring and course correction limit regression.

There are many chart options for performance dashboards. Important things to consider when creating charts include the following:

- *Frequency of data reporting.* Present data in appropriate intervals based on the nature of the process (e.g., daily, weekly, monthly). Where possible, use the lowest possible interval for more rapid identification of issues, for example, tracking daily patient throughput in the emergency department. Metrics like 30-day readmissions should be reported monthly.

- *Targets.* Use performance goals/targets as a comparison. Base targets on known best practices (i.e., top decile, top quartile, mean, median, or internal benchmark). Without an appropriate comparison, it is not possible to assess whether the current performance is acceptable or requires intervention.

- *Display.* Keep charts clean and simple. Adjust the scale (*y*-axis) to reflect the appropriate range of performance. Additionally, include an arrow to indicate the desired direction of change. This arrow enables quick assessment of progress compared with expected directional movement along the *x*-axis.

- *Lagging and leading metrics.* As discussed in Chapter 1, the lag measure represents the desired result, whereas the leading metrics are variables that the team can directly affect.

Table 7.2 Performance update table.

As of date	Metric	Target	Actual	Variance	Reason for variance	Action plan

Run charts are an effective way to show performance of operational and satisfaction metrics over time. The charts in Figure 7.12 display the daily length of stay (in minutes) and patient satisfaction over the course of a month. Bar graphs provide a similar visual and might be more effective in certain instances because of their ease of interpretation or display (Figure 7.13). Pie charts are simple displays for compliance or other data that emphasize a segmentation or proportion of results (e.g., yes, no). These graphs provide a straightforward assessment of the current state and make opportunities obvious (Figure 7.14).

Figure 7.12 Run chart examples.

Monthly patient throughput times

Figure 7.13 Bar chart example.

Quality control dashboard

Figure 7.14 Pie graph example.

Summary tables, like Table 7.3, provide a consolidated view of metric performance. If charts are too cumbersome or space is an issue, tables are an easy solution. These tables are referred to as scorecards or dashboards and may contain more than 10 performance metrics depending on the area. The considerations outlined earlier apply to these tables as well. The direction of desired performance and current state should be obvious. Using colors provides an added visual cue for quick assessment of favorable or unfavorable performance.

Table 7.3 Performance dashboard example.

		Current	As of date	Target	Variance
Patient satisfaction	▲	90.3%	Dec 14	92.0%	−1.7%
Length of stay (minutes)	▼	82.2	Dec 14	86.5	−4.3%

Case Study: Operating Room Performance Dashboards

The perioperative department applied lean improvement strategies across the entire value stream. As part of the evolution of the department, leadership employed a performance dashboard to evaluate the daily progress of operating room (OR) operational metrics to ensure streamlined patient flow. A comprehensive review of previous Jefferson OR projects was published by the American Society for Quality (ASQ 2013). Using the OR information system, leadership developed a tracking dashboard that monitors four performance indicators: (1) cases completed and in progress, (2) OR turnover by floor, (3) on time to holding area (HA) for first-case starts, and (4) on-time first-case starts. Figure 7.15 is an example of the OR performance dashboard.

These data represent indicators for efficiency within the daily OR patient flow. As you can see, there is a focus on first-case starts. If the day starts off slow and behind schedule, there is a compounding effect on the remainder of the day. For the OR, it is critical to start on time and efficiently turn operating rooms over to enable continuous flow.

Figure 7.15 Performance dashboard example in the OR.

⚠️ CHAPTER CHALLENGE

Go on a gemba walk through a department (it can be your department) and look for signs that remind or tell employees to be careful. Signs can be an indicator of a process problem and that root cause has not been properly addressed. Are there any root causes not being addressed? Are there any opportunities to apply error-proofing?

QUESTIONS

1. Why do you need to identify root causes before developing a solution?
2. How is a tool like the fishbone diagram used to diagnose key issues?
3. How can you learn from errors?
4. What processes in your area can apply error-proofing? Are error-proofing tactics already in place? Are they effective? Can they be replicated or adapted for other processes?
5. What is the progression of problem solving? Why is prevention at the top?
6. What are ways in which humans can make errors? How do you address or anticipate these concerns?
7. Why is performance feedback an important part of sustainability?
8. What types of information (data, charts, etc.) are provided in your area with regard to performance versus target? If there are not any, why not? What should they be?
9. What are the different ways in which sustainability can be threatened? How can you counter these scenarios?
10. Why do you need to include targets with performance dashboards?

Chapter 8
Executing a Project through Lean DMAIC

Knowing is not enough; we must apply. Willing is not enough; we must do.

– Goethe

The first seven chapters provide the conceptual model for executing lean improvements. The five principles of lean are critical in systematically identifying opportunities for improvement and developing effective countermeasures. This chapter covers the project management framework for executing lean improvement projects. Similar to Six Sigma, creating a lean process follows the DMAIC structure (define, measure, analyze, improve, control) (Bicheno and Holweg 2008). We will review the key deliverables within each phase and discuss the importance of a systematic approach to performance improvement. The structured checklist-driven approach to improvement enables consistent outcomes.

Lean improvement projects emphasize the collaboration of content and process experts. Individuals who do the work where the problem lives are responsible for helping develop solutions and fixes (Graban 2012). Lean practitioners are responsible for facilitating the problem-solving process, leveraging the expertise and experience of the employees who work the process (Aij et al. 2013). Chapter 9 details the facilitation approach. The lean DMAIC checklist allows individuals to execute projects in a systematic, structured way.

KAIZEN

Kaizen is a Japanese term that means "change for good" (Imai 1997). A rapid improvement event (RIE) is a type of facilitated kaizen focused on changing a process for the better. The focus is incremental process improvement. RIEs can range from two hours up to three days depending on the problem complexity and project scope. However, kaizen and rapid improvements occur more commonly on the front lines, where the work happens (Graban and Swartz 2012). Kaizen represents any opportunity to change for the better—not just formal improvement projects.

The kaizen mentality and approach follow the format of the plan-do-check-act (PDCA) cycle. Walter A. Shewhart developed the PDCA model. The model emphasizes piloting improvements, reviewing the impact, refining, and then repeating (Figure 8.1) (Langley et al. 2009). A future state defines what direction to go based on the current state. An implementation plan outlines key tasks for moving toward the future state. Progress and impact are evaluated during and after implementation. The iterative cycle consists of the following:

- *Plan:* Define the objective. Prepare for the improvement changes/actions to be implemented. Identify who will do what, how, and when. Define the expected outcomes of the changes.
- *Do:* Implement the planned changes.
- *Check:* Evaluate the impact of the implemented changes against the expected outcomes. Did the changes have the desired effect? Does the process need to be further refined?
- *Act:* Make refinements to the changes, plan the next iteration of experimentation, and then implement the revised changes and assess their impact compared with expectations.

Figure 8.1 PDCA cycle.

Of the four phases of the PDCA cycle, check is probably the most important. In the check phase, the effectiveness of the plan and execution are evaluated, asking:

- What are we trying to accomplish? Why?
- What is the expected outcome?
- How will we know it is an improvement?
- What worked or did not work? Why?
- What do we need to refine to achieve our goals?

The PDCA model aligns with a lean concept called improvement kata. Kata is a Japanese word that means the description and practice of detailed choreography of patterns and movements (Lean Enterprise Institute n.d.). Traditionally from martial arts, practicing kata provides the systematic framework for people to tackle problems. Popularized by the book *Toyota Kata* (Rother 2010), the four-step model

(Figure 8.2) defines the structured approach from problem/goal identification to intervention implementation. The improvement kata approach isolates the next target condition as the incremental improvement step. The next target condition represents an advancement from the current state that begins to resemble the desired future state. Incremental improvement strategies make transformation efforts manageable and less overwhelming. Remember, don't boil the ocean.

Understand the direction	Grasp the current direction	Establish the next target condition	PDCA toward the target condition
What problem are you trying to address?	What is the current state? Are there patterns?	What is your objective (future state)?	PLAN / DO / CHECK / ACT

Figure 8.2 Improvement kata model.

The questions to ask when implementing the improvement kata model are as follows (Rother 2010):

1. What problem are you trying to address?
2. What obstacles or barriers are preventing you from reaching your goal?
3. Which obstacle or barrier (choose only one) are you going to address?
4. What is your next step (PDCA cycle) and what do you expect to happen?
5. When are you going to the gemba to see what you have learned and what you need to do next?

The PDCA model is powerful. Implement something (pilots and trials work best), evaluate the impact, and refine as needed. Review results and ensure process compliance. Reassess and redesign after changes are hardwired, seeking a new level of performance, and "rinse and repeat." Sometimes you pilot new ideas only to find that what you were doing previously worked best. Each effort is a learning opportunity to identify the strengths and limitations of the intervention and use that knowledge to improve the next experiment (Langley et al. 2009).

Figure 8.3 depicts the scope and frequency of problems an organization likely experiences. System- and organization-level improvements are lower in frequency. These processes and problems are complex in nature and involve various value streams and functional areas. The scope is broad and comprehensive. Department- and team-level opportunities are multifaceted. Opportunities involve only a few (or one) functional departments or teams. The most abundant opportunities are at the frontline level (Graban and Swartz 2012). Processes and problems at the front line tend to be straightforward and less complex. The power of lean is leveraging this section of the pyramid. By empowering staff to solve problems at the source, these small improvements (kaizen) have a compounding effect across the organization.

System/organizational level
Complex processes and problems crossing various value streams and functional areas

Department/team level
Multifaceted processes and problems involving core departments or teams. Narrower in scope than system/organization level efforts.

Frontline level
Straightforward and often less complex processes and problems

Figure 8.3 Types of kaizen.
Source: Adapted from Liker 2004.

> *Focus on the most important issues and opportunities. The more goals and projects you try to pursue, the less likely you are to achieve them. Be deliberate and intentional with your resources (i.e., time, people, supplies, equipment, energy). Remember, there are always far more good ideas than there is the ability to execute them.*

LEAN DMAIC MODEL

The lean DMAIC model is a checklist-driven, systematic approach used to deploy the roadmap. The overlay of DMAIC on the roadmap depicts how the checklist applies the lean principles to a project (Figure 8.4).

- *Define:* Establish the scope and clearly define the problem to be addressed
- *Measure:* Document and validate the current state using process maps, data, and analysis to quantify current capability
- *Analyze:* Analyze data and identify opportunities
- Improve: Utilize the lean fundamentals, flow, and pull to implement countermeasures for the identified opportunities
- *Control:* Emphasize sustainability and process and outcome quality

The Five Principles of Lean

Define value	Map the value stream	Establish flow	Implement pull	Strive for perfection
Determine scope	Map current state	Determine customer demand	Create a pull system	Identify root causes
SIPOC	Process mapping	Takt time calculation	Pull system	5 Whys/ fishbone
Define value through customer's	Collect and analyze data	Balance the process	Reduce batching	Error-proof process
DEFINE	**MEASURE/ ANALYZE**	**IMPROVE**		**CONTROL**
VA/NVA activity	Process analysis	Workload balance	Single-piece flow	Error prevention
Identify waste	Establish lean fundamentals	Standardize the work	Manage inventory	Sustain improvements
Waste walk	5S, layout, and visual management	SOP	Kanban system	Performance dashboards

Figure 8.4 Roadmap with DMAIC overlay.

Remember, kaizen (change for good) is an ongoing process. Lean is the relentless pursuit of waste reduction. Checklists, like other processes and systems, should be continually evaluated and improved to ensure they drive quality and efficiency. You do not want these types of documents to be static. For example, when the lean DMAIC checklist was first developed at Jefferson, it was six pages long. There was a lot of detail for everything that needed to take place. After each RIE, the teams would evaluate the checklist and discuss what was missed and unused. Over the course of six years, the list narrowed to a single page, which continues to be refined. Keep notes as you apply the tool. Document tasks you might have missed or details that were overlooked. Include your own revisions on details and steps to consider in advance based on prior or new experiences. The DMAIC checklist helps provide project management structure (Hina-Syeda et al. 2013). You can apply the checklist to non-lean projects, bypassing tools or activities that do not apply; however, the framework is the same.

The lean DMAIC checklist includes deliverables and logistics for initiating, planning, executing, and closing lean improvement projects (Figure 8.5). The appendixes contain a detailed review of all tools and templates provided. The time frame for each phase is an approximate guideline for how long the planning, execution, and control/close processes take. Depending on the scope and resource availability, the project might vary significantly. Use your organizational knowledge and experience to determine what works best for you.

Lean DMAIC Checklist

Project name: _____ **Date last revised:** _____

Date of event: _____ **Facilitators:** _____

DEFINE Phase Checklist
5–6 weeks before event

- [ ] Assign facilitator team roles
    – Leader, communications, logistics
- [ ] Kickoff meeting with sponsor(s)
    – Define problem/goal
    – Identify individuals to interview/draft communication plan
- [ ] Review current IS or other projects in area
    – Review potential/upcoming IS changes
- [ ] Conduct voice of customer (VOC) interviews
- [ ] Conduct a waste walk
- [ ] Develop high-level process map
- [ ] Begin project charter
- [ ] Assess change readiness using profile tool
- [ ] Use systems and process profile tool
- [ ] Schedule event (location/date/times)
- [ ] **Close DEFINE phase**

MEASURE Phase Checklist
4 weeks before event

- [ ] Review previous rapid improvement events, kaizens, or other projects
- [ ] Formulate data collection plan (if needed)
- [ ] Conduct process value analysis
- [ ] Conduct workflow value analysis
- [ ] Create current state value stream map (VSM)
- [ ] Determine event improvement metrics (2–3)
    – Identify data sources
    – Collect and graph baseline data
    – Calculate potential financial impact
- [ ] Consolidate VOC interviews into key themes
- [ ] Select team of process experts/stakeholders (ideal size is 6–8)
- [ ] Complete project charter
- [ ] Assess equipment, IS, and facilities support requirements
- [ ] **Close MEASURE phase**

ANALYZE Phase Checklist
3 weeks before event

- [ ] Perform data analysis
- [ ] Determine key stakeholders
    – Conduct stakeholder analysis
- [ ] Develop vision statement and elevator speech

1–2 weeks before event

- [ ] Confirm event location, time, and attendance
    – Confirm sponsor attendance at kick-off
- [ ] Prepare team information packet
    – Charter, VOC summaries, other relevant documentation
- [ ] Complete rapid improvement event agenda
- [ ] Prepare needed supplies (flip charts, markers, tape, sticky notes, PowerPoint, handouts, etc.)
- [ ] **Close ANALYZE phase**

IMPROVE Phase Checklist
Event duration 2 hours to 3 days

The Rapid Improvement Event

- [ ] Prepare event room (1hr before start)
    – Post all flip charts, prepare supplies
- [ ] Kickoff (sponsor welcome)
- [ ] Current state validation—where we are today and what we need to do to get to future state

Problem-solving process:

- [ ] 1. Brainstorm issue/barriers
- [ ] 2. Filter and prioritize
- [ ] 3. Brainstorm potential solutions
- [ ] 4. Filter and prioritize
- [ ] 5. Develop action plan
- [ ] Develop recommendations
- [ ] Develop communication plan
- [ ] Finalize Control phase action plan
    – Determine Control phase meeting schedule, time, and location
- [ ] Create sponsor/process owner report-out
    – Review Control phase action plan
    – Present recommendations
    – Discuss next steps
- [ ] Report out to sponsor(s) and process owner(s)
- [ ] **Close IMPROVE phase**

CONTROL Phase Checklist
4–8 weeks after event

1 week after

- [ ] Review communication plan/deliverables
- [ ] Monitor event metrics
- [ ] Control phase team meeting

2 weeks after

- [ ] Monitor event metrics
- [ ] Control phase team meeting

3–4 weeks after

- [ ] Monitor event metrics
- [ ] Control phase team meeting
- [ ] Develop control plan with sponsor(s) and process owner(s) to monitor sustainability
- [ ] Calculate any financial impact
    – Cost savings/avoidance, etc.
- [ ] Conduct process analysis (before/after)
- [ ] Conduct change readiness profile (before/after)
- [ ] Begin kaizen A3 report

5 weeks after

- [ ] Project handoff
- [ ] Finalize kaizen A3 report
- [ ] Send thank-yous to participants
- [ ] **Close project and CONTROL phase**

6–8 weeks after

- [ ] Formal results presentation/sharing

Checklist key
- 🟩 Complete
- 🟨 In progress
- 🟥 Not started

NOTES:
_____
_____
_____
_____
_____
_____
_____
_____
_____
_____

Figure 8.5 DMAIC checklist.

Checklist key
- 🟩 Complete
- 🟨 In progress
- 🟥 Not started

The checklist is a standard work and visual management tool. Tasks do not have to be completed in a stepwise fashion. You can complete deliverables in the define phase while working on tasks in measure and/or analyze. The checklist key provides an easy status update on all items. The box next to the phase deliverable should be color-coded according to its completion status.

Define Phase

Appendixes A and B describe tools presented here in further detail. The define phase initiates the project (Figure 8.6). Once the scope is defined, the define phase checklist is employed. The work put into the first three phases (define, measure, and analyze) will pay big dividends downstream, reducing rework and other issues (Toussaint and Gerard 2010). The focus is on processes, not outcomes. If the focus is on improving the correct process, outcomes will follow. It is like the analogy of losing weight: if you focus on the process (burning more calories than you consume), the weight reduction will follow. An additional note: before engaging in an improvement project, make sure the area under evaluation is within your circle of control. If you do not have the ability to change it (e.g., another department's process), you will have to assess your effectiveness in influencing the desired change; otherwise you could be fighting a losing battle.

DEFINE Phase Checklist
5–6 weeks before event
- [ ] Assign facilitator team roles
    –Leader, communications, logistics
- [ ] Kickoff meeting with sponsor(s)
    –Define problem/goal
    –Identify individuals to interview/draft communication plan
- [ ] Review current IS or other projects in area
    –Review potential/upcoming IS changes
- [ ] Conduct voice of customer (VOC) interviews
- [ ] Conduct a waste walk
- [ ] Develop high-level process map
- [ ] Begin project charter
- [ ] Assess change readiness using profile tool
- [ ] Use systems and process profile tool
- [ ] Schedule event (location/date/times)
- [ ] **Close DEFINE phase**

Figure 8.6 Define phase checklist.

Assign Facilitator Team Roles (Leader, Communications, Logistics)

An improvement team, especially one led by lean practitioners, needs defined roles. These individuals serve as the core team driving the project. Ideally, at least three individuals are assigned to the team in order to distribute the workload. The leader is responsible for delegating project tasks to the team. The communications person manages the communication plan. The logistics person oversees the coordination of tasks required to schedule and host an improvement event.

Kickoff Meeting with Sponsor(s)

The project sponsor is typically the person with decision-making authority (e.g., vice president or director). The kickoff meeting is between the improvement team and the sponsor. The problem and objective of the project are reviewed and agreed upon. The sponsor provides a list of individuals for the team to interview and include in the improvement event. The sponsor identifies the process owner, the individual with direct day-to-day oversight of the functional areas affected by the project. Lean projects typically have several process owners since the project flows horizontally across functional departments. The team also drafts the communication plan.

Communication Plan

The communication plan defines the groups of stakeholders that need to be kept informed throughout the DMAIC project phases (Snee and Hoerl 2003). For each specified group there is a key message about the project or impending change that needs to be articulated. Depending on the group, the delivery mechanism and frequency of providing communication will vary. For example, clinicians typically prefer communication through huddles rather than email. The person responsible for delivering the message is from the improvement team or the sponsor.

Review Current Information Systems or Other Projects in Area

It is important to do an environmental scan of previous, current, or upcoming projects related to the effort. Are there projects that you can leverage? Are there individuals or teams of importance that you can include? This will help reduce the likelihood of rework, redundant projects, or counterproductive efforts.

Conduct Voice of Customer Interviews

Voice of customer (VOC) interviews are critical for understanding the context of the problem. Since a variety of stakeholders are usually involved, shadowing is a great way to learn the process (Pande and Holpp 2002). Remember to "go and see, ask why, and show respect" (Womack 2011). If you do not understand the issues that staff are dealing with, how can you help support and empower them to resolve them? Talk with employees and look beyond surface issues. Drill down to the root causes (5 Whys), and look across the value stream (Graban 2012). Ask the following questions during VOC interviews: (1) What is working? (2) What is not working? (3) What frustrates you at work? and (4) If you could change one or two things, what would you change and why?

Conduct a Waste Walk

The waste walk is an observational assessment of process inefficiencies at the gemba. The improvement team allocates time to observe the process and employee flow and documents all DOWNTIME wastes observed.

> **Waste walk questions**
> - How does the process work?
> - How do you know if it is being performed correctly?
> - How do you know when an error occurs?
> - What do you do when a problem arises?
> - What cues are there to indicate you need to do something?
> - Do you do tasks the same way as others?

Develop a High-Level Process Map

Draft a high-level process map using the project scope.

Begin Project Charter

The project charter is the contract between the improvement team and the sponsor. The charter includes the scope, problem, and objective. Additional information includes what data are used, individuals of value, and anticipated issues or barriers to address. To begin, complete page 1 of the two-page charter.

Assess Change Readiness Using Profile Tool

The change readiness profile tool assesses the current environment of the targeted improvement area (Figure 8.7) (Palmer 2004). The six domains (detailed in Chapter 10) evaluate the current, transition, and future state components to leading change. Through VOC interviews or a survey, the improvement team can estimate the area's level of change readiness.

Use Systems and Process Profile Tool

Another tool used to determine the impact on change is the systems and process profile (Figure 8.8). This assessment tool evaluates the potential effect a change could have on various elements like staffing, information systems, and resources. This tool, along with the change readiness profile, provides a better understanding of the environmental current state and enables the improvement team to identify vulnerable areas and leverage strengths.

Figure 8.7 Change readiness profile tool.

What is the impact of the following items when it comes to changing the system/process?

Figure 8.8 Systems and process profile tool.

Schedule Event (Location, Date, Times)

The logistics leader works with the sponsor to determine the date and duration of the improvement event. As described earlier, the event could be two hours or up to three days depending on the project scope and problem complexity.

Close the Define Phase

The define phase closes once all applicable deliverables have been completed.

Measure Phase

Tools presented here are further described in Appendices A and C. The measure phase introduces data collection (Figure 8.9). The following deliverables help paint a picture of where opportunities for improvement exist within the process. Improvement event participants are also identified.

Review Previous Rapid Improvement Events, Kaizens, or Other Projects

If the problem was previously addressed, review what that team did. Lessons learned and strategies applied will provide insight as to how you can move your team forward. If there were similar projects in other areas, you might be able to adopt and adapt their improvement approach. Also, remember that kaizen happens everywhere. Talk with staff and see if they have previously tried to solve the problem. Solutions and lessons learned are generated by more ways than just projects. Where possible, do not reinvent the wheel.

MEASURE Phase Checklist

4 weeks before event

☐ Review previous rapid improvement events, kaizens, or other projects
☐ Formulate data collection plan (if needed)
☐ Conduct process value analysis
☐ Conduct workflow value analysis
☐ Create current state value stream map (VSM)
☐ Determine event improvement metrics (2–3)
  –Identify data sources
  –Collect and graph baseline data
  –Calculate potential financial impact
☐ Consolidate VOC interviews into key themes
☐ Select team of process experts/stakeholders (ideal size is 6–8)
☐ Complete project charter
☐ Assess equipment, IS, and facilities support requirements
☐ **Close MEASURE phase**

Figure 8.9 Measure phase checklist.

Formulate Data Collection Plan (if needed)

Providing data to drive improvements is critical. How can you get better if you do not even know how you are doing in the first place? How will you know where your vulnerabilities and strengths are? We have to arm people with actionable information and then hold them accountable for the outcomes. Develop a data collection plan if there are no information systems or automated data collection tools in place. This can be an interim log to calculate baseline performance. A post-improvement audit will occur in the control phase to assess the impact of change.

Conduct Process and Workflow Value Analyses

Using the Microsoft Excel–based tools, conduct time study observations following the process and employee flow. As described in Chapter 3, process value analysis is one of the most powerful lean diagnostic tools.

Create Current State Value Stream Map

Using the high-level SIPOC and process value analysis observations, complete the current state VSM. Remember to include waiting in between steps.

Determine Event Improvement Metrics (Two or Three)

Improvement metrics should reflect the operational performance of the area (Lawal et al. 2014). The metrics should align directly with the problem and objective. Using the appropriate chart (see "Performance Dashboards" in Chapter 7), collect and graph baseline data. The baseline is the foundation from which to assess the impact of planned changes. If applicable, calculate the financial impact of any change (e.g., overtime or rework reductions).

Consolidate VOC Interviews into Key Themes

Sort key themes that were consistent throughout the VOC interviews conducted by the improvement team. Themes usually include lack of communication; unavailable information, tools, and equipment; poor coordination between or within teams; issues with information systems; and no accountability. The themes might indicate potential root causes.

Tools presented here are further described in Appendix A and Appendix C. The measure phase introduces data collection. The deliverables help paint the picture of where opportunities for improvement exist within the process. Improvement event participants are also identified.

Select Team of Process Experts/Stakeholders

Involving stakeholders is critical to the success of any improvement or change effort. You have likely experienced a project stall or fail because the right people were not included. Lean thinking comes from a horizontal perspective. Who is involved upstream and downstream? Include all parties across the continuum of a process. For example, when improving patient flow in the operating room, include the departments that see the patient first (i.e., admissions/registration, pre-procedure nursing), the operating room itself, and the areas that may see the patient after surgery (i.e., nursing unit, recovery unit). Horizontal thinking breaks the vertical "silo" approach. The ideal number of improvement event participants is six to eight individuals, not including the improvement team facilitators.

Complete Project Charter

Finalize the charter by completing page 2 of the template.

Assess Equipment, Information Systems, and Facilities Support Requirements

Depending on the scope, area, and problem, assess whether ad hoc support services will be needed during the scheduled improvement event.

Close the Measure Phase

The measure phase closes once all applicable deliverables have been completed.

Analyze Phase

Tools presented here are further described in Appendices A and D. The analyze phase includes analysis of collected data as well as final logistic planning for the improvement event (Figure 8.10).

Perform Data Analysis

Using data, determine opportunities for improvement. What are the key drivers of the problem? If you are not comfortable with data analysis, seek help from individuals with this skill set. Data analysis will help verify and target root causes.

> **ANALYZE Phase Checklist**
>
> *3 weeks before event*
> ☐ Perform data analysis
> ☐ Determine key stakeholders
>   –Conduct stakeholder analysis
> ☐ Develop vision statement and elevator speech
>
> *1–2 weeks before event*
> ☐ Confirm event location, time, and attendance
>   –Confirm sponsor attendance at kickoff
> ☐ Prepare team information packet
>   –Charter, VOC summaries, other relevant documentation
> ☐ Complete rapid improvement event agenda
> ☐ Prepare needed supplies (flip charts, markers, tape, sticky notes, PowerPoint, handouts, etc.)
> ☐ **Close ANALYZE phase**

Figure 8.10 Analyze phase checklist.

Determine Key Stakeholders

Use VOC and process observations to conduct a stakeholder analysis with the improvement team. Identify individuals or groups that support the project and those who oppose it. If there is resistance to the effort, develop a strategy to win their support or, at the very least, address their concerns and limit the negative impact they might cause. Project success is contingent on leveraging the leaders and influencers within the improvement area. Build a guiding coalition to help communicate and disseminate changes rapidly.

Develop the Vision Statement and Elevator Speech

The elevator speech provides a concise summary that defines the project, objective, and what staff can do to help. This becomes a consistent message delivered between the improvement team and the sponsor throughout the life cycle of the project. When combined, the vision statement provides the destination and direction of the improvement strategy, while the elevator speech outlines the script to communicate important aspects of the change (i.e., what, when, how, what you can do to help, how it affects you).

Confirm Event Location, Time, and Attendance

The logistics person confirms all required resources are available (e.g., audio/visual equipment, food/snacks, and supplies such as sticky notes, markers, and flip charts). The sponsor undertakes the improvement event kickoff to set expectations.

Prepare Team Information Packet

The improvement team shares information gathered and analyzed through the first three project phases. The charter, VOC summary, and other relevant analyses

150 *Chapter Eight*

are distributed to the improvement event participants. This information provides context for where identified opportunities exist and the current state baseline.

Complete Rapid Improvement Event Agenda

The agenda details are in Appendix A.

Close the Analyze Phase

The analyze phase closes once all applicable deliverables have been completed.

Improve Phase

Appendices A and E further define the tools presented here. The rapid improvement event (or improvement event) is the problem-solving portion of the project (Figure 8.11). The first three phases provided a detailed understanding of the current state through VOC interviews, observations, and process analysis. Now with an assigned team of process experts, the improvement team is ready to facilitate the problem-solving process. Chapter 9, "Facilitating Rapid Improvements," provides a systematic approach to develop a high-impact action plan.

Prepare Event Room (One Hour before Start)

Verify that all needed supplies are ready in advance of the participants arriving.

Kickoff

Led by the sponsor, participants get an overview of why the project was selected, what the objective is for the improvement event, and the expectations for their participation and commitment into the control phase.

Current State Validation

The team reviews the informational packet with the participants. Remember that some participants may not understand process maps or other basic lean concepts like VA versus NVA activity. Depending on the level of knowledge, you might need to provide a simple introduction or tutorial on concepts and terms. This can also be done in advance of the improvement event.

Problem-Solving Process

The five-step problem-solving process is explained in Chapter 9. The steps are: (1) brainstorm issues and barriers, (2) filter and prioritize, (3) brainstorm solutions, (4) filter and prioritize, and (5) develop and implement an action plan.

Develop a Communication Plan

Once the action plan is developed, create or revise the vision statement and elevator speech. Briefly explain what is changing, why, and how it will happen. Remember that the improvement event participants are representing their area or discipline. Implementing improvements requires the commitment of all employees within the affected area. Therefore, it is essential to communicate (and over-communicate) with everyone not directly included in the development of the action plan.

> **IMPROVE Phase Checklist**
> *Event duration 2 hours to 3 days*
> **The Rapid Improvement Event**
> ☐ Prepare event room (1hr before start)
>   –Post all flip charts, prepare supplies
> ☐ Kickoff (sponsor welcome)
> ☐ Current state validation—where we are today and what we need to do to get to future state
> Problem-solving process:
> ☐ 1. Brainstorm issue/barriers
> ☐ 2. Filter and prioritize
> ☐ 3. Brainstorm potential solutions
> ☐ 4. Filter and prioritize
> ☐ 5. Develop action plan
> ☐ Develop recommendations
> ☐ Develop communication plan
> ☐ Finalize Control phase action plan
>   –Determine Control phase meeting schedule, time, and location
> ☐ Create sponsor/process owner report-out
>   –Review Control phase action plan
>   –Present recommendations
>   –Discuss next steps
> ☐ Report out to sponsor(s) and process owner(s)
> ☐ **Close IMPROVE phase**

Figure 8.11 Improve phase checklist.

Finalize Control Phase Action Plan

Before completing the improve phase, determine how the action plan will be implemented and monitored. Determine when and where to hold the weekly control phase meetings. Standing meetings (where you literally stand in a circle) are most effective. The meeting should occur as close to the affected area as possible and should be brief and direct, focusing on status updates and next steps.

Report Out to Sponsor(s) and Process Owner(s)

Upon completion of the action plan and control phase planning, the improvement event participants should report out to the sponsor and process owner. If there are recommendations that require approval or feedback, this is the time for the team to make the pitch.

Close the Improve Phase

The improve phase closes once all applicable deliverables have been completed.

> **Improvement Team Reflective Questions**
>
> *The following are suggested questions to reflect on when facilitating a rapid improvement event.*
>
> *Day 1 Review:*
> - What did you observe the team doing today?
> - What would you do differently and why?
> - What lean concepts (tools/principles) is the team working on, and do they need help?
> - What must be done by the end of day tomorrow?
>
> *Day 2 Review:*
> - What obstacles did you observe with the team seeing waste?
> - What specifically did you do that worked well? Why?
> - What was today's biggest challenge? How did you deal with it?
>
> **Participant Reflective Questions**
>
> *Day 1 Review:*
> - What are your observations of the process?
> - What workarounds exist?
>
> *Day 2 Review:*
> - What are the key wastes you observed?
> - What are the root causes of these wastes?
> - What changes have you tried or will you try?
> - How do you plan to communicate these changes?
> - Did you communicate to all people affected by the changes?
> - How are you going to sustain the new process?

Control Phase

Tools presented here are further described in Appendices A and F. The final project phase is the control phase (Figure 8.12). This phase consists of executing the action plan that was developed in the improve phase as well as formally closing the project and handing off the outstanding action items and tasks to the sponsor and process owner. The challenge in the control phase has more to do with the beginning/middle of the project than the close. Most times the operational handoff is an after-thought. If you don't plan for risk mitigation, resource allocation, metric monitoring, and ongoing discussion/review, then you should not expect sustained results. You need to hardwire these components to ensure progress can be maintained; it is not easy.

Review Communication Plan/Deliverables

The communications leader ensures execution of the communication plan throughout this phase of the project. At this point changes are being made to the process. Communication and feedback are critical.

CONTROL Phase Checklist
4–8 weeks after event

1 week after
☐ Review communication plan/deliverables
☐ Monitor event metrics
☐ Control phase team meeting

2 weeks after
☐ Monitor event metrics
☐ Control phase team meeting

3–4 weeks after
☐ Monitor event metrics
☐ Control phase team meeting
☐ Develop control plan with sponsor(s) and process owner(s) to monitor sustainability
☐ Calculate any financial impact
  –Cost savings/avoidance, etc.
☐ Conduct process analysis (before/after)
☐ Conduct change readiness profile (before/after)
☐ Begin kaizen A3 report

5 weeks after
☐ Project handoff
☐ Finalize kaizen A3 report
☐ Send thank-yous to participants
☐ **Close project and CONTROL phase**

6–8 weeks after
☐ Formal results presentation/sharing

Figure 8.12 Control phase checklist.

Monitor Event Metrics

Data updates continue throughout the control phase. Figure 8.13 shows the baseline data (gray) compared with the post-intervention data (blue) and the target. The team communicates performance updates to the affected area on a regular basis, serving as a feedback loop.

Control Phase Team Meeting

The weekly team meetings involve the improvement team, improvement event participants, sponsor, process owner, and any stakeholder that needs be included. The team reviews the control phase action plan, and participants provide updates on assigned items.

Develop Control Plan with Sponsor(s) and Process Owner(s) to Monitor Sustainability

Before concluding the control phase, the improvement team develops a control plan with the sponsor and process owners. The control plan includes strategies for ongoing verification of process compliance, data collection and dissemination, and longer-term refinement of the changes. This is an important transition plan, focusing on hardwiring effective changes.

Figure 8.13 Example of run chart, post-improvement.

Calculate Any Financial Impact

Where applicable, calculate any cost savings, revenue enhancement, or cost avoidance resulting from project. Utilize internal expertise to evaluate and estimate the financial gains. Assessing the impact of improvements can be challenging. Many organizations look for the dollar savings that improvement projects generate, but there are other indicators that show quality output gains (e.g., efficiencies realized, increases in staff/patient satisfaction), all of which are important.

Conduct Process Analysis and Change Readiness Profile (Before/After)

The process analysis (before and after) shows the new distribution of VA to NVA activities. The change readiness profile demonstrates any changes in the work area environment as they relate to change management factors. Results of these analyses support the potential positive impact of the project.

Project Handoff

At the conclusion of the control phase, the improvement team hands off the project to the sponsor and the process owner. The action plan may not be complete, so it is the responsibility of the sponsor and the process owner to oversee its execution. The improvement team formally closes and hands off the deliverables and assignments so it can move on to the next project.

Finalize Kaizen A3 Report

The A3 report is a standard project documentation template that describes the project's story (Figure 8.14). This becomes the main document for sharing lessons learned and results (Jimmerson, Weber, and Sobek 2005). Organizations can accelerate improvements by sharing such information so similar areas and work processes do not encounter the same problem or issue (Sobek and Smalley 2008). The term A3 refers to the paper size (11 inches × 17 inches). It is a tool that was developed in the late 1960s by Toyota as a standard format for problem solving, proposals, plans, and status reviews (Bicheno and Holweg 2004; Lean Enterprise Institute n.d.).

EXECUTING A PROJECT THROUGH LEAN DMAIC 155

Project title
Participant names

Background	**Countermeasures** (implemented or proposed)	**Results** (metrics to follow/baseline data)
Provide context about the area (organization, department, workspace) under review. What are the core processes/outputs? What is interesting about this project?	Describe the countermeasures applied or proposed. Explain how the countermeasure addresses the problems identified as well as the expected outcomes.	Provide performance dashboard (pre/post if applicable) of metrics described in the problem statement and objectives. Results should link throughout the A3 report. If an improvement was made, indicate when it occurred so it is easy to see before/after. Indicate the desired direction of the data (i.e., higher is better).
Problem statement	**Pictures/process maps**	
What problem is being addressed? How did you validate the problem? What implications/consequences exist if the problem is not resolved?	Provide a current state process map. What are the main issues and gaps in the process? What section are you targeting and why? Provide a future state map to demonstrate the impact of countermeasures on the process. What is different and why?	**Next steps**
Project/proposal objective		What activities will be required for implementation? Who will be responsible and by when? What other issues/barriers need to be addressed?
How do you define success? What specific goals and outcomes define success (e.g., performance metrics)?		

Figure 8.14 Example of a kaizen A3 report.

156 Chapter Eight

Send Thank-Yous to Participants

Improvement event participants took time from their workday to help contribute to the project. Be sure to thank them for their time and efforts during both the event and the control phase. Success and sustainability rely on engaged staff who feel their contributions are valued.

Close the Project and Control Phase

The control phase closes once all applicable deliverables have been completed.

Formal Results Presentation/Sharing

Several weeks after the close of the control phase, the sponsor and the process owner provide an update on the project's success and sustainability of results. This is a great opportunity to check (refine) and act (from PDCA). Continuous improvement encourages the frequent review of implemented solutions to ensure they are having the desired, favorable impact. Update the A3 report with final results and distribute it to all appropriate stakeholders.

Case Study: Patient Flow through the Short-Procedure Unit (SPU)

Content from ASQ publication *"Let It Flow: Improving Perioperative Patient Flow using Lean Improvement Strategies"* (Delisle and Jaffe 2015)

The largest volume of surgeries occurs on Jefferson's Center City campus. The OR is a setting abundant in opportunities for improvement. System inefficiencies can lead to suboptimization of OR utilization, thereby decreasing revenue generation. Delays, from patient arrival to entering the preoperative holding area, have an impact on the ability to start scheduled OR procedures on time. Due to high surgical volumes, delays in first cases have a cascading effect on the entire schedule, bottlenecking the pre- and post-procedural areas. These delays have fiscal consequences and are a primary source of patient and employee dissatisfaction.

The project was conducted for 32 of Jefferson's main ORs. On the day of surgery, the patient flow process begins with checking in at admissions and ends after surgery, where the patient is either discharged to home or admitted to an inpatient bed. In order to impact meaningful, incremental improvement, the project scope narrowed to only include patient flow from patient check-in at admissions through arrival at the holding area (HA) (Figure 8.15).

The study design was a pre/post-intervention assessment. The project used the DMAIC framework (define, measure, analyze, improve, and control). The primary outcome measure was the time from patient check-in to arrival at the holding area. The patient flow process in the pre-intervention analysis was 54.1 minutes.

Prior to a scheduled RIE, certified lean leaders conducted voice of customer (VOC) interviews and process analysis observations. These deliverables established the baseline current state. VOC interviews were conducted with more than 20 staff from all associated areas (registration, SPU, HA, OR, transportation, administration, etc.). The key themes of issues inhibiting process efficiency identified through the VOC interviews and observations were: (1) scheduling, (2) registration delays due to location of department, (3) transportation of patients from SPU to HA, and (4) lack of coordination of activities within the SPU. The inputs from the interviews and process analysis served as the basis for improvement.

Figure 8.15 Current state process map for OR patient flow.

Process analysis showed a large proportion (more than 60 percent) of NVA activity (Figure 8.16). Within the current state of the process, 43.3 percent of the process time involved the patient waiting for something to happen (i.e., waiting for a nurse, physician). An additional 8 percent of the time was committed to patient travel from location to location. In patient flow studies, waiting and transportation are typically the most pervasive forms of waste in the process. These results were expected due to the complexity of the process, geography of work areas, and organizational structure (i.e., admissions, transportation, and OR staff having different reporting structures and managers).

Figure 8.16 Value analysis breakdown for OR patient flow.

After the current state VOC and process analyses were completed, the lean team entered the improve phase of the project. The lean practitioners facilitated a four-day RIE with a multidisciplinary group of staff from registration, SPU, HA, and OR (together known as the team). The goal for the team was to develop and pilot countermeasures to address and eliminate identified waste and issues.

During the event, the lean leaders led a structured problem-solving process. Participating staff brainstormed barriers and issues that drive inefficiency. The salient issues were prioritized through consensus voting. The priority issues were inefficient patient flow logistics and lack of workflow coordination within the SPU. These issues became targets for improvement. The team developed solutions through structured brainstorming and additional site visits to the work area. There were three core solutions that required detailed action planning:

1. Patient registration moved from the admissions department to SPU at the bedside. This process change removes the need for patients to check in multiple times (previously at admissions then at SPU) (Figures 8.17 and 8.18).

158 Chapter Eight

Figure 8.17 Post-intervention process for OR patient flow.

Figure 8.18 Improvement team piloting changes.

Improvement team piloting registration at the bedside with mock patients

2. The SPU charge nurse (responsible for patient flow monitoring) was relocated and tasks were standardized. The charge nurse role is integral in managing flow and assigning nurses to patients based on priority and need. The role rotates between three individuals, which necessitates a standard approach to documentation and responsibilities. The added structure enables staff to work efficiently while the charge nurse monitors the flow of patients, nurses, and registrars.

3. The SPU patient interview processes were streamlined to accommodate the integration of registration staff. The patient interview process performed by the nurse was lengthy. The "need to know" information was identified and rescripted. This standardized the approach and freed up time for the registrars to complete the admission prior to the patient's surgery preparation.

After the improve phase, the solutions were hardwired into daily operations. The control phase included weekly monitoring of action plan progress as well as data updates and reporting. Figure 8.19 provides the pre-/post-intervention monthly processing time trends, including the pre-intervention. Post-intervention data demonstrate a statistically significant improvement in mean processing time from pre-intervention of 54.1 minutes (95 percent confidence interval 53.3–54.8 minutes) to post-intervention 46.1 minutes (95 percent confidence interval 45.3–46.9 minutes, p = 0.000).

Figure 8.19 Monthly average of SPU processing time.

The process value analysis graph depicts the distribution of VA to NVA activities (Figure 8.20). Post intervention, the percentage of VA activities increased from 40 percent to 49 percent, which was a direct result of reducing and eliminating NVA activities such as transportation and waiting.

Figure 8.20 Process value analysis before and after intervention.

⚠ CHAPTER CHALLENGE

Develop a project plan using the lean DMAIC checklist. Outline the deliverables with an associated timeline. Execute the plan. What was your experience using the structured approach? Was the checklist helpful? Are there components that need to be added or removed based on your experience?

QUESTIONS

1. What does the kaizen mentality represent?
2. What does everyday kaizen mean?
3. How does the PDCA cycle work? What is the significance of check and act?
4. Why do projects require structured phases?
5. What benefit does a project checklist provide? How can you use this in your area of responsibility?
6. Why are VOC interviews important? Who should you talk to when starting a project or process evaluation?
7. What kind of information can a change readiness profile give you? Why is this useful?
8. Why do you need to perform observations and process analyses?
9. Who should be included in a rapid improvement event? Why?
10. What is the importance of weekly control phase team meetings?
11. Why do projects need to be handed off to sponsors and process owners?
12. How are kaizen A3 reports used to communicate project success and lessons learned?

Chapter 9
Facilitating Rapid Improvements

A plan is an experiment you run to see what you don't understand about the work.

– Steven Spear

Rapid improvement events (RIEs) are an effective management approach that accelerates the pace of change. The RIE ranges in duration from two hours to three days or longer, depending on the scope of the project and complexity of the problem. RIEs involve process experts and stakeholders (usually 6–12 individuals) who are brought together to solve a problem and implement an action plan. The approach expedites the normal business approach of forming committees or working groups that can take months to solve a problem. The rate of change is as important as the scope of it. If you rush something, you will generate strong resistance. If you go too slowly, you will lose momentum. The balance of scope, rate of change, and stakeholders involved lead to project success or failure.

When implementing improvements, the lean term is kaizen. Kaizen is not just a facilitated improvement event but also any improvement made to address a problem. Both the previous chapter and this chapter describe how to manage improvement projects and facilitate teams. However, these concepts are just as applicable to daily improvements made at the gemba. Kaizen should happen everywhere, all the time. It is essential to ingrain the kaizen mindset of continuous improvement. The focus is always on delivering value to customers. Without customers, there is no purpose to exist as a company.

> **Advice for RIEs**
> - Kaizen should not happen to people; it happens through people.
> - Facilitators are there to help point the team in the right direction (where the opportunities lie). The team develops the solutions.
> - Completing a few objectives is significantly better than partially starting many.
> - Sometimes you have to explain the obvious because the distribution of common sense is not even.

Projects ripe for the rapid improvement approach share common characteristics:

- The problem and goal are clearly defined
- They are within your scope of control
- They can be fixed quickly (i.e., solutions can be implemented within 30–60 days)
- They will eliminate unnecessary work and/or reduce costs
- They require strong leadership support and buy-in from key stakeholders
- They are aligned with organizational values and strategic initiatives

Effective RIEs include clearly specified roles and responsibilities:

- *Sponsor:* Leadership position (e.g., vice president, director) with decision-making authority over area of focus. This individual is accountable for the success of the effort and helps remove barriers to action plan implementation. The sponsor helps drive results through oversight and support.
- *Process owner:* Person with managerial oversight (e.g., manager, supervisor) who is responsible for implementation and sustainability of the action plan.
- *Participants:* Process experts that provide content expertise and context to solve the problems and issues being addressed. These individuals also help develop and implement the action plan and build staff buy-in and engagement.
- *Facilitator:* Individual with responsibility to lead participants through the problem-solving process. He or she partners with the team to drive action plan implementation.

FACILITATION GUIDELINES

Facilitated meetings for RIEs should follow the same guidelines as earlier regarding roles, responsibilities, and ground rules. Establishing team roles helps clarify expectations and ensures that the problem-solving process can be efficiently managed (Andersen, Rovik, and Ingebrigtsen 2014). Since RIEs are short in nature, it is important to have delegated tasks and timelines. These are some common roles within RIE teams:

- *Lead facilitator:* This person guides the group through problem-solving activities to achieve objectives and ensures everyone participates and stays focused.
- *Process checker:* This role is for a co-facilitator. The process checker maintains focus on agreed-upon processes used and helps the participants apply tools correctly. He or she also assists the lead facilitator.
- *Scribe:* The scribe is responsible for recording ideas verbatim on sticky notes, flip charts, or other provided materials. The role of scribe is assigned to a participant.
- *Timekeeper:* The timekeeper monitors time during small group activities and provides updates to keep the team on track. This is another important role

during an RIE. The assigned time allocation for activities should be closely followed to ensure the RIE meets its intended objective in the set time period.

- *Presenter:* Again, for group-based activities, the presenter leads the presentation of the group's work. He or she is responsible for concisely summarizing the activity outcome.

Ground rules provide participants with expectations for how to behave and what to expect during an RIE. Ground rules describe how the RIE will run, how participants are expected to interact, and what behaviors are acceptable or unacceptable. They help teams self-manage and self-correct. Examples of ground rules include the following:

- Start and end on time
- Cell phones and pagers should be set on vibrate
- Vegas rules—what is said in the room stays in the room
- Have an open mind, leave cynicism at door
- One person speaks at a time

Facilitators provide an opportunity at the start of the RIE to review ground rules and ask participants to add others to the list. The best way to ensure compliance with ground rules is to provide participants an opportunity to define what they will be.

> *The parking lot is a tool that helps keep discussions focused. Typically, a flip chart or document is posted in the room of the RIE and is used to store issues and ideas that have been captured on sticky notes. The parking lot is used when topics come up that: (1) are outside the project scope, (2) contain issues that need to be addressed by a different group of stakeholders, or (3) require questions, comments, or follow-up at a later point in time. This tool helps the team stay the course and meet the RIE objectives in the allocated time.*

THE KAIZEN PROBLEM-SOLVING PROCESS

Facilitating RIEs requires a structured problem-solving approach called the kaizen problem-solving process (Figure 9.1). This five-step process leads to the identification of key issues, development of effective solutions, and implementation of a well-defined action plan. The five steps are:

1. Brainstorm issues and barriers
2. Filter and prioritize issues and barriers
3. Brainstorm solutions
4. Filter and prioritize solutions
5. Develop and implement the action plan

Figure 9.1 Five-step kaizen problem-solving process.

A set of tools accompanies each step to help facilitate the process. The following section reviews the five steps and associated tools. Note that only a select number of tools are presented. As stated in the introduction, there are many ways to accomplish a task, but this book presents the most effective approaches based on years of experience facilitating rapid improvements.

Step 1: Brainstorm Issues and Barriers

The first step of the kaizen problem-solving process is to brainstorm issues and barriers (Figure 9.2). Before discussing solutions, first identify the root causes to address. Solution development is premature if the root cause is unknown. Sometimes we search for answers without knowing the right questions. It is hard to be patient and take a step back. Think less like a firefighter and more like a fire prevention engineer. A firefighter chases down fires to put them out. An engineer designs sprinkler systems and uses specific materials to reduce the likelihood of a fire ever occurring. That is how we need to think about improvements.

Figure 9.2 Step 1: Brainstorm issues and barriers.

Brainstorming is a divergent activity. This means any idea is accepted. During this step, you want the participants (content and process experts) to provide any potential issue or barrier that might contribute to the problem you are trying to solve. The goal is to capture as many ideas as possible regarding the topic at hand.

Tools to Use During Step 1

Three brainstorming tools can be used during this step: (1) silent brainstorming, (2) free-for-all, and (3) the fishbone diagram.

Silent Brainstorming

- *How to do it:* Participants have 5–10 minutes of silence for this individual activity in which they write their ideas on sticky notes (one idea per note). Once everyone has written down his or her ideas, the facilitator leads the report out, a brief presentation summarizing the team's work. Each person reads one idea aloud. The facilitator takes the sticky note and places it on a blank flip chart. If other participants have the same or a similar idea, the facilitator consolidates them. The report out rotates one person, one idea at a time, until all ideas have been shared.

- *When to use it:* Silent, individual activities are a great way to diminish any dominating personalities or to provide shy, introverted personalities an opportunity to share their thoughts.

- *What it looks like:* The picture on the left in Figure 9.3 shows the team members reporting out on their ideas. The picture on the right depicts the facilitator consolidating issues and barriers by theme.

Figure 9.3 Examples of improvement teams brainstorming.

166 *Chapter Nine*

Free-for-All

- *How to do it:* The free-for-all is a dynamic brainstorming activity. The facilitator poses the question of what issues and barriers contribute to the problem, and all participants openly share their ideas. It is important to assign at least one scribe during the free-for-all so all documentation is captured. Another important consideration during this activity is the ground rules. Remember to encourage open, respectful dialogue.

- *When to use it:* This open, collaborative activity works well with groups whose members are comfortable with one another. If participants are able to leave their titles at the door and exercise an open mind, the free-for-all can be highly engaging and productive.

- *What it looks like:* Similar to silent brainstorming, the free-for-all yields a flip chart with consolidated issues and barriers.

Fishbone Diagram

- *How to do it:* Chapter 7 details the fishbone diagram.

- *When to use it:* This tool provides more structure to brainstorming than either silent brainstorming or the free-for-all. The fishbone is effective if participants are slow to discuss issues and barriers or do not know where to begin. The added structure enables participants to compartmentalize the issues and barriers into predefined themes (i.e., personnel, materials/supplies, measurement, method/processes, machine/equipment).

- *What it looks like:* Figure 9.4 shows an example of a completed fishbone diagram.

Figure 9.4 Example of a fishbone diagram.

Step 2: Filter and Prioritize Issues and Barriers

The second step of the kaizen problem-solving process is to filter and prioritize the issues and barriers (Figure 9.5). Step 2 is one of the most critical components of the problem-solving model. You have to differentiate between issues and barriers within your control and those outside your control before you can develop solutions.

Filtering and prioritizing are convergent activities. During this step, the participants help determine which issues and barriers can be directly addressed. Subsequently, participants prioritize these issues and barriers based on the ones with the largest impact on the problem. The goal is to narrow issues and barriers to only those that we can influence.

Tools to Use During Step 2

Step 2 has two phases: (1) filter and (2) prioritize. Filtering requires one tool, the in-control/out-of-control activity. Prioritization can be done through dot voting or consensus voting.

Phase 1: Filter—In or Out of Control

- *How to do it:* After the issues and barriers have been collected in step 1, the next step is to filter them. The facilitator takes one issue at a time and asks the participants whether it is "within our control" or "outside our control." The facilitator simply asks the question and moves the sticky note accordingly. The participants are responsible for categorizing the issues based on the knowledge, experience, and scope of work. If an issue or barrier seems to be partly within our control and partly outside our control, break the issue or barrier into smaller pieces. Ask participants to specifically identify those elements that are within our control and document them on a new sticky note. There should not be any sticky notes straddling the line.

- *When to use it:* Immediately after step 1.

- *What it looks like:* The flip chart should have two boxes, one inside the other (Figure 9.6). The inner box defines elements that are in control. All issues

Figure 9.5 Step 2: Filter and prioritize issues and barriers.

168 *Chapter Nine*

and barriers determined to be within the group's control are placed there. Correspondingly, the issues and barriers that are outside the group's control are placed along the outside region.

- *Hint for categorizing issues and barriers:* While performing the in-control/out-of-control activity, facilitators continue to recategorize issues and barriers by theme (e.g., staffing, technology, process, communication). The identified issues and barriers are typically symptoms of underlying root causes. The themes provide a general summary of these symptoms and may define the potential root cause of the problem. The facilitator creates the categories and writes each one on a new sticky note and displays it above the cluster of issues and barriers. Participants review and approve the categories before phase 2. The flip chart in Figure 9.7 shows the sticky notes sorted by theme.

Figure 9.6 In-control/out-of-control template.

Figure 9.7 Example of categorizing issues and barriers.

Phase 2: Prioritize Issues and Barriers

Once the issues and barriers have been sorted (according to whether they are within or outside our control) and categorized by theme, the next step is to prioritize them. Prioritization occurs only for issues and barriers determined to be within the group's control. During this phase, participants vote on what theme/category within their control has the most significant impact on the problem. Generally, two or three prioritized themes result from the voting activity. Depending on the breadth and complexity of the prioritized themes, the facilitator might choose to focus on one or two for solution development (steps 3–5).

Dot Voting

- *How to do it:* Each participant receives four dots. The dots can be stickers, pieces of paper, or made with markers. Participants use the dots to vote on the theme/category that has the biggest impact on the problem. Participants do not vote on the individual issues or barriers identified. This is why it is important to categorize after filtering. Participants use their dots as they deem appropriate. Dots can be evenly distributed (four dots for four categories) or concentrated (four dots for one category or three dots for one and only one dot for another). The theme/category with the most dots is the priority for steps 3–5.

- *When to use it:* Dot voting is an individual activity. Participants are encouraged to go up to the flip chart and vote regardless of what their peers are considering. The dot voting strategy aims to reduce group bias.

- *What it looks like:* Figure 9.8 shows various teams using dot voting. The picture on the far right shows the dots surrounding the identified categories (orange sticky notes).

Consensus Voting

- *How to do it:* Consensus voting is a group-based activity. The identified categories are discussed with the participants. The facilitator leads the discussion until there is agreement around the priority category of issues and barriers.

Figure 9.8 Examples of improvement teams voting.

- *When to use it:* This approach is effective if there is general consensus and a clear theme throughout step 1. Similar to the free-for-all brainstorming activity, this can be a dynamic activity that requires facilitation.

- *What it looks like:* Consensus can be shown through a simple show of hands.

Step 3: Brainstorm Potential Solutions

The third step of the kaizen problem-solving process is to brainstorm solutions (Figure 9.9). By now, the prioritized category of issues and barriers has been identified as the root cause. The team is now ready to begin solution development. As noted earlier, there might be one or two prioritized themes/categories that will be addressed during this step.

Brainstorming solutions is a divergent activity. All ideas are welcomed. As with step 1, you want the participants to share any and all ideas that could address the root cause. The objective of step 3 is to gather as many solutions as possible. Solution development entails the following (Silverstein, Samuel, and Decarlo 2009):

- *Substitutions*—replace existing process with improved approach
- *Combinations*—leverage and combine steps to improve quality and efficiency
- *Adoption and adaption*—adopt and adapt proven best practices
- *Modification*—change the approach/steps to yield different results
- *Elimination*—remove process steps that produce errors or inefficiencies

Guidelines for Solution Development: Spear's Four Rules

Solution development requires creative insight and a logical approach for implementation. The guiding rules for this problem-solving step come from Steven Spear. Spear developed four rules based on observations at Toyota manufacturing plants. These rules serve as the foundation for solution development (Jimmerson 2010; Spear 2005):

1. Activities are clear and well defined. Everyone knows what he or she is supposed to do, when, and how long it should take.

2. Steps are simple and direct.

3. Flow is simple and direct. The process has as few steps and people are needed to complete.

4. Problems are dealt with in a timely and direct manner.

> *In most areas with opportunities for improvement, the common source of issues is the violation of Spear's first rule. Staff cannot communicate and coordinate efforts effectively without clear expectations.*

Figure 9.9 Step 3: Brainstorm solutions.

Tools to Use During Step 3

Four tools can be used during step 3: (1) silent brainstorming, (2) free-for-all, (3) direct issue-to-solution brainstorming, and (4) reverse engineering. The silent brainstorming and the free-for-all tools are conducted in the same way as described in step 1.

Direct Issue-to-Solution Brainstorming

- *How to do it:* Direct issue-to-solution brainstorming is the most effective of the solution development tools. Participants work in small groups of three or four people. Each group receives the sticky notes from the prioritized theme/category. Then, each individual note is placed in a column on flip chart paper or on a table or desk. The group brainstorms solutions to the specific issue. During this process, the group might identify a general solution that addresses several issues at once.

- *When to use it:* This tool is the suggested approach for simple, effective solution development. It provides a linear path from issue to solution, which tends to appeal to most participants.

- *What it looks like:* Figure 9.10 shows the flow of direct issue-to-solution brainstorming. First, the prioritized theme is selected. Second, the individual issues that compose the theme are placed in a column. And third, corresponding solutions are developed for each individual issue.

Reverse Engineering

- How to do it: The reverse engineering tool provides a different approach to problem solving. Rather than developing solutions based on the identified root causes, the reverse engineering approach takes issue identification to the next level. During this activity, the participants discuss all the ways in which they can ensure the problem persists. Once the group brainstorms ways to achieve this, they shift the focus toward solving the new problems identified.
    - For example, if the problem being addressed is a loud nursing unit, one way to ensure the condition persists is to implement a "talk loud" policy that requires staff to shout during all interactions. To counter the "talk loud" policy, the team might develop a visual management solution that obviates the need for verbal communication, thus reducing the noise level.

172 Chapter Nine

Figure 9.10 Example of direct issue-to-solution brainstorming.

- *When to use it:* This tool is highly effective when groups are struggling with creative ideas.

- *What it looks like:* Figure 9.11 depicts the flow from prioritized problem to ways in which it can persist, leading to a corresponding solution.

Step 4: Filter and Prioritize Potential Solutions

The fourth step of the kaizen problem-solving process is to filter and prioritize the solutions (Figure 9.12). Selecting what you get involved with is tricky. We live in a resource-scarce world, including our own resources (e.g., time, effort, money). There will always be more good ideas than time and resources to implement them (McChesney, Covey, and Huling 2012). We have to prioritize by what will give us the biggest bang for our buck. The convergence of solutions through filtering and prioritizing leads to a high-impact action plan (step 5). The goal is to narrow solutions to those that are effective.

Figure 9.11 Example of reverse engineering.

Figure 9.12 Step 4: Filter and prioritize solutions.

Tools to Use During Step 4

The main tool used during step 4 is the payoff matrix. Depending on the results of prioritization, the group might have to use dot or consensus voting to further refine the selection. Another tool that helps segment solutions is the Lamina (pronounced la-mine-ah) tree of low-hanging fruit.

Payoff Matrix

- *How to do it:* The payoff matrix is a simple and highly effective tool that is based on an x-axis and a y-axis. The x-axis is "ease of implementation," which is defined as easy or difficult. The y-axis is "impact on problem," which is defined as low or high. The facilitator asks a presenter from each group to read aloud their solutions from step 3. For each solution, the facilitator asks the participants, "How easy is this to do?" and "What is the potential impact on addressing the problem?" As with the in-control/out-of-control tool, the participants determine the appropriate quadrant. The goal is to differentiate and isolate solutions:

  – High impact, easy to implement: These are the types of solutions we are looking for. Ideas that fall into this category provide the biggest impact at a relatively low cost and with little effort.

  – High impact, difficult to implement: Solutions that fall into this category require careful consideration. It is important to understand the reason for it being categorized as difficult to implement. Are the difficulties in resource requirements (e.g., staffing, new equipment), culture, or behaviors? Depending on the factors, the team might decide to table the solution or develop a recommendation for the sponsor to provide guidance or make decisions.

  – Low impact, easy to implement: These solutions are known as "just-do-its"—simple ideas that have a minimal positive impact and consume little or no resources.

  – Low impact, difficult to implement: Solutions in this category should be ignored altogether. The value of the payoff matrix is in identifying the high-impact solutions. Avoid anything that is difficult with a minimal impact.

- *When to use it:* The payoff matrix is used after all solutions have been brainstormed.

- *What it looks like:* Figure 9.13 shows the four quadrants. The green quadrants indicate solutions worth pursuing for step 5, the orange quadrant (high/difficult) represents solutions that require further consideration and refinement, and the red quadrant (low/difficult) should be avoided.

> *There will always be more problems and good ideas to tackle than the time, money, and energy to address them. Though we have great intentions to do wonderful things, it is not possible or realistic to expect it all. Prioritization is essential, and you need to have the ability to identify and exploit the "levers" that have the biggest impact to drive outcomes.*

Lamina Tree of Low-Hanging Fruit

- *How to do it:* The Lamina tree tool stores the low/easy solutions known as the just-do-its. Since just-do-its are simple, straightforward ideas, they do not require thorough action plans. Therefore, the Lamina tree of low-hanging fruit serves as a temporary placeholder for these ideas.

- *When to use it:* The Lamina tree is used after the solutions have been prioritized by quadrant. The Lamina tree holds solutions from the low/easy quadrant. The solutions act as leaves on the tree—the more the better. Once action plans are developed for the high/easy and select high/difficult solutions, the solutions on the tree are assigned an action plan.

Figure 9.13 Payoff matrix.
Note: For more information on the matrix, visit http://www.mindtools.com/pages/article/newHTE_95.htm.

- *What it looks like:* Figure 9.14 shows a before-and-after view of the Lamina tree. (The Lamina tree of low-hanging fruit was developed by Caroline Lamina, a Jefferson lean leader [Figure 9.15].)

Figure 9.14 Example of Lamina tree of low-hanging fruit.

Caroline (Carrie) Lamina, anatomic pathology manager in the Clinical Lab and a Jefferson lean leader since 2010, facilitating a swimlane map. Carrie developed the tree of low-hanging fruit, hence the name.

Figure 9.15 Inventor of the Lamina tree.

Step 5: Develop and Implement Action Plan

The final step of the kaizen problem-solving process is to develop and implement the action plan (Figure 9.16). The action plan details how tasks will be accomplished based on a set timeline.

Tools to Use During Step 5

The two tools used during step 5 are the action plan worksheet and the control phase action plan.

Figure 9.16 Step 5: Develop and implement an action plan.

Action Plan Worksheet

- *How to do it:* The action plan worksheet defines how to execute the prioritized solutions. The participants take the selected solutions (high/easy and some high/difficult) and complete the worksheet.

- *When to use it:* Once the payoff matrix is complete, the prioritized solutions are removed from the flip chart. Participants can be broken into smaller groups to complete this tool.

- *What it looks like:* The action plan worksheet has two components: the action plan and recommendations. The action plan (Table 9.1) is used for tasks or solutions that do not require sponsor approval. Recommendations (Table 9.2) are used to provide a business case for sponsor review and decision. Each table provides specific information on the solution. "What" is the solution identified in step 4. "How and why" provides the steps to complete the task/solution, along with the explanation for why it is being done as part of the project. "Resources needed" includes staff, equipment, supplies, and leadership support. "Expected outcome" outlines what will result from this solution. Ideally, the expected outcome is quantitative (i.e., performance metrics). Anytime we put a countermeasure in place for a problem, we must measure (through observations and/or metrics) or check to see that the problem truly has been solved. The last two components, "Who" and "By when," define the responsible person and timeline for completion. The recommendation table also has "What decision needs to be made?" as an item. This helps facilitate the discussion between the RIE team and the sponsor.

Table 9.1 Action plan template.

What	How and why	Resources needed	Expected outcome	Who	By when

Table 9.2 Recommendation template.

What	How and why	Resources needed	Expected outcome	What decision needs to be made?	By when

Control Phase Action Plan

- *How to do it:* The control phase action plan is a Microsoft Excel–based tool used to document post-RIE activities. The facilitator and the process owner help manage post-RIE implementation of action items. As described in the section "Control Phase" in Chapter 8, the control phase action plan serves as the agenda for weekly status update meetings.

- *When to use it:* The action plan worksheet is transferred to this tool. The control phase action plan is updated weekly and disseminated to the project team.

- *What it looks like:* The Microsoft Excel tool tracks updates using both a stoplight indicator (red = not started, yellow = in progress, green = complete) and supporting text for updates. Figure 9.17 is a blank template of the tool. Appendix C provides details for using the tool in Microsoft Excel.

Figure 9.17 Control phase action plan screenshot.

The kaizen problem-solving process keeps discussions moving toward action. Each step has a specific objective that leads to a high-impact solution. Steps are completed in succession and cannot be skipped. You should not go from step 4 (developing solutions) back to step 1 (brainstorming issues and barriers). This is how things do not get resolved! After each step is complete, the facilitator gets consensus that the step is finished, and the team moves forward to the next one.

Remember along the way that problem-solving is a team sport. As a facilitator, you do not want to leave people behind. Ensure a level of consensus (or at least common understanding) before moving forward on discussion items. The facilitator's job is to leverage and optimize the knowledge and experience of the team. This five-step process positions them to do so.

> *Do you have to take this formal approach? No. The five-step framework is a guide to problem-solving. If a problem needs immediate attention, think through the process to determine the most effective solution. Remember the four rules of solution development.*

FACILITATOR'S ROLE IN GROUP DYNAMICS

A facilitator acts like an orchestra conductor. The facilitator works with experts and forms teams to collaboratively solve problems. A good conductor harnesses the skills of many to create a unified piece of music. Similarly, a good facilitator can extract and leverage the knowledge and contributions of individuals and coordinate a focused improvement effort. Improvement teams typically run through the five stages of team development: forming, storming, norming, performing, and adjourning (Table 9.3) (Tuckman 1965). The facilitator has four main roles during this process:

1. Creating and maintaining a collaborative group environment
2. Building rapport
3. Establishing and upholding expectations for behavior (ground rules)
4. Keeping progress moving forward

The forming stage represents the beginning of the project work (when the RIE team comes together). The facilitator helps shape expectations, establish ground rules, and define the approach and agenda for the initiative. Team formation includes introductions, allowing members to learn more about each other in terms of their roles, responsibilities, and a few personal topics (e.g., favorite travel destination, hobby). During this stage, the facilitator lays the groundwork to build rapport and trust with the group. This enables open discussion and collaboration throughout the problem-solving process.

As conversations move into the current state issues and barriers, individuals begin challenging each other and jockeying for position. The storming stage can be emotional and frustrating. During this time, the facilitator role switches to a coaching capacity. The facilitator needs to adeptly manage conflicts, uncover root causes, and guide the team forward in the problem-solving process. It is important to focus on objective data and issues so teams can avoid interpersonal conflict such as blaming, shaming, and/or disrespecting one another. Depending on the issue at hand, tension can be high, and the facilitator needs to be mindful of the dynamics between individuals and the overall team. When managed successfully, the team can acknowledge opportunities and agree on a path forward toward solution development. Chapter 10 dives into the key strategies and tools that enable effective change leadership.

Norming occurs when individuals within the team begin to build rapport and competitive cohesion. The facilitator shifts to a supporting role, enabling the team a degree of autonomy to establish roles and develop solutions. The ground rules become a tool for the team to self-manage while they form a clear solution and action plans. This process lays the foundation for longer-term commitment to the action plans and project success as well.

Table 9.3 Stages of group dynamics.

Stage	Description	Facilitator's role	Problem-solving step
Forming	• Kickoff • Introduction of project, process, and what to expect • Might have lack of clarity about purpose or problem • Individuals may not know each other	**Direct** • Clarify roles and expectations • Provide structure • Manage discussions	**Step 1** Brainstorm issues and barriers
Storming	• Disagreements, frustration, and/or challenging people's ideas	**Coach** • Facilitate communication • Surface and address issues • Manage conflict	**Step 1** Brainstorm issues and barriers **Step 2** Filter and prioritize issues and barriers
Norming	• Leverage ground rules • Build rapport and relationships • Competitive cohesion develops ("We are the best")	**Support** • Support and consultation as needed • Passive, enabling team to establish internal roles	**Step 3** Brainstorm solutions **Step 4** Filter and prioritize solutions
Performing	• Clarity and agreement on goals • Constructive confrontation • Creative idea sharing	**Support** • Same as above	**Step 5** Develop and implement action plan
Adjourning	• Planned project close • Recognition for participation and contributions	**Delegate** • Provide handoff instructions	**Project close**

As the team moves into the action plan development phase, team members collectively begin performing. The performing stage occurs when team members leverage each other's strengths and take a unified approach to accomplish the stated goal. Implementing action plans requires collaboration, support, and commitment to address barriers and make decisions. When the team is in the performing stage, they drive accountability for task completion and follow-through. The facilitator provides support and reinforces the importance of action plan ownership and ongoing communication.

Lastly, the adjourning stage represents the conclusion of the project/initiative. The facilitator directs handoff conversations between the team and sponsors to ensure all tasks have assigned owners and associated timelines. The facilitator works with the sponsor to organize a recognition effort (e.g., certificate of achievement, pizza party, broadcast communication, thank you card) for all participants. Once all handoff items are addressed, the team can disband. Adjournment provides a formal close to the individuals' responsibilities on the team, though they may carry forward new roles and tasks as defined by the project.

> *The facilitator's focus is on process: organization, communication, roles, behaviors, and decision-making. Team members focus on content.*

CHAPTER CHALLENGE

Facilitate a small group discussion or project team through the five-step kaizen problem-solving process. What tools do you find to be effective? Which tools are challenging or require practice? How was the facilitation approach received by your colleagues? What was the end result?

BONUS CHALLENGE:

Incorporate Spear's four rules into a meeting or project you are working on. How was it received? What value do the rules contribute?

QUESTIONS

1. What characteristics make a good RIE?
2. What roles need to be defined for an RIE?
3. Why are ground rules established? How do they contribute to the improvement team members self-managing each other?
4. What is the benefit of having a structured problem-solving approach?
5. Before this chapter, did you have a clearly defined way to solve problems?

6. Why is there an emphasis on divergent thinking during step 1, brainstorm issues and barriers?
7. What is the significance of sorting issues and barriers into those that are within your control and those that are outside your control?
8. What happens if you try to address an issue or barrier that is outside your control?
9. How can Spear's four rules be applied to your work area? Are there processes or tasks that violate any of the rules? If so, what can you do to address them?
10. Why is the payoff matrix an essential tool prior to action plan development? Who determines the priorities?
11. How can you apply the problem-solving process to informal efforts?
12. What are the responsibilities of the facilitator when leading any type of RIE or even a meeting?
13. How do the stages of group dynamics affect the facilitator's role? What phase is the most vulnerable?

Chapter 10
Leading Change

What we do is important. But how we do what we do is even more important.

– Nick Saban

Identifying how to change a process is easy; the hard part is getting people to understand the need for change and then act on it. Leading change is a difficult, uphill struggle that we all encounter in everyday life. This chapter covers the components of effective lean management and strategic change leadership, and provides insight from Jefferson's lean leaders.

Change occurs when something moves from its current state to a new future state (Figure 10.1). During the change, there is a transition period. The transition state is the time period in which the performance gap from the current state to the future state shortens. The current state defines what exists today in terms of processes, culture, and expectations. Employees are comfortable with predictable, consistent processes. The future state presents the unknown. It may be undefined and, as a result, cause hesitation, insecurity, and uncertainty. Spanning the current and future states is the transition. Transition states can be disorganized and tumultuous and can create inefficiencies. This turbulent time is the critical turning point in driving positive, sustainable change.

When a process/workflow changes it requires thought, which takes more time and energy. Think back to when you switched from a tactile touch phone to a smartphone. At first, you had to stop and think about everything you were

Figure 10.1 Change model.

doing. You could no longer feel the buttons, so you had to look at what you were typing. But at some point, it became automatic. It required hardwiring the new way. The transition was most likely difficult due to the change from tactile buttons to a sensitive touch screen. You became less productive and made more mistakes as you adjusted. But over time you became facile and more efficient. This example highlights the importance of managing the transition state. The transition requires patience, reassurance, education, communication, and support to make a successful leap to the future state.

Transforming workflows and changing a team/organization's energy toward forward momentum requires leadership commitment. Leaders need to prioritize, resource, and focus to achieve lasting results. Core to the leadership commitment is alignment. Leaders must get everyone rowing in the same direction if they want to take advantage of scale, resources, and employee contributions. It requires a balance of being clear with the direction/goals and realistic with the team's ability to execute and affect change.

The scale of improvements and transformations vary. Change happens at macro and micro levels (Table 10.1). In reality, there are both organizational and individual states of change. Both levels require attention and thought into the strategy to improve the likelihood of success.

LEAN MANAGEMENT

> *"Seek first to understand, then to be understood."*
>
> – Stephen Covey

To further promote and sustain continuous improvement, the right systems need to be in place. The lean management system comprises two main components: standard work and discipline (Mann 2010). This system provides the structure from which all lean improvement strategies can be successfully developed and deployed. An underlying philosophy in the system is discipline to adhere to standard work and accountability.

Table 10.1 States of change at the macro and micro levels.

State	Macro level (organization, department, etc.)	Micro level (individual)
Current	How things are currently being done today	How I do my job today
Transition	How to shift from today's work to future needs	How my job will change
Future	How things will be done tomorrow	How I will fit into this new way of working

As with any system, tools and concepts accompany the lean management philosophy to create discipline and achieve results. Positive results will follow if processes are managed effectively (Chan et al. 2014). The leadership challenge is to set the tone, manage expectations, and hold staff accountable for performance (Aij et al. 2013; Kaplan et al. 2014).

Leaders have a pivotal role during the transition state of change. Leaders must communicate, coach, and remove barriers during this time in order to reduce resistance and static inertia. Communication is an integral component of leadership. During the transition state, employees need a degree of reassurance from decision-makers and leaders. Employees want to understand the reason for change as well as the urgency behind it. Additionally, employees look for what is in it for them. At a personal level, what about the change will likely get employee buy-in? Since change happens at an individual level, employees need to personally commit to changing their role in the process and help move toward the future state. Leaders must also communicate how the change will occur, which is essentially the components of an action plan (i.e., who, what, how, why, and by when).

As a coach, a leader must help employees manage the transition. Leaders might need to meet with staff individually and develop strategies to address personal barriers to change (e.g., lack of knowledge or skill set in the new environment). Training and education enable staff to quickly adopt new processes and reduce the time from the current state to the future state (Graban and Prachand 2010; Langley et al. 2009). The transition state is an active period that requires frequent touch points between leadership and staff to ensure barrier removal. Resistance is a natural response to change. Active change management includes strategies to reduce or limit resistance while keeping forward progress.

> *A lean leader is someone who has the technical skills to drive process improvement and interpersonal skills to support change management. Lean leaders focus on continuous improvement, gemba walks, empowering staff to solve problems, and system/process issues (asking why, not who).*

Leader Standard Work

Leader standard work is a core element of lean management. As described in Chapter 5, standard work is the basis for improvement. The responsibility of following standards does not exclude leaders. For a person in a leadership or managerial role, standard work translates to daily checklists and regular expectations. Leader standard work is the linchpin of change management. The main components of leader standard work are gemba walks and huddles.

Gemba walks are a way to learn by seeing. The closer a leader's oversight is to the staff at the gemba, the more frequently he or she should walk (Mann 2010). Learning to see involves looking for process variation and flow disruption, wastes, and underlying issues that limit productivity and quality. Gemba walks require going to see the actual process, learning through observation, and asking questions

(Womack 2011). When a problem arises, a good lean manager does not respond, "Come to my office and let's talk about it," but rather, "Show me." Gemba walks remove assumptions about what is happening and require verification (Liker 2004). Gemba walks also do more than just verify issues; they help build rapport and understanding between leaders, their staff, and customers.

Gemba walks are not meant to be used solely for problems. This activity is an ongoing responsibility and leadership best practice. It helps in anticipating and preventing issues as well as verifying and solving identified problems. Leaders will sometimes implement a change without understanding the actual current state and operations of a process. As a result, the process can become more cumbersome, can become inefficient, and can increase quality-related issues—the opposite of the intention. Leaders are responsible for going to see what actually happens, engaging staff in learning about their struggles, and soliciting ideas for improvement.

Huddles are an effective way to communicate with staff. Huddles are short, standardized meetings that involve individuals from a department or team. Typically, they occur before the start of a shift or during a transition/handoff of shifts. A huddle should have a standard agenda that includes the following (Mann 2010):

- *Performance dashboard updates:* Review of key metrics progress compared with target and expectations

- *Things to be aware of:* Review of any anticipated issues or problems as well as expected customer volume and staffing issues

- *Open discussion:* Discussion of any concerns or opportunities for improvement

Staff members or the manager of the area can lead huddles. The following are questions to ask at every huddle:

1. How are we doing?

2. What opportunities do we have to improve?

3. What are we doing to improve/address them?

Discipline

The best way to improve overall performance is to establish the expectations, provide the needed education and support to achieve them, and hold employees accountable for the results. Weight management offers a great analogy for discipline. If your goal is to lose weight, what do you need to do? The answer is simple: burn more calories than you consume. The trick is not which workout or diet fad to enroll in. Rather, it is having the discipline to burn more calories than you consume, which obviously means smart eating and exercise. People who maintain a healthy weight or who can lose weight and sustain their weight loss display the discipline to do so (not counting genetic factors). It is a matter of personal will and effort. Using this analogy, managers know what the key standard tasks are that they should be doing (e.g., gemba walks, communication). However, most leaders lack the discipline to do them.

Discipline requires a daily commitment to leader standard work (Kaplan et al. 2014). Gemba walks should be scheduled and regularly occurring, as well as spontaneous in nature. Leaders need to shift their focus from firefighting to fire prevention. Employee empowerment is central to this effort. Figure 10.2 segments roles and responsibilities for frontline staff, middle management, and senior leaders. Frontline staff have a primary focus on maintaining daily operations while participating in improvement efforts (Jimmerson et al. 2005). Middle managers should spend the majority of their time on improvement efforts. They have additional responsibilities to monitor daily operations and participate in strategy development and innovation. Senior leaders should spend the majority of their time on strategy and innovation while contributing to improvement efforts. Lean management emphasizes the need to empower the frontline staff to problem solve at the source (Jimmerson et al. 2005). If senior leaders and middle managers are too busy fighting fires and troubleshooting at the daily operations level, there is no one setting the direction and strategy for improvement.

Empowering employees means giving them the education and tools to become problem solvers. Then, leadership needs to create a working environment that enables and promotes active problem solving (Toussaint and Gerard 2010). There needs to be an asserted effort to develop the skill sets and competencies of staff and then empower them to improve their work. Process change is simple and straightforward. The hard part is dealing with people and the myriad reactions to change (from acceptance to passive resistance to active resistance/ sabotage). Empowering staff is a scary thing for leaders because it takes control out of their hands. It is, however, liberating to delegate tasks and responsibilities to competent staff, giving the leader more freedom to concentrate on priority issues, improvement projects, and strategic initiatives.

> *Leaders need to provide staff the "what" but empower staff to determine the "how." It is the responsibility of leaders to provide direction, but the staff makes it come to life (with leadership support behind the scenes).*

Figure 10.2 Segmenting roles and responsibilities.

LEADING CHANGE[2]

The transition from the current state to the future state makes all the difference. Sustainable change is not possible without a strategic approach to manage individuals through the transition (Lighter 2013). There are strategies that position a successful change initiative. The approach models John Kotter's article "Leading Change: Why Transformation Efforts Fail" (Kotter 1995). Kotter identified various reasons that initiatives and projects failed, based on common mistakes made by leadership, which align with the three states of change. This section highlights the main considerations and tools to apply to overcome each of Kotter's barriers to change before, during, and after a transition (Figure 10.3).

Change requires an understanding of the interpersonal dynamics and culture of a team/organization. The culture represents the behavioral norms and values of a group, both visible and invisible (Kotter 1996). A well-defined strategy and execution plan will not work without an approach that acknowledges and addresses culture. We do not live in a bubble; therefore, change needs to be viewed holistically.

Driving change through a team/organization requires strong leadership. Leadership and management can be viewed as separate functions and skills. Successful change requires both, though leadership is the critical component. According to Kotter, transformations require 70-90 percent leadership and only 10-30 percent management (Kotter 2001). The following provides a breakdown of management versus leadership:

- Management: Tends to be reactive, focused on tasks like planning, budgeting, staffing, and problem-solving

- Leadership: Tends to be proactive, focused on setting a clear vision, aligning people and resources, and providing motivation and inspiration to overcome obstacles and achieve goals

Change happens *through* people, not to people. The future state represents something new and different, and for many people that can leave a lot to the imagination. Change brings uncertainty, insecurity, and a vague sense of what to expect. All of this leads to hesitation to engage, passive resistance, or even

Current state
1. Create urgency for change
2. Establish the guiding coalition

Transition state — Performance gap
3. Define and communicate the vision
4. Remove barriers
5. Provide feedback on progress

Future state
6. Hardwire changes

Figure 10.3 Change model with leadership responsibilities.

---

[2] Content contributions from Shane Flickinger, MHA, FACHE, CLSSBB.

deliberate attempts to halt or derail the initiative. When you think of organizational change management, you have to remember that the organization is a collection of individuals. Change happens at the individual level and is translated to teams and "teams of teams," which make up the broader organization. For each person there is an impact that he or she needs to reconcile in order to buy in.

A person's willingness and ability to accept and embrace change can be segmented into three categories: rational, emotional, and environmental. There are some common surprises about leading people through change (Heath 2010):

- *Rational.* Resistance can be due to a lack of clarity. If people do not know what direction they are headed, they may end up going in circles. A clear vision and direction are essential in providing guidance and alignment.

- *Emotional.* Exhaustion can be mistaken for laziness. Change can be difficult and taxing on mental and emotional resources. As people adapt to new changes, it may sap their energy more quickly, and this can lead to mental and physical exhaustion.

- *Environmental.* The perception of a "people" problem usually is a situational problem. If the work setting, workflows, organizational structure, and other similar factors are not aligned, people will not be able to adapt to a change. If you want people to behave differently, make sure the environment is set up for a path of least resistance.

Successful change leadership requires a clear direction, defined action plan, execution, and an engagement strategy to build and sustain momentum (The Advisory Board Company 2011). It is important to understand varying factors that lead to the perception of resistance so you can dive deeper to understand the reality of the situation. Change happens at the individual level, and people are complicated! The following section outlines the change leadership framework that facilitates behavior change at an individual and team level. Successful change requires behavior change: see/visualize the problem, feel a sense of urgency, and change behaviors to address issues and opportunities (Kotter and Cohen 2002).

The change readiness profile tool (Chapter 8, Figure 8.7) provides the framework to assess an initiative's readiness and gaps to drive positive change. Six domains define the key areas that need to be addressed to ensure successful implementation and sustainability. The following section details each domain.

> *Depending on the scope and complexity of a change initiative, you may choose to go through the stages formally using the tools/templates provided or use it as an informal guide. The key is developing the awareness and appreciation for each stage of change. For example, you will be more successful simply by understanding the importance of stakeholder engagement, whether you do a formal stakeholder analysis or not.*

1. Create Urgency for Change

Without a need or sense of urgency for change, it is nearly impossible to shift static inertia to dynamic. Sometimes leaders have to make the fear of doing nothing appear more dangerous than the fear of the unknown. Using the burning platform analogy, if the platform is ablaze and disintegrating rapidly, you will jump off, even though you are afraid that sharks or other dangers might be in the water, because the option of staying on the platform is no longer viable. Getting people on board with the idea of change is challenging but essential. Overcoming inertia is the most difficult step (Womack and Jones 1996).

Establishing urgency requires a clear understanding of the current state as well as the future state direction. Change can be framed as a threat or opportunity (Figure 10.4). The threat vs. opportunity matrix provides a tool to capture short- and longer-term considerations. The goal is to identify the major threats to be mitigated and opportunities to be leveraged. This brainstorming tool can help teams determine what is within their control and what will resonate with others as it relates to the urgency to change.

The importance and criticality of the situation should be articulated, developing a dissatisfaction with the status quo and building momentum toward action (General Electric Company 2006). Showing current performance can help people visualize the need for change. For example, you can show future projections/trends if things do not change, highlight worst-case scenarios for continuing business as usual, or demonstrate gaps between high performers and your organization/team. Messaging around urgency needs to vary based on audience. Depending on the individuals and teams, you need to message a need for change in a way that resonates broadly. To achieve this, key points should emphasize the following (The Advisory Board Company 2011):

- *Logic*. Contains a straightforward set of information founded in logic and data, including: fact-based assessment of a situation, opportunities/solutions proven by best practices and research, cause-and-effect relationships, and return on investments.

	Threat	Opportunity
Short-term		
Longer-term		

Figure 10.4 Threat versus opportunity matrix.

- *Values*. Appeals to the organization/team's mission and values, highlighting the norms of behavior and ethics.

- *Emotion*. Emphasizes the impact on feelings such as suffering/misfortune, joy/fulfillment that the change represents.

A disconnect in priorities can lead to a lack of engagement and appreciation in a sense of urgency. This is especially true when working on change initiatives that span multiple departments and stakeholders. Everyone at work has their own priorities and responsibilities based on their role and supervisor's direction. When it comes to driving a change initiative, it is important to understand how the urgency resonates with others. Though the need for change is clear to you and the team, other stakeholders may not understand or connect with the reason behind a change and therefore can be passive or resistant to your efforts. It is important to determine what barriers, stressors, and other factors are pulling your stakeholders' attention and resources.

The key to addressing resistant behavior and unsupportive/unengaged stakeholders is to find a way for them to connect to the "why" and clarify the benefits of changing. In other words, define "What's in it for me?" Change requires people to do things differently, so it is important to help them visualize a clear picture of the future and what their role looks like. It is not possible to define the future with certainty. The future state direction provides a roadmap to progress in which everyone can contribute.

Answer the following questions when evaluating the urgency of a change (Advisory Board Company 2011):

- Is this a priority (for me, my team/organization)?

- Do the benefits outweigh the costs?

- Do employees have the right skill set to execute?

- Do we have leadership support/commitment?

If you answered no to any of the questions, the initiative needs further analysis and realignment with organizational objectives. Overall, the majority of employees, more than 75 percent of the managers, and all the senior executives should embrace the need for change if it is going to be successful (Kotter 1996).

2. Establish the Guiding Coalition

To drive change, there must be a core group of individuals dedicated to the objective. The guiding coalition is the team responsible for generating momentum and building buy-in from their peers. A guiding coalition gives you strength in numbers. These individuals can help move everyone in the same direction and build the positive, forward momentum that is needed to change things as well as sustain the gains. You need people who are passionate about the end goal in order to generate engagement and buy-in with those around them.

There are hidden leaders who have tremendous influence. Identify and leverage their network. Hidden leaders drive organizations through the power of influence. Driving improvements does not happen in isolation. Leaders need to leverage one another and build support from their colleagues and senior management (Jones and Mitchell 2006). Work the formal and informal structures, politics, and dynamics of an organization. Influence becomes an integral skill with increasingly complex work environments (academic medical centers are among the most challenging due to the various aims with teaching, research, clinical care, etc.).

The guiding coalition needs to include individuals with authority (decision-making ability), expertise in various core operations, internal and external credibility, and leadership competencies (Kotte 1995). These characteristics capture the central elements of change leadership. The size and scale of the guiding coalition should coincide with the scope of the change initiative. For small changes within a team, you might need several key members. Broader organizational change may require hundreds if not thousands of people to build enough momentum. It is important to include key stakeholder groups to ensure their representation and engagement; these groups may include the following and should be included in the stakeholder assessment (analyze phase, reference Appendix A, Table A.7):

- Clinicians: physicians, advanced practice providers, nurses, pharmacists, technicians
- Support teams: facilities, housekeeping, IT, supply chain, patient access
- Senior management: VPs, C-suite, board of trustees
- Customers: patients/families, referring providers
- External organizations: vendors, payors, unions

3. Define and Communicate the Vision

The vision defines where the leader sees the organization or department going (Lighter 2013). Without a vision, the change initiative can disband into seemingly unintegrated tasks without an end goal. Employees cannot align their individual responsibilities and tasks with the organization's strategic objectives if the direction is not defined or communicated. A clear vision motivates people and teams to take action in the right direction.

Developing the vision requires leadership and management skills. From a leadership perspective, the vision needs to have an appealing future state and strategy that outlines how it can be realized. The management component includes a plan outlining specific actions and timelines as well as the resources (staffing, equipment, supplies, etc.) required to implement (Kotter 1996). Balancing leadership inspiration and management execution lies in the vision being aspirational *and* achievable. The more of/less of chart helps shape the vision in the early phases of the draft (Figure 10.5). To use this tool, briefly describe the change initiative vision/goal. Then list what actions and outcomes you expect to see more of and less of when the new vision is realized (General Electric Company 2006). Complete the tool in a group brainstorming fashion and share it with key stakeholders for validation.

Vision:	
More of...	**Less of...**

Figure 10.5 More of/less of chart.

A clear vision provides the basis for communication. It is important to articulate why the change needs to occur before outlining how it will be accomplished (Mauer 2002). At the individual level, employees need to feel connected to the need for change. They also need to believe that change will bring about positive outcomes. An elevator speech is an effective way to concisely communicate the urgency of change, the direction for the future state, and how employees can contribute to the stated goals. The format is simple:

- *Description*: Here is what the project/change initiative is about
- *Importance*: This is why it matters
- *Outcomes*: This is what success looks like in the future
- *Commitment*: This is what we need from you/how you can contribute

The development of a succinct, clear elevator speech is an important step in the communication process. Effectively deploying the message across a team/organization can be difficult. Large departments that operate 24/7 pose a unique challenge. Communication is challenging and more critical because you have to reach night-shift and weekend staff, as well as part-timers. This is why communication is so important. Failure to reach these individuals can cause a change effort to halt, be less effective, or fall apart. The communication plan, described in Chapter 8, Define Phase, provides the framework to develop a comprehensive approach to reach key stakeholders (Appendix Table A.7 depicts an example of the tool).

As noted earlier, staff can appear unengaged or unwilling to support a change initiative if the message is not clear. Change leadership requires employee engagement and contributions. You might be able to accomplish things through sheer force, but sustainability is unlikely, and you will probably develop a reputation that people won't want to work with you. Healthcare is a people-oriented business, and how you engage the people impacted by a change is an essential component to the execution strategy.

> *The common shortcomings when developing a compelling vision (Dye and Garman 2015):*
> - Lack of clarity: Employees do not understand what the future state looks like and what it means to them. Additionally, there might be a lack of understanding in how the organization/team will move from the current to future state.
> - Lack of meaning: The message does not resonate with staff, especially the critical stakeholders needed to move things forward. Individuals need to understand "what's in it for me?" so they know how they can contribute to the vision.
> - Lack of communication: It is not sufficient to communicate the vision once. Per the communication plan, it is essential to have a robust and ongoing communication strategy that leverages different ways of messaging (e.g., emails, huddles, team presentations, fliers, town halls). A bi-directional feedback loop with stakeholders will enable the change leadership team to refine messaging to better connect with staff.

4. Remove Barriers

One of the main roles for leaders is removing barriers and obstacles that impede progress. Barriers include organizational structure/hierarchy, limited skills or training, inadequate staffing or information systems support, and lack of supervisory support and commitment (Kotter 1995). These issues need to be anticipated and addressed to maintain progress. Once inertia becomes dynamic, it is critical to ensure limited resistance to maintain the established momentum. This is where leader standard work comes into play. Through gemba walks and huddles, leaders can anticipate issues and work with staff to strategically remediate and remove barriers. Resistance also arises when there is lack of agreement on the problem or the solution (Chalice 2007).

Employee resistance can occur unintentionally if you are not attentive to the interpersonal dynamics. Individual resistance expresses itself in different ways (Mauer 2002):

- *Intellectual*: Due to a lack of data and information, individuals might feel like they do not understand what the issue/problem is that needs to be addressed.

- *Emotional*: Due to feelings of fear and insecurity, individuals feel like the change will impact them negatively (i.e., loss of control, potential failure).

- *Personal*: Due to a lack of trust or belief in the change, individuals may not feel comfortable trusting the message/messenger based on prior history, differences in values, or other factors that lower trust between individuals and teams.

Other forms of resistance include organizational barriers. Some issues impact an individual's ability to fully engage and are outside of their control. These areas include organizational structure, training, IT systems, and supervisor support (Kotter 1996). Poor organizational structure design leads to lack of clarity in roles/responsibilities and inconsistent accountability. Silos can also create friction between departments/teams and make it more difficult to collaborate. Training may not be sufficient to give employees the skills required to contribute to changing workflows and responsibilities. Similarly, if the IT systems (e.g., electronic health record) are not designed and optimized to improve workflows, employees will be limited with what they are able to accomplish. Lastly, without local-level support from supervisors, employees may not be supported and empowered to embrace a new change.

Leaders need to prioritize and align structures, systems, and processes to position people for success at all levels depending on the barrier and its impact on the change initiative. The in-control/out-of-control tool described in Chapter 9 (Figure 9.6) should be used to determine which of the identified barriers can actually be addressed.

5. Provide Feedback on Progress

The transition state can take weeks, months, or even years. The future state can appear so distant and unattainable that employees lose sight of the goals and energy dissipates. To counter this effect, it is essential that staff receive consistent feedback. Benefits of acknowledging success and progress include the following:

- Validation of efforts and potential sacrifices
- Recognition and appreciation of staff contributing to change
- Reinforcement and encouragement of vision and progress made to date
- Limited pushback from resistors or other individuals who are not supportive of the change

Review key metrics to assess progress leveraging leader standard work and performance dashboards. Celebrate accomplishments, both large and small, along the way. Employees can be disengaged if there is not closure in this feedback loop. These short-term wins remind staff of the progress made to date and help communicate their status along the transformation journey. A "short-term wins" strategy is an effective way to systematically inject positive energy into the change initiative. Short-term wins provide proof that a change initiative is making progress (e.g., scorecards), rewards teamwork and contributions, and keeps senior leaders engaged (Kotter 1996). Without a short-term win strategy, the change initiative is at risk for complacency and regression.

The short-term wins plan enables the change leadership team to develop a strategy for building and sustaining momentum (Table 10.2). Using the tool, the team defines the appropriate action items/deliverables that need to be achieved through the change initiative transition state (General Electric Company 2006). These milestones mark important progress toward the future state. Using KPIs and other measures, the team can capture wins, usually defined as incremental improvement and positive trends in performance. Importantly, the tool outlines how to celebrate the short-term win. Wins can be celebrated in a variety of ways: email update, award/certificates of achievement, intranet postings/highlights, individual/team shout-outs at department meetings and huddles. The main point with short-term wins is to build teamwork, a sense of accomplishment, and positive reinforcement that everyone's effort is making a difference. Short-term wins need to be visible, unambiguous, and link to the change initiative vision.

Table 10.2 Short-term wins plan.

What (action items)	Who (owner)	Measurement (KPIs)	How it will be celebrated	By when

6. Hardwire Changes

Leader standard work is crucial in hardwiring gains. Hardwiring improvements comes with discipline and accountability. Leaders need to consistently perform gemba walks and ask everywhere: (1) What is the process? (2) How can you tell it is working? (3) What are you doing to improve it? A true transformation occurs at many levels in many forms. A new paradigm might require different skills and a new mindset that are not currently available. Hardwiring improvements is one of the most challenging responsibilities.

Department/team interdependence can further complicate hardwiring gains and ensuring sustainability (Kotter 1996). Depending on the scope and scale of the initiative, there could be several to dozens of interrelated and interdependent teams involved. Changes in one area inevitably will impact other areas, known and unknown. Failing to understand and appreciate the concept of interdependence can lead to significant barriers and challenges. Alignment of departments/teams is achieved through the organizational structure design, alignment of priorities, integration of workflows, and standardization of roles, KPIs, and goals.

Throughout the transformation journey of the change initiative, it is important to consolidate gains and simplify structures, systems, and processes. Interdependencies will continue to exist, though the team should focus on streamlining and standardizing these components (remember Spear's 4 rules, Chapter 9, step 3). An effective framework to decentralize alignment across teams, especially if they are spread geographically, is a tight-loose-tight model (Ulvnes 2015):

1. *Tight*: Define what needs to be accomplished in clear terms (purpose). The vision provides objectives that are straightforward and quantitative in nature. All departments/teams should understand how success and progress will be measured over time. Departments/teams use the vision to align their action plans (step 2 below).

2. *Loose*: Based on the overarching vision, the "loose" component addresses how the work gets done (implementation). The loose model represents the need to allow room for creativity and flexibility based on the department/team's size, context, politics, and other relevant factors. You cannot and do not want to micromanage the implementation of all changes. The loose concept decentralizes and empowers local leaders to own their role in the change initiative.

3. *Tight*: The loose, decentralized approach for how work gets done still requires oversight for results. The third step (tight) defines what is being measured for success. The KPIs, both outcomes and process measures, provide objective data to drive accountability.

The tight-loose-tight model provides creative space for teams to have autonomy on the *how* and be held accountable for the *what*. It is an especially effective approach when the change initiative is broad in scope and complexity.

During the phase of leading change, it is important to reassess key systems and processes. Early in the initiative, the team uses the system and process profile tool (Figure 8.8). This tool should be reevaluated once changes are made to assess ongoing barriers and gaps. These barriers and gaps may evolve over time based on the impact of changes. Sustainability relies on a consistent effort to mitigate risks, reduce barriers, and facilitate bidirectional feedback on performance.

Changing culture with existing people poses another real challenge. If leaders train, educate, support, and hold staff accountable for their performance, staff will take care of the results (Graban and Prachand 2010). Without a solid, unified leadership front, sustainability and progress are likely to fail. Changing the work environment is the challenge. Without hard work and discipline, nothing can be accomplished. To be excellent and strive for perfection, you must have the discipline, day in and day out, to do the right things, the right way, every time. Getting better is an ongoing journey and at times a struggle. But if you are persistent and disciplined, you will achieve your results.

> *Vision and innovation are important, but structure and discipline are critical (Kenney 2011).*

LESSONS FROM JEFFERSON LEAN LEADERS

Since 2008, Jefferson has certified more than 125 individuals as lean practitioners (known as lean leaders at Jefferson). Lean leaders hold full-time positions throughout the clinical, operational, and academic departments within the organization. Positions held include physicians (attendings, fellows, and residents), nurses, pharmacists, respiratory therapists, and administrators. These employees were trained through the TJU College of Population Health Operational Excellence program and participate in lean projects throughout the organization post-certification.

There have been more than 100 formal lean projects at Jefferson over the years. Some lean leaders have been in the program since its inception, while others are newly certified. To provide readers with insight from the wealth of experience accumulated at Jefferson, the lean leaders answered the three questions listed below. Their lessons learned shed light on the importance of discipline, persistence, and dedication to improvement. The transition from "doing lean" to "becoming lean" is subtle and happens over time. Lean leaders say it takes more than a year before things begin to come naturally. Project experience and content refreshers help hardwire lean thinking.

What advice do you have for individuals who want to execute lean projects?

- "It is very important to clearly identify the problem before jumping to solutions. Lean projects must be focused on eliminating waste and identifying value-adding processes through the eyes of the customer. Remember, do not try and 'boil the ocean.'" – Brian Glynn, RRT, MS-HQS, director, enterprise business intelligence

- "Stay committed and focused. There are still a number of people who do not believe in the benefits of lean. Do not let them discourage you." – Roseann Pauline, MBA, change agent, supply chain management

- "Be prepared to face resistance. People are scared of change and fear you are assessing their individual performance. As a lean leader you need to support, reassure, and guide those participating during the entire process." – Steven Gudowski, RRT, associate director of respiratory care quality and safety

- "Ensure you have buy-in from management and leadership. You will need their support to help you build results into the culture of your organization." – Nicole Jastrzembski, BS, RN, senior business continuity analyst

What has been a key lesson learned in your engagement with the lean program at Jefferson?

- "Put it all on the table—the good, the bad, and the ugly." – Carole Harvey, patient access trainer

- "Trust the lean process to work." – Caroline Lamina, anatomic pathology manager, clinical laboratory

- "Sometimes you need to put your ideas and opinions aside to allow teams to build their own solutions. But you still need to use your experience to guide them toward a good outcome." – Andrew Wierzbieniec, MHSA, director, business development

- "You must be prepared to meet resistance and develop a change management plan. Lean projects often result in a change to a process, which can lead to fear and trepidation. Engaging front-line staff in the process will help overcome this resistance." – Brian Glynn, RRT, MS-HQS, director, enterprise business intelligence

- "Not all staff will be supportive or engaged. Some will challenge the principles of lean. Be persistent and work toward engaging those who are interested in making changes." – Jenny Bosley, RN, MS, clinical nurse specialist, performance improvement

- "Lean needs to be more than head knowledge; it needs to be part of your soul—how you live and look at life every day. To make lean a viable part of your personal or organizational culture, lean needs to be a passion…always striving to be the best at getting better." – Robert Bartosz, MHA, director of finance and business planning

If an organization wanted to begin a lean journey, how do you suggest it get started?

- "Pick a few highly motivated people with great attitudes and make them lean leaders. Those few will use lean themselves and teach others in the process. This will be the start of a new lean culture at your institution." – Steven Gudowski, RRT, associate director of respiratory care quality and safety

- "The best way for them to get started would be to engage their staff. Communication is key. They should also offer lean courses to the staff to give them an opportunity to see how being lean can positively affect their organization." – Lisa Liciardello, BSN, RN, administrative charge nurse, perioperative nursing

- "I would suggest to not start off attempting to 'boil the ocean.' Instead, begin the journey by identifying small wins, such as creating standards, because without these no improvements can occur." – Leigh Elko, MS, PMP, RRT, practice optimization manager

- "Demonstrate to employees that they will actually have the opportunity to impact their daily work by improving processes that will lead to better job satisfaction and customer satisfaction. Process improvement is a journey, not a destination." – Thomas J. Louden, director of managed care reimbursement and contract compliance

Everything You Need to Know

This book can be summarized into the most salient points using the numbers 5-8-4 (Figure 10.6). If you comprehend and can apply the components of 5-8-4, you will be a successful problem solver and lean leader. The tools and templates provided enable you to put these concepts into action in an integrated and effective way.

The "5" represents: (1) the five lean principles, (2) the concept that everything is 5S, and (3) the kaizen problem-solving process. First, the five lean principles provide the roadmap for creating a lean process. This framework is the model for executing lean improvements. The components within each principle describe key deliverables and considerations. Second, a core takeaway of this book is that everything is 5S. The 5S approach is a systematic way to improve physical layout and system/process design. Finally, the kaizen problem-solving process is a standard approach focused on identifying the root causes within your control and developing and implementing high-impact solutions.

The "8" represents the eight wastes. To identify the root causes, you must have a thorough understanding of these wastes. The eight DOWNTIME wastes are the focus of lean thinking. Once you identify your customer and define value, you can begin to identify, isolate, and eliminate the NVA activity. Waste reduction and elimination is at the core of lean.

Lastly, the "4" represents Spear's four rules: (1) activities are clear and well-defined, (2) steps are simple and direct, (3) flow is simple and direct, and (4) problems and issues are dealt with in a timely and direct manner. The rules provide the framework for solution development. The point is that the new solution is not more complicated than what currently exists. Integrating the 5-8-4 components provides the structure and systematic approaches necessary to drive meaningful change.

Figure 10.6 Lean thinking summarized as 5-8-4.

The future of healthcare is unknown. Delivery models and organizational structures will change in response to shifts in reimbursement and customer requirements. Lean thinking has a pivotal role in leading the way. Cost reduction and resource allocation will continue to drive decisions, making quality improvement paramount (Al, Feenstra, and Brouwer 2005; Slobbe et al. 2011). Doing things correctly the first time helps reduce operational costs through less rework and fewer inefficiencies. Using the lean thinking philosophy for the underlying leadership system, as described in Chapter 1, aligns organizational goals with individual employees. The purpose, process, people approach promotes empowering employees to own and improve their work in order to achieve higher-level objectives. Lastly, the horizontal lean perspective (i.e., patients, products, materials, and equipment flow horizontally across functions) enhances coordination and collaboration across stakeholder groups. A systems-based viewpoint and management approach positions organizations to support and improve population health and broader health system strategies.

CHAPTER CHALLENGE

Implement leader standard work as part of your daily responsibilities (even if you do not have a formal leadership role or staff reporting to you). Conduct daily gemba walks. What are you learning from staff? What system/process issues exist that inhibit their work or threaten quality?

BONUS CHALLENGE

Implement huddles in your work area. Start regular, structured meetings to discuss current state issues and performance and anticipated concerns. How are the huddles improving communication? What improvements have been realized as a result?

QUESTIONS:

1. Why is it important to manage the transition state of change?
2. What happens if the future state is not defined and the vision is unclear?
3. How does leader standard work support continuous improvement and sustainability?
4. What is the result of leaders who do not conduct gemba walks or facilitate huddles?
5. Why do senior leaders and middle management need to focus more on improvements and strategy than on daily operations? Why is empowering front-line staff difficult?
6. What elements of leading change can be difficult in your organization/ department/ work setting? Why?
7. How can you develop and communicate a sense of urgency? What is the significance in doing so?
8. Who can be members of your guiding coalition for positive change? What characteristics do they share? How can they leverage one another?
9. Why is performance feedback necessary during the transition state?
10. How are changes and improvements hardwired?
11. How does culture affect change efforts?
12. Which of the lessons learned shared by Jefferson lean leaders resonates with you? Why?
13. How can the 5-8-4 concept be deployed in your organization/department/ work setting?

BONUS QUESTION

What will you do differently now that you are a lean thinker?

Chapter 11
Pandemic Preparedness: A COVID-19 Case Study

Failure to prepare is preparing to fail.

– Ben Franklin

In the fall of 2019, a novel coronavirus began spreading throughout China. The virus quickly invaded countries throughout the world, creating a global pandemic. Formally known as severe acute respiratory syndrome coronavirus 2 (SARS-CoV-2), COVID-19 is in the same family of viruses as the common cold and flu (Centers for Disease Control and Prevention 2020b). Due to the contagious nature of the disease and the mortality rate within the older population and individuals with co-morbid conditions, the COVID-19 crisis crippled the global economy and led to significant loss of life. At the time of this writing, there are no clinically proven treatments or vaccines for COVID-19, though scientists, researchers, and clinicians are working hard to find a solution (Centers for Disease Control and Prevention 2020b). In absence of a treatment or vaccine, communities across the world are utilizing measures such as performing hand hygiene, wearing face masks in public, and practicing social distancing to slow and reduce virus transmission.

Geographic and temporal clustering of outbreaks create variation in virus expression across communities, states, countries, and broader regions (Cavallo, Donoho, and Forman 2020). As a result, it is difficult to model and anticipate how the virus will interact with the environment and impact the healthcare delivery system. The surge in COVID-19 cases throughout the United States creates a significant strain on critical supplies such as personal protective equipment (PPE) (gowns, gloves, face shields, disinfectant). Demand for these supplies is 100 times higher than normal according to the World Health Organization (Tyrrell et al. 2020). Additionally, healthcare organizations are faced with unprecedented staffing challenges intertwined with the complexity of COVID-19 critically ill patients, the societal impact of social distancing, and personal risk of exposure to individuals and their families.

Pandemic responses are complicated given the nature and scale of infection. Pandemics affect the ecosystem, cutting across boundaries, impacting all sectors of business, and interrupting social norms. Outbreaks are highly variable and impact communities, patient populations, and healthcare facilities in different ways.

Therefore, a response requires a holistic approach to manage, mitigate, and control factors that can be influenced (Centers for Disease Control and Prevention 2020a).

Senior leaders in healthcare organizations need to participate in the planning and preparedness process (Mason and Friese 2020). Aside from the poor clinical outcomes and deaths associated with outbreaks, the potential longer-term impact on an organization's financial health can be catastrophic, especially for hospitals. Hospitals already operate on low margins due to the current reimbursement system and ongoing increases in labor, supplies, and medications. Exacerbating the issue, outbreaks produce a surge in medical cases, inundating the emergency department and critical care units. In response to the increased demand for high-acuity staffing and PPE supplies, hospitals may reduce or halt elective procedures, which can negatively impact the case mix index, increase variable costs, and increase length of stay (Tyrrell et al. 2020). Despite federal and state government support, some organizations may not be able to recoup the financial losses sustained during the crisis.

The following section outlines a pandemic preparedness approach leveraging lean thinking as the foundation. The checklist and details provide a framework from which to adapt to your organization's context and unique needs. Concepts, tools, and deliverables come from lessons learned in similar outbreaks such as H1N1 and Ebola (Deloitte 2020). Future outbreaks cannot be predicted. However, scenario planning and operational preparedness can improve outcomes if/when another one occurs (Centers for Disease Control and Prevention 2020c). Depending on the nature of the outbreak, this framework should supplement (not replace) guidance from federal, state, and local officials (Tyrrell et al. 2020).

PANDEMIC PREPAREDNESS DMAIC CHECKLIST

Leveraging the DMAIC model presented in Chapter 8, the pandemic preparedness DMAIC checklist (Figure 11.1) synthesizes information from trusted sources that include the Centers for Disease Control and Prevention (CDC) and the World Health Organization (WHO), among others. Pandemic responses are not improvement events or projects; however, the DMAIC model can be applied as a planning tool to ensure timely and effective activation. The following information will reference tools throughout the book and the appendices, as well as introduce new concepts. The checklist contains areas of focus including (Deloitte 2020):

- Scenario planning
- Communication strategy
- Crisis response and management
- Resource optimization: supply chain, staffing, facilities
- Care alternatives: telehealth, alternative sites of care
- Financial analysis and reporting
- Health and enterprise risk analysis

Pandemic Preparedness DMAIC Checklist

Project name: _____ Date last revised: _____

Core team: _____

DEFINE Phase Checklist
- ☐ Assign preparedness planning team roles
- ☐ Kick-off meeting w/ sponsor(s)
- ☐ Draft communication plan outline
- ☐ Review scenario planning
- ☐ Determine crisis response & management teams
- ☐ Conduct voice of customer (VOC) interviews
- ☐ Conduct waste walk
- ☐ Develop high-level process map for key workflows
- ☐ Assess change readiness using profile tool
- ☐ Use systems & process profile tool
- ☐ Close DEFINE phase

MEASURE Phase Checklist
- ☐ Review previous outbreak events for lessons learned
- ☐ Formulate data collection plan
- ☐ Conduct process and workflow value analyses
- ☐ Consolidate VOC interviews into key themes/ risks
- ☐ Conduct supply chain management assessment
- ☐ Develop staffing resource strategy
- ☐ Create surge plan
- ☐ Determine incident activation and considerations
- ☐ Close MEASURE phase

ANALYZE Phase Checklist
- ☐ Perform financial analysis and reporting
- ☐ Perform data analysis
- ☐ Conduct stakeholder analysis
- ☐ Determine staff training needs & deployment strategies
- ☐ Conduct FMEA
- ☐ Close ANALYZE phase

IMPROVE Phase Checklist
Incident Response Activation
- ☐ Activate the emergency operations plan
- ☐ Evaluate current state of equipment, staffing, supplies, capacity
- ☐ Evaluate response plan and determine key decisions/timelines
- ☐ Communicate with staff, patients, visitors, and key partners/organizations
- ☐ Close the command center/plan for return to normal operations
- ☐ Close IMPROVE phase

CONTROL Phase Checklist
- ☐ Continue response team status update meetings
- ☐ Calculate financial impact
- ☐ Conduct pre/post KPI analysis
- ☐ Conduct comprehensive debrief with key stakeholders
- ☐ Close CONTROL phase

NOTES:
_____
_____
_____
_____
_____

Checklist key
- 🟩 Complete
- 🟨 In progress
- 🟥 Not started

Figure 11.1 Pandemic preparedness DMAIC checklist.

Define Phase

The define phase includes deliverables that help outline the scenarios, scope, and scale of a response (Figure 11.2). Like improvement projects, action items in define, measure, and analyze are foundational to ensuring alignment and coordination of resources in a timely and organized manner. As shared in Chapter 8, be mindful of what is within your circle of control. You cannot fix or address many variables that have a major impact on your plans and response. It is important to understand what these factors are and define appropriate mitigation approaches for them.

DEFINE Phase Checklist
☐ Assign preparedness planning team roles
☐ Kick-off meeting w/ sponsor(s)
☐ Draft communication plan outline
☐ Review scenario planning
☐ Determine crisis response & management teams
☐ Conduct voice of customer (VOC) interviews
☐ Conduct waste walk
☐ Develop high-level process map for key workflows
☐ Assess change readiness using profile tool
☐ Use systems & process profile tool
☐ **Close DEFINE phase**

Figure 11.2 Define phase checklist.

Assign Preparedness Planning Team Roles

The pandemic preparedness work needs to be coordinated by a core group of individuals with defined roles. The preparedness planning team should comprise an identified leader and key contributors who are responsible for managing:

- Planning/coordination
- Operations
- Human resources/staffing/employee support and wellness
- Supply chain
- Infection control/prevention
- Communication

Other ad hoc roles can round out the team based on needs and circumstance. Ahead of the sponsor kickoff meeting, this team should convene to review the DMAIC checklist and determine the next steps.

Kickoff Meeting With Sponsors

The sponsor of an effort such as this should be someone with decision-making authority at an executive level (e.g., senior vice president, chief operating officer, chief medical officer). The kickoff meeting includes key representatives from senior leadership across all functions (nursing, operations, physicians, supply chain, pharmacy, support services, communications). For pandemic planning, the goal of this effort is to develop a robust and agile preparation strategy that can be quickly activated in the event of a major outbreak. Along with the sponsor, the team will review the key partners, departments, and individuals who need to be included in the various planning and activation workgroups.

Given the nature of outbreaks, a response requires a holistic approach that extends beyond the walls of an organization. Senior leaders need to manage the preparation and response along the care continuum, which requires partnership and coordination with other local, community, and private-sector groups in order to optimize and streamline resources (Tyrrell et al. 2020).

Draft Communication Plan Outline

The communication plan is a living document that details which stakeholders need to be informed and engaged throughout the DMAIC phases. As previously described, the communication plan provides specific information regarding key messages, delivery mechanisms, and frequency by stakeholder group. This level of specificity ensures effective communication and feedback loops to internal and external groups (Chopra et al. 2020).

As we are learning with COVID-19, outbreaks are dynamic. Information changes daily if not hourly, requiring ongoing and consistent communication. The following outlines key messages to highlight:

- *Internal:* This includes: signage, phone trees/message systems, emails, fliers, town halls, policy/procedure updates, and other forums used to inform staff, visitors, and other individuals who enter the facility (Centers for Disease Control and Prevention 2020a). Additionally, since outbreaks impact everyone, healthcare professionals are at risk both at home and at work. Caring for sick patients increases the risk of exposure to staff as well as their families, which can be overly concerning (Mason and Friese 2020). The internal communication plan should include information on what to do if you are exposed and public information resources and updates (like departments of health or the CDC). The communications plan should include an internal intranet landing page for all updates, useful links (e.g., CDC, WHO websites), education/training materials, and statistics. To supplement the intranet site, a daily broadcast email update can ensure a consistent cadence of communication to all staff. Managers can review this information during daily huddles and shift changes with staff to reinforce key messages.

- *External:* A robust communication plan includes mechanisms and forums outside of the organization. The external communication plan consists of interactions with partnering/neighboring health systems, local/state/federal agencies, public health authorities, community organizations, and other supporting companies (e.g., food, delivery, transportation, sanitation services). The community should have information on what to do if they have been exposed and how to utilize the organization's services (Tyrrell et al. 2020). For example, public messages should highlight the importance of avoiding the emergency department for non-life-threatening issues to reduce unnecessary exposure risk (U.S. Department of Health & Human Services 2020).

> IMPORTANT: You should have a comprehensive list of key contacts (name, title, phone, email, address, etc.) for the local health department, state health department, local/regional/state healthcare coalition (if applicable), and relevant partners/community organizations (i.e., long-term care facilities, skilled nursing facilities, hospitals, emergency medical services, fire and rescue, funeral homes).

Review Scenario Planning

Scenario planning provides iterations in scale, timeline, and complexity. Outbreaks vary greatly, a pandemic being the most pervasive and complex. It is important to conduct a variety of disaster planning exercises that enable the organization to stress the system and determine risk points. Many organizations already participate in local and state-level disaster planning drills (e.g., mass casualty, severe weather). The pandemic preparedness work should leverage preexisting structures and processes (Cavallo, Donoho, and Forman 2020). The preparedness team is responsible for coordinating scenario drills/exercises (simulations, tabletop discussions, etc.) and facilitating debrief sessions to capture lessons learned. These drills occur on a regular basis to ensure continuous readiness.

In addition to determining scenarios and exercises, the team needs to inventory past, current, and future projects that might impact the pandemic preparation and response strategy. For example, are there major IT projects (like an electronic health record (EHR) upgrade or rollout) that could impact clinical documentation and information sharing? Is there a construction project underway that impacts ingress/egress into the facility? Depending on your situation, these initiatives and considerations need to be accounted for in the planning and risk mitigation process.

Determine Crisis Response and Management Teams

The crisis response and management teams comprise key stakeholders within and outside of the organization. The preparedness planning team works with senior leadership to create or update the required teams to plan and oversee emergency response activation. The framework for the planning and activation teams follows recommendations from the Federal Emergency Management Agency's (FEMA) National Incident Management System (NIMS). Your organization's emergency operations plan (EOP) is the basis for the crisis response and management during a pandemic.

- *Planning team:* This group of multidisciplinary individuals (10-15 members) includes representatives from the following areas: administration, infection control, nursing, medical staff, emergency management, public relations, human resources, facilities, occupational health, critical care, emergency care, support services, and legal (Centers for Disease Control and Prevention 2020a). The planning team works through the details of the DMAIC checklist and reports status updates through the preparedness planning team. As a best practice, teams create smaller workgroups for focused planning and preparation, including (Chopra et al. 2020; FEMA - National Incident Management System):

    – *Operations:* Patient throughput, triage, staffing, and facilities management

    – *Infection control/prevention:* PPE training, disease and infection prevention education, exposure investigations/tracking, reporting

    – *Capacity planning:* Emergency department (ED)/intensive care unit (ICU) capacity, alternative sites of care, critical care expansion areas (e.g., post-anesthesia care unit (PACU), elective procedure guidelines, testing sites, telehealth)

- *Supply management:* PPE, medications, equipment, other essential or at-risk supplies
- *External team:* Members serve as organizational representatives for regional coalition, public health, local healthcare providers, etc.

- *Activation team:* Activating a response team requires clear roles and responsibilities. Given the dynamic nature of outbreaks and the complexity of healthcare organizations, a pandemic response needs to be well-coordinated and agile. The organization should have an incident management activation policy/procedure that details specific roles and logistics (U.S. Department of Health & Human Services 2020). Activation calls for the opening of an incident command center to centrally manage and coordinate myriad activities in real time. In activation mode, the planning teams outlined previously shift to implementing and monitoring the plans. Depending on the nature and evolution of the outbreak, other individuals/groups may be pulled in.

Conduct VOC Interviews

The voice of customer (VOC) interviews help the team understand the current state from a qualitative perspective. When focusing on pandemic preparedness, the VOC needs to include targeted questions to identify strengths, weaknesses, and blind spots within and across all departments. The following are examples of VOC interview questions:

1. How can you flex staffing (up or down) to adjust for volume? What challenges do you have with the current staffing model that might negatively impact operations in the event of a surge?

2. What supplies and equipment are critical to your department/unit/team's function? How reliable is the supply replenishment and equipment maintenance/repair process?

3. In the event of a surge due to an outbreak, what are your two or three biggest concerns? Where do you need help?

Conduct a Waste Walk

The waste walk assessment helps determine process inefficiencies that could be exasperated in a surge state. Key workflows need to be evaluated and refined to streamline activities and better utilize resources. The DOWNTIME waste matrix provides the details and tools for reducing waste.

Develop High-Level Process Map for Key Workflows

Outbreaks, like COVID-19, create significant operational issues. For example, an influx in ED patients creates a backlog in the ED waiting room, which is a patient safety risk. Additionally, slow discharge processes on the inpatient side reduce bed availability for patients boarding in the ED. These inefficiencies compound as cases surge, stressing the system and staff while creating an untenable patient safety risk. Using lean tools and techniques, improvement teams should evaluate and streamline the major workflows that are likely to be stressed during an outbreak. These include patient throughput (triage, ED, OR, critical care), supply chain (inventory management, replenishment, sourcing), staffing (pool resources, overtime, credentialing), and lab processing, among others.

Assess Change Readiness Using Profile Tool

Outlined in Chapter 10, the change readiness profile tool depicts the organization's state of readiness for an outbreak. The tool is populated based on VOC interviews, data analysis, and other relevant information.

Use Systems and Process Profile Tool

The systems and process profile evaluates the outbreak's potential impact on areas like staffing, information systems, and resources. Paired with the change readiness profile, these tools offer an assessment of potential vulnerable environmental and organizational factors. The pandemic preparedness team uses this information to direct the planning teams.

Close the Define Phase

The define phase closes once all applicable deliverables have been completed.

Measure Phase

The measure phase focuses on determining baselines for key performance indicators and resources such as staffing, supplies, equipment, and beds (Figure 11.3). In addition to developing a pandemic dashboard, organizations can utilize outbreak predictive models to anticipate volume surges and supply demand peaks.

MEASURE Phase Checklist
- ☐ Review previous outbreak events for lessons learned
- ☐ Formulate data collection plan
- ☐ Conduct process and workflow value analyses
- ☐ Consolidate VOC interviews into key themes/ risks
- ☐ Conduct supply chain management assessment
- ☐ Develop staffing resource strategy
- ☐ Create surge plan
- ☐ Determine incident activation and considerations
- ☐ **Close MEASURE phase**

Figure 11.3 Measure phase checklist.

Review Previous Outbreak Events for Lessons Learned

The pandemic preparedness DMAIC checklist is a tool based on previous lessons learned from other outbreaks such as H1N1, Zika, and Ebola. These past experiences provide insight into what worked well and what needs to be done differently moving forward to obtain better results. Effective preparation includes reflection and learning from past errors, omissions, and successes. The preparedness planning team and core workgroups should conduct an environmental scan of similar outbreaks locally, regionally, and globally. There are strategies and tactics that can be leveraged and transferred within and across industries for future pandemic outbreaks. As the COVID-19 situation evolves, teams should actively and continuously assess what is working well and what needs to be addressed, using the PDCA framework outlined in Chapter 8.

Formulate Data Collection Plan

Depending on the nature of the outbreak, it may not be easy to determine all data needs at this point. However, there are key performance indicators (KPIs) that can be tracked consistently to highlight clinical and operational challenges. The pandemic dashboard (Table 11.1) shows recommended KPIs based on lessons learned from COVID-19 (Centers for Disease Control and Prevention 2020a; Chopra et al. 2020).

In addition to developing a dashboard to track these KPIs, the team needs to define protocols for identifying, monitoring, and reporting outbreak confirmed patients (Centers for Disease Control and Prevention 2020a). This includes tracking any hospital-associated transmissions to patients and staff. The KPIs outlined previously provide a good starting point for monitoring organizational

Table 11.1 Pandemic dashboard.

Area	KPI
Operational	<ul><li>Bed utilization</li><li>ICU utilization</li><li>ED boarding</li></ul>
Clinical	<ul><li>Number of suspected patients (under investigation)</li><li>Number of confirmed patients (inpatient and outpatient)</li><li>Number of confirmed deaths</li><li>Number of confirmed patients discharged from inpatient unit</li><li>Lab result turnaround time</li></ul>
Supply chain	<ul><li>Equipment utilization (e.g., ventilator)</li><li>PPE utilization (gowns, gloves, facemasks, disinfectant, etc.)</li><li>Medication utilization (disease/treatment specific)</li></ul>
Staffing	<ul><li>Number of staff confirmed with disease</li><li>Number of staff exposed</li><li>Number of staff returned to work</li></ul>

performance during an outbreak. The nature of the disease will determine specific KPIs to track. For example, since COVID-19 can lead to respiratory failure, many patients require use of ventilators in critical care. The high volume and long duration of ventilator use creates a supply/demand issue for the machines.

Conduct Process and Workflow Value Analyses

Based on the priority workflows identified in the define phase, improvement teams use the Microsoft Excel–based tools to conduct time study observations following the process and employee flow. Ongoing continuous improvement efforts enable effective emergency response activation.

Consolidate VOC Interviews Into Key Themes/Risks

VOC interviews validate data trends and bring forward issues that data do not reveal or measure. Key themes, such as poor communication and lack of data, inform the planning and response teams. The feedback gathered through VOC adds context to the current state of strengths and risks as well as baseline KPI performance. These themes may also point to underlying root causes that are producing system and process quality problems.

Conduct Supply Chain Management Assessment

The principle "pull" focuses on just-in-time inventory. Hospitals continue to work hard in reducing inventory and lowering supply-related costs. However, managing a lean operation can compromise the organization's ability to respond to an epidemic surge (Cavallo, Donoho, and Forman 2020). To this end, it is imperative to conduct a comprehensive supply chain management assessment. The COVID-19 pandemic highlighted significant supply chain challenges from a global to local perspective, especially related to PPE availability and usage. The team needs to determine what supplies are vulnerable based on utilization, ease of acquisition, etc. and develop corresponding contingency plans (U.S. Department of Health & Human Services 2020). To ensure appropriate supplies during an outbreak, organizations should plan to have a minimum eight-week supply of essential patient-care supplies and equipment (Centers for Disease Control and Prevention 2020a).

During the COVID-19 outbreak, PPE supplies were exhausted rapidly, forcing the CDC to loosen guidelines (Advisory Board 2020a). For example, N95 respirators were traditionally a "one-time use" PPE supply. Guidelines evolved based on national and global supply shortages, resulting in recommendations for providers to maintain a single N95 respirator throughout a week of work. The conservation and reuse guidelines need to be developed for the organization in alignment with local, state, and federal protocols for storage, cleaning, and disinfection (Mason and Friese 2020). Organizations can outline a progressive conservation strategy using lessons from the early PPE challenges that COVID-19 created in March/April 2020.

Drug shortages are persistent regardless of an outbreak (Tyrrell et al. 2020). Depending on the disease, its rate of transmission, and treatment regime, medication supplies are at risk. To effectively and holistically manage key supplies, a centralized supply team should manage the inventory and the distribution of supplies (Advisory Board 2020a).

Develop Staffing Resource Strategy

Like supplies, staffing is an essential resource to operations. Staffing strategies need to be determined well in advance of an outbreak to ensure agility and flexibility as the situation evolves. The following outlines key staffing considerations before and during an outbreak:

- *Preparation:* All clinical staff need to complete annual fit testing (i.e., N95 respirators) (Mason and Friese 2020). The infection control/prevention team also provides appropriate education and job-specific training, so staff understand disease-specific details such as symptoms, infection control practices, and treatment protocols (Centers for Disease Control and Prevention 2020b).

- *Staffing capacity:* Outbreaks are not "business as usual"; therefore, normal staffing ratios and plans may not suffice (Chopra et al. 2020). Healthcare workers have an increased exposure risk, which can lead to staffing gaps/shortages due to quarantine and treatment periods (Cavallo, Donoho, and Forman 2020). Aside from clinical staff, surges require upstaffing core support areas such as environmental and food services (Tyrrell et al. 2020). Following are COVID-19 best practice staffing strategies to increase capacity (Centers for Disease Control and Prevention 2020a; Advisory Board 2020c):

  – Designate staff responsible for caring for suspected/confirmed outbreak disease patients. This limits the number of potential staff members exposed to patients. Plans need to be in place in the ED as well as critical care and nursing units.

  – Engage union/labor leaders to discuss staffing responsibilities, hours of operation, and other changes impacted by an outbreak.

  – Reallocate clinicians from non-emergent/essential areas. Consider reallocating surgeons/anesthesiologists to other clinical areas if elective procedure volume drops significantly. Flex outpatient staff into the acute care setting.

  – Train (upskill) nurses to work in critical care areas (for example, PACU nurses move to ICU).

  – Engage retired clinicians and medical/nursing students to join the workforce.

  – Extend nurse traveler/agency contracts and update nursing ratios to expand bed coverage.

  – Expedite credentialing for healthcare personnel from other organizations/states in conjunction with revised state and federal credentialing and practice guidelines.

- *Policies:* Healthcare workers are at high risk for exposure, creating potential staffing challenges. In addition, these employees have families at home who are also impacted by the outbreak. As seen with COVID-19, the closing of schools and implementation of social distancing measures creates an added pressure for many families. Without childcare options, some employees are not able to work. The organization should update policies related to work from home, sick leave, and absenteeism to reduce confusion and stress (Centers for Disease Control and Prevention 2020a). There must be clear exposure criteria and detailed plans for employee quarantine requirements (Chopra et al. 2020). Policies are likely to require frequent updates during the outbreak timeframe, adapting to the ever-changing circumstances.

- *Emotional support/wellness:* Employee safety and wellness is a top priority during the planning and activation phases (Advisory Board 2020b). COVID-19 impacts all people in many ways. For the healthcare workforce, these individuals share a significant burden to care for an unusually high volume of critically ill patients. Overwork, stress, emotional wear, among other factors, can lead to serious distress (Tyrrell et al. 2020). It is necessary to develop a comprehensive behavioral health/wellness support plan to help staff manage the stress and grief experienced during an outbreak like COVID-19 (U.S. Department of Health & Human Services 2020).

Create Surge Plan

Epidemic and pandemic outbreaks overwhelm the healthcare delivery system (Cavallo, Donoho, and Forman 2020). An important task during the preparedness phase is anticipating the response to volume surges. There are a variety of strategies organizations use to successfully create capacity for critical care, provide alternative sites of low-acuity care, and leverage technology for virtual/remote visits. Following are some key considerations when determining the surge plan:

- *Space:* The space plan needs to be flexible to accommodate specific patient needs, depending on the nature of the outbreak. All space should be considered when evaluating the emergency operations plan, including clinical and non-clinical areas. Plans should include treatment space for suspected/confirmed patients, critical care needs, testing sites and supply staging areas, among others.

    - *Clinical space:* In addition to servicing outbreak patients, the clinical space strategy includes maintaining services for at-risk patients who do not have the outbreak disease such as pregnancy, dialysis, and cancer (U.S. Department of Health & Human Services 2020). For outbreak-specific needs, the clinical care area must have the required resources to support patients. This might include general medical/surgical nursing unit setups or require specific features/functions/equipment to effectively isolate infectious patients. As an example, COVID-19 patients require negative pressure rooms to reduce exposure risk of airborne particles. The facility and clinic teams need to inventory and evaluate the negative pressure rooms, as well as determine alternatives, if patient volume exceeds capacity. Areas like the ED can utilize a geographic model in which suspected/confirmed outbreak patients are colocated in a "hot" zone while non-outbreak patients are in a "warm" or "cold" zone. Creating distinct zones enables staff to remain dedicated to specific patient populations, thereby reducing staff exposure. The protocol for managing outbreak patients needs to include triage processes that are appropriate for their point of entry (i.e., ED, outpatient clinic, direct admission) (Centers for Disease Control and Prevention 2020a). Lastly, the plan includes contingencies in the event of rapid increases in mortalities. The facility's morgue capacity can quickly be exceeded, requiring plans to leverage temporary morgues and collaborating with local organizations.

- *Non-clinical space:* Clinical care needs are high during an outbreak. As such, it is important to optimize space throughout the facility (and across facilities where possible). Non-clinical space can be repurposed to meet different operational and clinical needs during the emergency response. As an example, administrative and conference space can be repurposed for supply/equipment staging. Parking lots can be used as drive-through testing sites. Other space for consideration includes nearby hotels, college dormitory beds, or gyms (Advisory Board 2020c). It is important to inventory all potential space and develop a systematic approach for repurposing. Ideally, prioritize space that is closest to clinical areas.

- *Bed capacity:* The bed capacity plan aims to free at least 30 percent of inpatient beds, accommodating a potentially swift influx of patients (Chopra et al. 2020). The bed management department provides the complete inventory of all beds by type (med/surg, critical care, etc.), specialty beds/units, and periop (pre-op, PACU), among others. Surge planning includes conversion of beds to meet patient demand, namely, adding critical care capacity to the system (Advisory Board 2020c). Table 11.2 provides a high-level outline for the surge plan. The plan outlines actions/responses by department before and during a surge state. A comprehensive approach like this requires significant coordination and collaboration across the system. The table is not exhaustive; therefore, add relevant departments/actions and revise the list as needed.

- *Alternate sites of care:* Outbreaks are the result of contagious viruses. To limit exposure, the response plan includes alternate sites of care. This approach provides access to healthcare services without the exposure risk of face-to-face contact and/or close proximity to suspected/confirmed outbreak patients. Non-urgent elective procedures and outpatient visits should be rescheduled during the peak of the outbreak response. Elective urgent surgical procedures and inpatient diagnostic studies can shift to the outpatient setting where possible (Centers for Disease Control and Preparedness 2020a). Telehealth provides virtual access to providers through mobile devices. The telehealth option enables outpatient clinics to continue new and established patient visits. Since the technology required to support an expanded telehealth model can be complicated and expensive, it is important to understand the current capabilities and future considerations in order to adjust for a surge in virtual visit volume.

- *Entry/exits:* To reduce the flow of traffic within a facility, the plan must include a comprehensive strategy for ingress/egress. There should be a limited set of defined entrances for staff and visitors/patients during the outbreak response period (Centers for Disease Control and Preparedness 2020a; U.S. Department of Health & Human Services 2020). Other measures may need to be considered; for example, with COVID-19, organizations assigned nurses to conduct symptom screening at all entrances. Visitor and vendor restrictions must be evaluated. To reduce unnecessary exposures, only essential personnel should be on-site and in patient care areas. All individuals in the facility (staff, visitors, patients) may be required to wear face masks as well.

Table 11.2 Surge plan.

Department	Action/Response
ED	• Add hallway spots • Convert rooms to semi-private • Cancel nonessential education/training, meetings, or other activities to allow nurses to staff on the floor • Give charge nurse/nurse educators clinical assignments • Revise staffing assignments (update ratios) to cover patients in ED, boarding, and in waiting room
Nursing	• Open all inpatient nursing units to maximum capacity • Open all semi-private beds • Repurpose specialty beds for nonspecialty patients • Cancel nonessential education/training, meetings, or other activities to allow nurses to staff on the floor • Give charge nurse/nurse educators clinical assignments • Revise nurse-to-patient staffing ratio to increase coverage
Medical staff	• Prioritize rounding on ED boarders and confirmed/potential discharges • Expedite discharge documentation/orders before 11:00 a.m. • Cancel nonessential education/training, meetings, or other activities
Case management	• Facilitate discharges within ED and observation units • Provide medical staff/nursing with list of potential discharges • Evaluate extended recovery cases for potential discharge
Perioperative	• Increase staffing to cover PACU and extended recovery patients • Cancel or limit nonemergent elective procedures • Prioritize inpatient cases and add-ons for pending discharges
Ancillary/procedural areas	Including, but not limited to: radiology, rehab, cath lab, endoscopy, CVIR • Prioritize procedures, studies, and evaluations for pending discharge patients • Cancel or limit nonemergent elective procedures • Assess staff redeployment strategies to clinical areas in need
Patient flow: bed management/transfer center	• Prioritize bed placement for ED and PACU boarders • Review and prioritize next-day direct admissions and elective procedures • Evaluate and hold all external transfers to ED, except for trauma/ACS patients
Laboratory	• Send phlebotomy staff to ED/periop areas to assist with specimen collection and deliver
Respiratory	• Send staff to ED/periop areas to deliver ordered nebulizer treatments

(continued)

Table 11.2 Surge plan.

Department	Action/Response
Pharmacy	• Inventory and communicate status of key medications/drug supplies • Source alternative treatments/medications to accommodate demand
Linen services	• Increase deliveries of clean linen and increase pick-up times of soiled linen, prioritizing ED and inpatient discharged patient rooms
Transport	• Deliver additional beds to all units expanding capacity (as outlined above in ED/nursing actions)
Food services	• Provide extra meals/supplies to ED and PACU for boarding patients • Increase rounding frequency for dirty-tray pickup in ED
EVS	• Increase rounding frequency for room cleaning • Prioritize room cleaning for ED admissions and inpatient discharges • Reassign staff allocated to nonclinical space assignments
Facilities	• Prioritize facility and equipment repairs impacting clinical operations • Prioritize repair of broken beds/stretchers
BioMed	• Prioritize repair of biomedical equipment (e.g., infusion pumps)
Supply chain	• Assign ED point person to serve as liaison for ED supply chain • Increase frequency of ED supply room inventory to restock as needed • Provide additional supplies in ED/PACU to accommodate boarding patients • Inventory and communicate status of key supplies and at-risk items • Source alternative supply providers to accommodate demand
Administrative leadership	• Round on clinical units to evaluate staff needs/concerns as well as operational flow • Communicate updates and important information at a regular cadence (e.g., daily at midnight) • Facilitate leadership meetings with the above groups to discuss status updates, issues/concerns, and next steps. • Cancel all nonessential meetings/activities • Verify all departments initiated their surge plan

Determine Incident Activation and Considerations

As described in the define phase, the incident activation structure and process follows your organization's EOP. The NIMS defines specific roles, responsibilities, and processes to follow during an incident response. The activation team holds regular status update calls with key stakeholders. During a call, the pandemic dashboard KPIs are reviewed and departments provide brief updates. Frequency may vary from multiple times per day to once per week, depending on the circumstance. Throughout the incident response and in conjunction with local/state/federal authorities, adjust the service restriction plans based on staff, supply, and/or medication shortages (U.S. Department of Health & Human Services 2020).

Close the Measure Phase

The measure phase closes once all applicable deliverables have been completed.

Analyze Phase

The analyze phase dives deeper into the current state assessment for pandemic response preparedness (Figure 11.4). Work done in this phase helps inform mitigation and response strategies tailored to your organization.

ANALYZE Phase Checklist
- ☐ Perform financial analysis and reporting
- ☐ Perform data analysis
- ☐ Conduct stakeholder analysis
- ☐ Determine staff training needs & deployment strategies
- ☐ Conduct FMEA
- ☐ **Close ANALYZE phase**

Figure 11.4 Analyze phase checklist.

Perform Financial Analysis and Reporting

The incident response plan includes the limitation/cancellation of non-urgent elective procedures. As discussed in the chapter introduction, reducing elective surgical procedures can have a devastating impact on an organization's financial health. In collaboration with the finance department, the team performs a variety of financial analyses to understand the potential revenue impact of a sustained outbreak incident response. Variable expenses, from supplies and medications to staffing, also expect to increase dramatically. The EOP should be accompanied by the financial assessment so senior leaders understand the potential impact and decision points as well as determine priority services to restart.

Perform Data Analysis

KPIs are outlined in Table 11.1 of the measure phase. Using various scenarios, data analysis incorporates the utilization rate of supplies and other resources, estimating supply days on-hand and identifying potential weak points in the system.

Conduct Stakeholder Analysis

The broad impact and response of an outbreak involves myriad stakeholders. The team needs to assess internal and external stakeholders. Engagement strategies are tailored based on the level of resistance/support to the incident response strategy. As a living document, the communication plan reflects the specific needs of stakeholder groups and aligns with the stakeholder analysis.

Determine Staff Training Needs and Deployment Strategies

Before an outbreak occurs, it is important to understand the systems/processes you will need to leverage or accelerate. The next pandemic outbreak cannot be predicted. When it occurs, staff will undoubtedly need to be trained in the disease (i.e., signs, symptoms, progression, transmission) and methods to mitigate and treat it. Developing a training program and supporting technology takes time. Time is not a resource we have during a pandemic. The training strategy outlines the logistics and framework required to quickly develop and deploy education to relevant staff during a dynamic outbreak situation. This includes content development, technology to disseminate learning modules and track completion/compliance, physical training space (as appropriate), and a list of required participants (e.g., clinical versus non-clinical positions). The real-time training plan supplements the annual mandatory education that is part of the EOP.

Conduct FMEA

Failure modes and effects analysis (FMEA) is a process analysis tool used to evaluate potential failures in a design, product, or service (Tague 2005). The failure mode represents a way in which an error or failure may occur. This proactive risk assessment challenges stakeholders to work through and address assumptions tied to plans. The goal of the FMEA is to identify, address, and mitigate major risks.

- *Description:* A proactive risk assessment tool used to evaluate a system/process design. The Word document template provides a framework to complete in a multidisciplinary team (Figure 11.5).

- *When to use it:* Before implementing a comprehensive or high-risk plan. Identify and address major risks and gaps. The tool requires input from many stakeholders and further vetting by subject-matter experts to validate assumptions and considerations. This should not be done individually.

- *Required?* Yes, especially for the pandemic preparedness plan.

The process for completing the FMEA tool is straightforward. The FMEA tool asks progressive questions based on severity, occurrence, and detection of failures.

1. Complete scoping information at the top of the template: FMEA scope, date of completion, physician leader(s), facilitators, participants.

2. Enter all process steps/inputs in the first column.

3. Starting at the top, respond to the following questions in the adjacent columns related to that specific process step/input:
   - In what ways can the process step or input fail?
   - What is the impact of the failure (customer or internal requirements)?
   - What is the severity (SEV)?
     – The severity ranking estimates the impact on the customer or organization. The estimate ranges from 1 = none to 4 = catastrophic.

- What causes the failure?
- How often is it likely to occur (OCC)?
    - This column estimates the probability of a failure occurring during the expected lifetime of the process/service. The estimate ranges from 1 = remote to 4 = frequent.
- What are the existing controls and procedures that prevent either the cause or the failure?
- How well can you detect the failure (DET)?
    - The detection column estimates the probability of the problem being detected and acted upon before it has happened.

4. Determine the risk priority number: Multiply SEV, OCC, DET.
    - To calculate the perceived risk and priority, multiply the severity, occurrence, and detection estimated numbers together. Once each row is complete, the team can rank-order the top priority risks.
    - For example: If a process step has a SEV score of 4, OCC score of 2, and DET score of 3, the risk score is: SEV x OCC x DET = 4 x 2 x 3 = 24.

5. Define the next steps. In the final column, outline what actions can be taken to reduce/mitigate the risk.

Close the Analyze Phase

The analyze phase closes once all applicable deliverables have been completed.

Improve Phase

The improve phase of the pandemic preparedness DMAIC checklist refers to response activation (Figure 11.6). In other words, when an outbreak occurs the organization will activate the EOP. The following section describes additional tasks and considerations during this phase. Using COVID-19 as an example, the response activation time period can range from weeks to several months. As an analogy, the organization is running a marathon (Advisory Board 2020b). It is important to keep the end goal of "business as usual" in mind while focusing on the next two miles ahead. This type of marathon does not have a predetermined route, and obstacles come from anywhere, requiring agility and flexibility in the plans and responses.

PANDEMIC PREPAREDNESS: A COVID-19 CASE STUDY 221

FMEA scope:							
Date of completion:							
Physician leader(s):							
Facilitators:							
Participants:							

Key process step or input	Potential failure mode	Potential failure effects	SEV	Potential causes	OCC	Current controls	DET	Risk score	Actions recommended
What is the process step or input?	In what ways can the process step or input fail?	What is the impact of the failure?	What is the severity?	What causes the failure?	How often is it likely to occur?	What are the existing controls and procedures that prevent either the cause or the failure?	How well can you detect the failure?	Multiply SEV, OCC, DET	What are the actions for reducing the occurrence of the cause, or improving detection?

LEGEND:

Analysis	Description	Rating (lower is better)
SEV: Severity	Estimate impact on customer or organization	1. **NONE** or **MINOR** patient outcome: No injury, increase in length of stay, or increase in level of care 2. **MODERATE** patient outcome: Increase length of stay or increase level of care. 3. **MAJOR** patient outcome: Permanent lessening of bodily functioning, disfigurement, surgical intervention required, increase length of stay, increase level of care 4. **CATASTROPHIC** patient outcome: Death or major permanent loss of function, surgery/procedure on the wrong patient or wrong part of body
OCC: Occurrence	Estimate probability of a failure occurring during the expected lifetime of the process/service	1. **REMOTE**: Unlikely to occur (may happen sometime in 5–30 years) 2. **UNCOMMON**: Possible to occur (may happen sometime in 2–5 years) 3. **OCCASIONAL**: Probably will occur (may happen several times in 1–2 years) 4. **FREQUENT**: Likely to occur immediately or within a short period (may happen several times in one year)
DET: Detection	Estimate probability of the problem being detected and acted upon before it has happened	1. **VERY LIKELY** or **AUTOMATIC**: Processes exist to readily detect a failure 2. **LIKELY**: Possible to occur without detection though rare 3. **DIFFICULT**: Unlikely to identify the failure when it occurs 4. **UNLIKELY** or **NOT POSSIBLE**: Unable to detect failures and respond accordingly
Risk Score	After ranking the severity, occurrence, and detection levels for each failure mode, the team will be able to calculate a risk priority number (RPN).	The formula for the RPN is: RPN = severity × occurrence × detection

Figure 11.5 FMEA tool.

> **IMPROVE Phase Checklist**
> **Incident Response Activation**
> ☐ Activate the emergency operations plan
> ☐ Evaluate current state of equipment, staffing, supplies, capacity
> ☐ Evaluate response plan and determine key decisions/timelines
> ☐ Communicate with staff, patients, visitors, and key partners/organizations
> ☐ Close the command center/plan for return to normal operations
> ☐ **Close IMPROVE phase**

Figure 11.6   Improve phase checklist.

Activate the Emergency Operations Plan

The EOP activates upon anticipation/confirmation of an outbreak. The decision to initiate the response teams and corresponding internal disaster codes lies with senior leadership in conjunction with local/state/federal officials. The activation team described in the define phase coordinates the operational command center and starts the cadence of status update calls and data reporting.

Evaluate Current State of Equipment, Staffing, Supplies, Capacity

The pandemic dashboard provides up-to-date information on KPI trends. Leaders across the organization are responsible for providing status updates and action plans, especially related to supply shortages and challenges. Data transparency promotes resource optimization and systems thinking, ensuring supplies, equipment, and staffing are allocated based on priority needs.

Evaluate Response Plan and Determine Key Decisions/Timelines

Work completed during the define, measure, and analyze phases should be evaluated for their effectiveness upon incident activation. The activation team verifies that key workflows and processes are working well (e.g., ED patient throughput, bed allocation/prioritization). Risks identified through the FMEA and VOC interviews are monitored closely. The financial impact assessment continues to be updated based on the specific outbreak. Staff training plans begin as information from sources like the CDC and WHO are made available.

Communicate with Staff, Patients, Visitors, and Key Partners/Organizations

The internal and external communication plans are underway. All communication mechanisms should be evaluated for their effectiveness and refined as indicated. The dynamic nature of the outbreak requires sharing updates from groups like the CDC. An emphasis should be made regarding success stories and teamwork. During the COVID-19 crisis, social media outlets saw an outpouring of positive stories and messages from clinicians at the front line. These experiences build solidarity within teams and throughout the organization and community.

Close the Command Center/Plan for Return to Normal Operations

Stabilization of the outbreak is a local consideration. Senior leadership, along with local, state, and federal authorities, need to determine what stabilization means. The KPIs should demonstrate a significant reduction in outbreak cases and supply utilization rates. Organizations run a risk of loosening restrictions (i.e., visitor restrictions, elective procedures, PPE conservation strategies) too soon. Deactivation of the command center follows the EOP outline. Returning to normal operations may happen in progressive phases over weeks or months, depending on many factors.

Close the Improve Phase

The improve phase closes once all applicable deliverables have been completed.

Control Phase

The control phase marks the stabilization period of the outbreak response (Figure 11.7). During this phase, the team monitors KPIs and operational workflows to ensure sustainability. Similar to improvement projects, the control phase should not be an afterthought but rather part of the early stages of planning. The activation team coordinates operational handoffs and the transition back to normal operations.

Continue Response Team Status Update Meetings

As part of the handoff process with operational owners, the activation team continues the status update calls. During these calls, KPIs and department status updates are reviewed to ensure ongoing improvement and sustainability. This accountability process verifies everyone is doing their part and that issues do not advance undetected. Ongoing data analysis enables the team to determine any favorable or unfavorable trends, prompting course corrections as appropriate. Before concluding the control phase, the activation team develops a control plan with the sponsors and process owners. The plan includes strategies to maintain process compliance, data reporting, and longer-term process refinements.

CONTROL Phase Checklist

- ☐ Continue response team status update meetings
- ☐ Calculate financial impact
- ☐ Conduct pre/post kpi analysis
- ☐ Conduct comprehensive debrief with key stakeholders
- ☐ **Close CONTROL phase**

Figure 11.7 Control phase checklist.

Calculate Financial Impact

The financial models are likely refined throughout the activation phase as the organization's financial leaders learn more about the impact on revenue and expenses. Upon reaching a steady state, this assessment informs strategies to increase revenue (e.g., restart elective procedures, operate ORs on weekends, open outpatient office visits) and reduce expenses (e.g., reduce OT, redistribute staff/resources).

Conduct Pre/Post KPI Analysis

Along with the financial assessment, the pandemic dashboard KPIs are analyzed. The pre/post analysis informs the next iteration of the EOP and pandemic response plan.

Conduct Comprehensive Debrief With Key Stakeholders

The debrief consists of scrutinizing deliverables completed during the define, measure, and analyze phases, as well as the activation. Using information gathered in the financial and KPI assessments, the team provides an overview of the key findings and trends. The broad stakeholder group reflects on what worked well, what did not work well or go according to plan, and, importantly, what should be done differently to respond to future outbreaks. Lessons learned integrate into the EOP and are shared broadly with staff. As noted previously, special attention should be focused on employee and team recognition during the outbreak response.

Close the Control Phase

The control phase closes once all applicable deliverables have been completed.

⚠ CHAPTER CHALLENGE

Reflect on your organization's COVID-19 experience.

QUESTIONS:

1. How well did your organization and teams within the organization perform during the COVID-19 outbreak? What were two or three strengths and two or three opportunities for improvement?

2. What supply chain issues/barriers impact your specific organization? What lean tools can be used to address/mitigate these issues?

3. What substitutes are available for the most-used PPE supplies?

4. What is your inpatient capacity (med/surg, critical care, isolation rooms) for your health system? What strategies were used to expand capacity?

5. How was non-clinical space repurposed? How can you leverage the lean fundamentals to optimize the physical environment?

6. Why are surge plans important to initiate ahead of a potential influx of outbreak patients?

7. How can you ensure the safety of front-line providers during an outbreak?

8. Why is the FMEA tool strongly encouraged as part of the pandemic planning process?

9. How can you ensure lessons learned are integrated into operations and future crisis response situations?

Appendices

The appendices provide instructions to support the tools and templates provided with this book. To access, visit https://asqassets.widencollective.com/portals/fe7xvmfj/(H1580)LeanHealthcare. The tools are organized by the DMAIC project phases (Figure A.1). Two documents live outside the folders: the lean DMAIC checklist and the rapid improvement event portfolio. These two documents drive rapid improvement execution. The five folders contain various tools and templates referenced in the lean DMAIC checklist. Remember, the checklist, portfolio, tools, and templates are suggested to help project execution and should be adopted and adapted to your organization, department, or work setting accordingly.

To support your use of the tools, a supplementary folder labeled "Appendix Examples" contains a case study project for improving patient flow in a physician's office. The case study employs all the tools described in the appendix to demonstrate the appropriate use. Refer to the examples as you use each template.

> *Save as a new file any tool or template you use. The tools and templates are "read only" so you cannot overwrite them.*

```
Name
    01_DEFINE
    02_MEASURE
    03_ANALYZE
    04_IMPROVE
    05_CONTROL
    Lean DMAIC Checklist
    Rapid Improvement Event Portfolio
```

Figure A.1 Organization of tool/template documents.

Appendix A
Rapid Improvement Event Portfolio

The rapid improvement event portfolio is a Microsoft PowerPoint document that contains consolidated project deliverables. The portfolio aligns with the lean DMAIC checklist. Teams can document and summarize all deliverables in one location. This reduces excessive numbers of electronic files, versions, and other document control issues. Portfolio slides are segmented by DMAIC phase and described accordingly.

HIGH-LEVEL PROJECT PLAN

Before the first define phase tool there is a high-level project plan template (Table A.1). The plan contains some of the major project deliverables along with comments and columns describing why the deliverable is important, who is responsible, and when the task needs to be completed.

DEFINE

Project Charter

Description: The project charter is a two-page document that defines the project (Figure A.2). The first page contains basic project information (title, sponsor, process owner, team members, facilitators, start date, and scope). Other components include the project description, problem, and goal as well as the potential benefits (Silverstein, Samuel, and Decarlo 2009). This page gives individuals a solid understanding of what the project objective is and how success is defined. The second page of the charter reviews data sources, projects that can be leveraged or acknowledged, individuals of value (to be contacted for voice of customer (VOC) interviews), and potential barriers to success. These elements provide a high-level environmental scan.

When to use it: At the project start with the facilitators and sponsor

Required? Yes

Table A.1 High-level project plan.

Deliverable/action	Comments	Why are we doing this?	By when	Who will lead it
Project charter	Need to discuss with sponsor/process owners	To determine what is in and out of scope and what the project objective is	12/29	T. Brady
Communication plan	Ensure this includes department/staff upstream and downstream of the process	To ensure all stakeholders know what to expect, what they need to do, how they can help, etc.	12/29	D. Ortiz
Develop high-level process map	30,000-foot view of the process	To depict the process at a high level	1/9	M. Vaughn
Voice of customer interviews	Need to coordinate and interview appropriate stakeholders of process	To identify key themes staff indicate are contributors to the problem and tie quantitative measures to these themes	1/16	M. Vaughn
Logistics	Schedule event, identify process expert team, finalize resource requirements, prepare team packet	To ensure schedule and deliverables line up	1/16	D. Pedroia
Change leadership	Conduct change readiness assessment, conduct stakeholder analysis		1/17	T. Brady

Data analysis	Determine key metrics to monitor/data to display (no more than five); provide narrative to support graphs	To quantitatively analyze and determine root causes of the problem	1/28	M. Vaughn
Finalize fishbone diagram	Use information from VOC, observations, and data analysis	To qualitatively analyze and determine root causes of the problem	1/29	M. Vaughn
Draft improvement event agenda		To outline how to use the time with staff to achieve our project objective	1/28	T. Brady
Facilitate improvement event	Gather team of staff to identify solution to key drivers of the issues	To develop a high-impact action plan for staff to implement over the next four weeks	2/2	T. Brady
Develop control phase plan	Action plan based on facilitated session	To assign, document, update, and hold staff accountable for key action items	2/2	M. Vaughn
Draft A3 report		To document project concisely so it can be shared across all areas of the organization	2/17	T. Brady
Present A3 report to sponsor and process owner		To communicate lessons learned and project outcomes	3/6	T. Brady

Page 1

Project title: Improving physician's office patient flow	
Sponsors: S. A. Moose and G. L. Lohman **Process owners:** V. Wllfork and J. Edelman **Team members:** R. Gronkowski, M. Hoomanawanui, R. Ninkovich, S. Vollmer, D. Revis **Facilitators:** T. Brady (lead), M. Vaughn, D. Pedroia (logistics), D. Ortiz (communications) **Project start date:** Dec. 29, 2014 **Project scope:** Physician's office visit from patient sign-in to checkout	**Project description/problem and goal:** **What is the problem or opportunity?** Patient throughput is inefficient. Patients wait (in waiting area or exam room) for extended periods of time. **What is the goal for the team?** Reduce patient throughput time and balance staff workloads. **Potential benefits:** **Why are you doing this?** Patient satisfaction scores are low and throughput times are too long. We are not providing excellent service to our customers and risk losing their business. **What are you expecting to come out of this?** Improved coordination and collaboration across all staff. Improved patient satisfaction. Reduced throughput time.

Page 2

What are the data sources?

Office information system (OIS) and patient satisfaction surveys

How will the data be collected?

Electronically through the OIS and patient satisfaction survey tool. Reporting is automated.

Are there other completed or active projects that can be leveraged? No other projects have previously addressed patient throughput and/or satisfaction.	**Individuals of value:** B. LaFell (office manager), B. Browner (medical assistant), N. Solder (physician), D. Hightower (registrar/scheduler), P. Chung (charge nurse)

Potential barriers to success:

High volume so it is difficult for employees to take time to work on improvement projects.

No financial resources (project must be budget-neutral).

Staff has worked here for a long time. Many processes are ingrained as "the way we've always done it."

Figure A.2 Project charter.

Communications Plan

Description: The communication plan aligns communication strategies with stakeholder groups (Table A.2). Each group has a specified key message tailored to its interests, responsibilities, or needs. The delivery mechanism and frequency correspond with the nature of the group and its workflow.

When to use it: Draft with the sponsor and use throughout the duration of the project

Required? Yes

Waste Observations

Description: The waste observation table accompanies gemba walks and consolidates the results (Table A.3). Observations are documented and accompanied by clarifying comments.

When to use it: During or after gemba walks

Required? Yes

Waste Diagnostic Tool

Description: Figure A.3 displays the waste diagnostic tool. This tool provides a visual display of the presence and impact of waste on process flow. Each waste is evaluated along a continuum from low to high impact. The white dot is moved along the row accordingly.

When to use it: During or after gemba walks

Required? No

High-Level Process Map

Description: The high-level process map outlines the project scope (Figure A.4). The tool is in a modifiable table form. Process steps are added or removed as needed. However, because it is high level, the process map should not exceed eight steps.

When to use it: Before the high-level process map SIPOC (next tool). The SIPOC tool described next uses the steps defined here.

Required? Yes

High-Level Process Map SIPOC

Description: The high-level process map SIPOC details internal process requirements (Table A.4). Every step has a supplier, input, output, and customer. There are specific elements within each process step that are critical to quality (CTQ) as determined by the customer of that step. CTQ represents the factors that contribute to quality within that particular step (e.g., completed form) (Snee and Hoerl 2003). The output of one step typically is the input to the following step (Silverstein, Samuel, and Decarlo 2009). For example, a surgery patient (input) will have an IV

Table A.2 Communication plan.

Group	Key message	Delivery mechanism (e-mail, phone, etc.)	Frequency	Person responsible to deliver
Patients	Changes in processes to create a better experience and meet patient needs.	Signage, newsletter	Once before improvement, once afterward	D. Ortiz (with process owners)
Administration	Changes in policy/procedure that impact workflow, coding, billing, scheduling, etc.	E-mail, weekly meeting	Weekly	D. Ortiz (with process owners)
Medical assistants	Changes in workflow, responsibilities related to discipline. What is changing, when, how, and why.	E-mail, daily huddle	At least once per week	D. Ortiz (with lead medical assistant)
Nurses	Changes in workflow, responsibilities related to discipline. What is changing, when, how, and why.	E-mail, daily huddle	At least once per week	D. Ortiz (with charge nurse)
Physicians	Changes in workflow, responsibilities related to discipline. What is changing, when, how, and why.	E-mail, daily huddle	At least once per week	D. Ortiz (with lead physician)
Registrars/schedulers	Changes in workflow, responsibilities related to discipline. What is changing, when, how, and why.	E-mail, daily huddle	At least once per week	D. Ortiz (with process owners)

Table A.3 Waste observations.

Waste	Observations	Comments
Defects	Missing information on patient chart (demographics, insurance). Schedule is inaccurate.	
Overproduction	Chart prep (paper).	Staff prepares almost double of what is required.
Waiting	Patients wait in waiting room/exam room. Staff waits for tasks/assignments/information.	A lot of waiting by everyone. Though it seems busy, it also appears that nothing is happening because of the waiting.
Nonutilized skill/intellect	Staff waits for tasks/assignments/information. Uneven workload balance.	Medical assistants seem to be doing a lot of extra, unnecessary work.
Transportation	Patients walk a good amount.	Cannot change this due to fixed office layout.
Inventory	Patients waiting in waiting room (work-in-process—WIP).	
Motion	All staff, but mainly medical assistants, move around a lot, looking for people, information, supplies, etc.	Layout issues, no storage organization, rework from missing information.
Extra processing	Double documentation in patient charts and scheduling log.	

Figure A.3 Waste diagnostic.

placed (process step = placing the IV, output = patient with IV). This patient (input = patient with IV) then receives medication like a general anesthetic (process step = administer medication, output = sedated patient). To complete this tool, you have to walk the process and follow the flow of the item (i.e., patient, specimen, form). Document the details of what occurs.

When to use it: After gemba walks and process observations

Required? Yes

| Enter office | Sign in | Get vitals | RN interview | Physician exam | Receive Rx | Check out |

Figure A.4 High-level process map.

Table A.4 High-level SIPOC.

Supplier	Input	Process step	Output	Customer What is critical to quality (CTQ)?
Patient	Insurance card and license	**Sign in**	Registered patient and activated chart	Accurate/up-to-date patient information
Patient	Registered patient	**Get vitals**	Vitals taken and documented in chart	Accurate recordings of vitals (height, weight, blood pressure, temperature)
Medical assistant/ patient	Patient with vitals taken	**RN interview**	Understanding of reason for visit, history, and physical	Accurate assessment of health
Nurse	Patient history/ physical and reason for visit	**Physician exam**	Determination of illness/issue, treatment plan	Accurate assessment of health
Physician	Determination of illness/issue, treatment plan	**Receive Rx**	Prescription slip	Accurate medication, dosage, etc.
Patient	Patient with Rx	**Check out**	Scheduled follow-up appointment, patient payment	Schedule availability, accurate copay amount

Change Readiness Profile

Description: The change readiness profile provides an environmental assessment of the area within the scope (Figure A.5). Each of the six domains is evaluated along a continuum based on the current leadership abilities. The white dots move up the column from low to high depending on assessment.

When to use it: After VOC interviews and gemba walks

Required? Optional, but strongly recommended

Based on the current state, what is the leadership's ability to do the following?

1 Create urgency	2 Establish coalition	3 Communicate vision	4 Remove barriers	5 Provide progress feedback	6 Hardwire changes

Figure A.5 Change readiness profile.

System and Process Profile

Description: A profile tool that is similar to the change readiness profile evaluates systems and processes. The system and process profile depicts the potential impact of change on system or process components (Figure A.6). As with the change readiness profile, each of the six domains is evaluated along a continuum. White dots move along the column from low to high impact.

When to use it: After VOC interviews and gemba walks

Required? Optional, but strongly recommended

Figure A.6 System and process profile.

MEASURE

Process Value Analysis Results

Description: Chapter 3 details the process value analysis tool (Figure A.7). This is a gemba-based tool completed through time study observations and analysis. Paste the results from the Microsoft Excel tool into the portfolio.

When to use it: Time studies are conducted after initial gemba walks and VOC interviews. Before closely watching the process, it is essential to understand the environment and build rapport with staff.

Required? Yes (if applicable)

Workflow Value Analysis Results

Description: Chapter 3 details the workflow value analysis tool (Figure A.8). Like the process value analysis tool, this tool is gemba based. Paste the results from the Microsoft Excel tool into the portfolio.

When to use it: Time studies are conducted after initial gemba walks and VOC interviews. Workflow value analysis typically follows process value analysis. The process value analysis results will direct lean practitioners to process steps that require additional evaluation.

Required? Yes (if applicable)

RAPID IMPROVEMENT EVENT PORTFOLIO   239

Figure A.7   Process value analysis results example.

Figure A.8   Workflow value analysis results example.

Current State VSM

Description: Chapter 3 describes value stream mapping (VSM) in detail. The current state VSM is a modifiable table-based process map (Figure A.9). Remember that there should be five to eight high-level steps and fewer than 15 midlevel steps. Consolidate the map if it is too detailed. The table has a section below each midlevel process step for entering the VA/NVA cycle time and first pass yield (FPY). The NVA row also contains a box to enter time spent waiting, which is located between each step. Lead time, overall FPY, and value-added ratio may be entered in the bottom right-hand corner.

When to use it: After building the high-level process map (Figure A.4) and SIPOC (Table A.4)

Required? Yes

Baseline Data for Key Metric(s)

Description: Improvement metrics should reflect the problem statement and objectives. Using the appropriate chart, as outlined in Chapter 7, paste the baseline data here.

When to use it: When data are available

Required? Yes

Voice of Customer Summary

Description: VOC interviews occur individually or in small groups. Throughout this process, key themes emerge. The table highlights these themes along with identifying the elements that are critical to quality (Table A.5).

When to use it: After completing VOC interviews, consolidate notes into more general themes and potential root causes.

Required? Yes

Voice of Customer More of/Less of

Description: Another VOC approach, the more of/less of tool, defines stakeholder expectations (Table A.6). During VOC interviews (or even after as part of summarizing), stakeholders are asked what they want more or less of from the process. This information sheds light on areas of opportunity (less of) and potential solutions (more of).

When to use it: Either during VOC interviews as part of the questions asked or afterward during the VOC consolidation

Required? No

Rapid Improvement Event Portfolio   241

| Enter office | Sign in | Get vitals | RN interview | Physician exam | Receive Rx | Check out |

	Enter office	Sign in	Called back	Vitals	RN interview	Physician exam	Receive Rx	Check out
VA	1				5	8	10	4
NVA		0	1	25	1	0	1	28	20	1	5
FPY %	100%	99%	99%	95%	90%	90%	96%	98%

Steps:

1. Document all steps and determine high-level steps
2. Fill in midlevel process steps
3. Document observed cycle times (Is it VA or NVA? Color in steps accordingly)
4. Estimate/document first-pass yield (with process experts)

Lead time *(total time):* 110 minutes
First-pass yield *(multiply all FPY):* 71.0%
Value-added ratio *(VA time/lead time):* 25.5%

Figure A.9 Current state VSM example.

Table A.5 Voice of customer summary.

Key theme	Critical to quality (CTQ) *What has a direct and significant impact on its actual or perceived quality?*	Comments
Coordination	There is limited coordination across disciplines. As a result, staff doesn't know when to do what or how long tasks should take. This leads to process delays.	Occurs for all disciplines
Visual management	No visual cues signaling any information. For example, once a patient is in the exam room, you do not know how long the patient has been in there, who the patient needs to see, or what is left to do prior to discharge.	
Communication	As with coordination, communication across staff is poor. Huddles are in place, which is good.	Not having visual cues adds to the confusion
Workload balance	Uneven workloads lead to delays in processing and bottlenecks (i.e., waiting for an employee to complete several tasks).	No prioritization process, therefore nothing can be expedited

Table A.6 Voice of customer more of/less of.

More of	Less of	Comments
Visual cues		
Performance metric overviews		Charts displayed in office for monthly performance compared with goal
Communication across disciplines		
Ownership in patient experience and teamwork		
	Finger pointing	Remove "blaming" culture
	Reactive to problems rather than proactive	
	"It's not my job" response	

ANALYZE

Stakeholder Analysis

Description: The improvement team conducts stakeholder analyses internally. Stakeholders are identified (through VOC interviews, observations, and gemba walks) and listed in the table (Table A.7). Each individual or group is evaluated on its level of support for or resistance to the change initiative. Target individuals or groups that are neutral, against, or strongly against using influence strategies based on their primary issues and concerns. Alternatively, for stakeholders who are strongly supportive, develop strategies to leverage their buy-in and engagement.

When to use it: After VOC interviews and gemba walks

Required? Optional, but strongly recommended

RACI Chart

Description: The RACI chart is another stakeholder tool used to determine how to appropriately include various individuals, departments, and groups (Table A.8). The list of tasks outlines basic project deliverables or phases. The top row consists of stakeholder groups. For each task, determine whether the stakeholder group is:

- Responsible for doing the work
- Accountable for completing the task (the responsible group typically reports to the accountable group)

- Consulted as content experts
- Informed of the outcomes

Depending on the categorization, place the corresponding letter (R, A, C, or I) in the cell. This tool helps identify roles and responsibilities throughout the change process.

When to use it: For projects that are multidisciplinary and complex in nature with many stakeholders

Required? Optional, but strongly recommended

Data Analysis Results

Description: Determine where the opportunities are through data analysis. Chapter 1 described the difference between lagging (outcomes) and leading (process measures) metrics. Data analysis should assess the impact of leading metrics. Do the data identify the key drivers of the problem? Copy and paste analyses into this section of the portfolio.

When to use it: After establishing baseline performance and identifying leading metrics

Required? Optional, but strongly recommended

Table A.7 Stakeholder analysis.

Stakeholder (name or group)	Strongly supportive	Supportive	Neutral	Against	Strongly against	Issues/concerns	Influence strategy
Patients	X					None	
Administration		X				None	
Medical assistants				X		Changes in workflow, responsibilities	Frequent communication, inclusion in problem solving, gemba walks to learn their challenges/issues
Nurses			X			Changes in responsibilities and holding staff accountable	Inclusion in problem solving
Physicians				X		No time to implement changes	Identify best time for facilitated RIE based on their availability
Registrars/schedulers	X					None	

Table A.8 RACI chart.

Tasks	Stakeholder (name or group)				
	Patients	Administration	Office manager	Medical assistants, RNs, physicians	Registrars/schedulers
Project definition		A	R		
IS technical assessment		I	R	C	C
Stakeholder analysis		I	R		
Project plan (Gantt chart)		A	R	C	C
Project implementation			A	R	R
Project results	I	A			

Fishbone Diagram

Description: Details for completing the fishbone diagram are in Chapter 7. The fishbone analysis qualitatively documents potential root causes of the problem (Figure A.10). The improvement team should populate the fishbone using VOC interviews, observations, and gemba walks.

When to use it: After VOC interviews, observations, and gemba walks, but it should be verified by content experts (employees working the process)

Required? Optional, but strongly recommended

Rapid Improvement Event Agenda

Description: Table A.9 outlines the RIE agenda. The agenda models the five-step kaizen problem-solving process and the improve phase checklist. Facilitators need to assign sections of the agenda to one another. The "details" column offers guidance and hints, while "materials needed" suggests supplies. The estimated time will vary depending on the duration of the RIE.

When to use it: After the duration of the RIE has been determined

Required? Yes

Figure A.10 Fishbone diagram example.

IMPROVE

Payoff Matrix

Description: The improvement team facilitates the payoff matrix (as described in step 4 of the five-step kaizen problem-solving process in Chapter 9). The payoff matrix slide on the portfolio holds the information developed by the team afterward (Figure A.11). Not all solutions developed will become action plan items. However, there is value in documenting all ideas, so individuals outside the improvement team can see other considerations and ideas.

When to use it: The payoff matrix is used after all solutions have been brainstormed. The portfolio slide can be populated in real time or after the RIE.

Required? Yes

Table A.9 RIE agenda template.

Title	Details	Materials needed	Estimated time
Kickoff	Goal/purpose of rapid improvement event	• Flip chart: parking lot	10 min
Intro, icebreaker	• Who the facilitators are/what we're doing • Who are you? Where do you work/what do you do?		10 min
Agenda	Review RIE agenda with participants • Current state review • Identify key issues/barriers • Develop action plan to implement future state	• PowerPoint	5 min
Current state review	Review charter, process map, data, Gemba walk observations	• PowerPoint	35 min
Step 1: Identify issues/barriers to achieving goals Step 2: Filter and prioritize	What are the biggest issues/barriers? Tools: 1) Silent brainstorming/group brainstorming/fishbone diagram–post-its 2) In/out of control 3) Dot voting	• Sticky notes • Flip chart: in/out of control	60 min
Step 3: Identify solutions Step 4: Prioritize based on impact	Based on prioritized issues/barriers, what actions/interventions can impact change? Tools: 1) Silent brainstorming/group brainstorming/direct issue-to-solution/reverse engineering 2) Payoff priority	• Sticky notes • Flip chart: payoff matrix	60 min
Step 5: Develop action plans and recommendations	Develop recommendations for next steps	• Action plan/recommendation template	45 min
Conclude session and report out	Determine next follow-up meeting (location/time/date) to review progress		20 min

High impact/easy to do	High impact/difficult to do
• Utilize visual cues (exam room flags) • Define roles and responsibilities through swimlane mapping • Survey patients on process change—solicit input on other suggestions for improvement • Do checkout upon sign-in	• Implement new information system to track financial and operational metrics • Implement financial incentives for staff based on performance to target
Low impact/easy to do (low-hanging fruit)	**Low impact/difficult to do**
• Post performance dashboard on weekly basis, review at huddles • Start employee-of-the-month award program for staff member creating/implementing positive change • Post changes as a result of patient feedback in the waiting room so patients can see that improvements are being made	• Hang signs in waiting area bathroom that define what patients need for checkout (i.e., credit card, cash)

Figure A.11 Payoff matrix template.

Action Plans and Recommendations

Description: Tables A.10 and A.11 provide the action plan and recommendation components described in step 5 of the five-step kaizen problem-solving process in Chapter 9. As with the payoff matrix, development of the action plan takes place during the RIE and is subsequently documented in the improvement portfolio. This portfolio slide is a means to document the plan and maintain a record of it along with other project deliverables.

When to use it: The action plan follows solution prioritization.

Required? Yes

Future State VSM

Description: Chapter 3 describes future state VSMs in detail. The VSM tool for the future state is the same as that for the current state (Figure A.12). Steps for creating the future state VSM are the same.

When to use it: The future state VSM construction occurs once the solutions/interventions have been selected.

Required? No, but helpful to accompany current state VSM for comparison

Table A.10 Action plan example.

What	How/why	Resources needed	Expected outcome	Who	When
Utilize visual cues (exam room flags)	Purchase flags to help indicate where patients are in the process	Exam room flags	Improved visual management, reduced motion, reduced LOS	R. Gronkowski	2/20
Define roles and responsibilities through swimlane mapping	Create future state swimlane map to illustrate new process flow	N/A	Clarity in staff understanding of roles/responsibilities	M. Hoomanawanui R. Ninkovich	2/18
Survey patients on process change, solicit input on other suggestions for improvement	E-mail electronic survey to solicit voice of customer	Survey	Identified opportunities for improvement	R. Ninkovich	2/23
Do checkout upon sign-in	Schedule follow-up appointment and collect copay upfront; reduces time for patient	N/A	Reduced LOS	D. Revis	3/9
Post performance dashboard on weekly basis, review at huddles	Print dashboard, post in break room, and review in huddles so staff know how they are doing	Dashboard	Staff awareness of performance	S. Vollmer D. Revis	2/23
Start "employee of the month" award program for staff members creating/implementing positive change	Staff-nominated employee, improves morale and encourages contributions to improvements	Small gift/award for selected individual	Improved staff morale	R. Gronkowski	3/2
Post changes as a result of patient feedback in the waiting room so patients can see improvements are being made	Print infographic of changes and results to communicate value-adding changes	Infographic	Improved patient satisfaction	S. Vollmer D. Revis	3/9

Table A.11 Recommendation example.

What (proposal)	How/why	Resources needed	Expected outcome	What decision needs to be made?	When
Implement new information system to track financial and operational metrics	Purchase IS software to enhance metric tracking and reporting	Finances to purchase, IT expertise to install and train	Accurate performance reporting	Approval to purchase	3/2
Implement financial incentives for staff based on performance to target	Determine targets and financial incentives for all staff, align office performance with financial incentives	Finances for incentive bonus structure	Aligned effort and improved collaboration toward common goal	Approval of finances for program	3/2

Enter office → Sign in, pay, schedule follow-up → Get vitals → RN interview → Physician exam → Receive Rx → Leave

	Enter office	Sign in, pay, schedule follow-up	Called back	Vitals	RN interview	Physician exam	Receive Rx	Leave
VA	1				5	8	10	4
NVA	0	3	18	1	0	1	16	12	1	1
FPY %	100%	99%		99%	95%	95%	95%	99%	99%

Steps:
1. Document all steps and determine high-level steps
2. Fill in midlevel process steps
3. Document observed cycle times (Is it VA or NVA? Color in steps accordingly)
4. Estimate/document first-pass yield (with process experts)

Lead time *(total time)*: 81 minutes
First-pass yield *(multiply all FPY)*: 82.4%
Value-added ratio *(VA time/lead time)*: 34.6%

Figure A.12 Future state VSM example.

CONTROL

Control Phase Action Plan

Description: Appendix F provides details of the control phase action plan.

When to use it: After the RIE as part of the control phase team meetings

Required? Yes

Lessons Learned

Description: Solicit input from improvement team members (facilitators and participants) and document their thoughts. Pose the following questions: (1) What are the key lessons learned from this RIE? (2) What advice do you have for someone ready to start an RIE? (3) What was the most gratifying part of the experience?

When to use it: After the RIE or after completing the control phase

Required? No, but suggested for documenting project experience

Kaizen A3 Report

Description: The A3 report, described in the "Control Phase" section in Chapter 8, consolidates the project into a concise summary (Figure A.13). Elements from the project charter, VOC summary, process maps, data analysis, payoff matrix, and action plan inform the report. There are two versions of the kaizen A3 report in the portfolio. The first slide is a blank template for the team to complete. The second slide is a reference that contains questions and considerations to guide the team. The portfolio houses all key project deliverables. However, the kaizen A3 report should be a standalone document that presents the salient project components.

When to use it: At the conclusion of the project

Required? Yes

RAPID IMPROVEMENT EVENT PORTFOLIO   251

Improving Physician's Office Patient Flow
T. Brady, M. Vaughn, D. Pedroia, D. Ortiz

Background
The physician's office has a large volume of patients during the workweek. Patients arrive throughout the day at a variable rate. The multidisciplinary team is responsible for uneven workloads, and staffing levels are lower than desired.

Problem statement
The patient flow process is constantly interrupted by waiting. The lack of staff coordination leads to bottlenecks and compounding delays. Patient and employee satisfaction are low. As the volume of patient visits continues to rise, the need to streamline process flow/throughput is paramount.

Project/proposal objective
The goal of the project is to reduce patient length of stay (LOS) from 110 minutes to 90 minutes. This will be achieved by identifying and eliminating non-value-adding (NVA) activity and enhancing coordination across all team members.

Team members
R. Gronkowski, M. Hoomanawanui, R. Ninkovich, S. Vollmer, D. Revis

Future state

	Enter office	Sign in, pay, schedule follow-up	Called back	Vitals	RN interview	Physician exam	Receve Rx	Leave
VA	1			5	8	10		1
NVA	0	3	18	1	0	16	12	4	1
FPY %	100%	99%	99%	95%	95%	95%	99%	99%

Countermeasures (implemented or proposed)
- Utilize visual cues (exam room flags)
- Define roles and responsibilities through swimlane mapping
- Survey patients on process change
- Do checkout upon sign-in
- Post performance dashboard on weekly basis, review at huddles
- Start "employee of the month" award program for staff members creating and/or implementing positive change
- Post changes as a result of patient feedback in the waiting room so patients can see improvements as they are being made

Results
Lead time: 110 minutes reduced to 81 minutes
First-pass yield: improved from 71% to 82%
Value-added ratio: improved from 26% to 35%
LOS and patient satisfaction above target

Monthly patient throughput times

Patient satisfaction scores

Next steps
Monitor results through weekly huddles.
Follow up with sponsors regarding proposed recommendations and patient feedback.

Figure A.13   Kaizen A3 report example.

Appendix B
Define Folder

DOWNTIME MATRIX

Description: The DOWNTIME matrix should accompany gemba walks and waste observations (Table A.12). It should also inform solution development.

When to use it: During observations, time studies, brainstorming issues and barriers, and solution development

LEAN ENGAGEMENT COMMUNICATION PLAN

Description: The lean engagement communication plan (Table A.13) is a comprehensive version of the communication plan presented earlier (Table A.2). The communications lead (from the facilitator team) is responsible for overseeing execution of the plan. Table A.13 defines specific deliverables, timelines, and expectations for a lean engagement. Teams should review the plan and adapt accordingly to meet the needs of the area under review.

When to use it: Before, during, and after the RIE

Required? Optional, but strongly recommended

Table A.12 DOWNTIME matrix.

Waste	Definition	Examples	Potential causes	Questions to ask	Countermeasures
Defects	Rework, errors, incomplete or incorrect information	• Medication errors • Process step not performed correctly • Missing information	• Lack of understanding of what "defect-free" means • Insufficient training	• Are tasks clearly defined (who, what, when, how)? • Are errors dealt with directly and promptly or passed along?	• 5S • Visual management • Standard work • Error-proofing
Overproduction	Producing more than what is currently needed (too much or too soon)	• Medications administered early to accommodate start schedule • Printing extra copies of information just in case	• No clear understanding of what is needed, when, in what quantity • Poor communication • Inconsistent process	• Are there more supplies prepared than needed? • Is the demand known?	• Workload balancing • Standard work • Checklists • Pull systems
Waiting	Delays, waiting for anything (people, paper, equipment, information)	• Delays in bed assignments • Delays in receiving information or communication • Waiting for next process steps to begin	• Poor understanding of time required to complete a task • No visual cues to indicate next step in the process • Delays compounding one another	• Are there bottlenecks/delays in the process due to obtaining information, supplies, etc.? • Are there clear expectations for how long process steps should take?	• VSM • Swimlane map • 5S • Workload balancing • Cross-train staff
Nonutilized skill/intellect	Nonutilizing staff skills or knowledge, poor workload balance	• No cross-training • Nurses transporting patients • Physical drawing labs	• Lack of well-defined process • Unclear or undefined roles and responsibilities	• Are employees cross-trained? • Are employees encouraged to suggest/implement improvements?	• Swimlane map • Workload balancing • Standard work

Transportation	Unnecessary movement of something being processed (e.g., forms, patient, specimen, equipment)	• Placing stretcher in hall and constantly having to move it • Transporting forms from building to building or electronically to several areas	• Poor physical layout • Poor system/process design	• Are forms, patients, or materials moved to temporary locations? • Is technology being leveraged to limit physical handoffs?	• 5S • Physical layout • Visual management • Standard work
Inventory	Excessive supplies, batch processing, work in progress	• Extra/outdated manuals • Excessive supplies • Obsolete equipment	• Supply/demand not well understood • Outdated supplies/equipment not discarded • Disorganized area, unclear what is necessary/unnecessary	• Is there extra equipment/supplies lying around? • Do forms, supplies, or patients wait in groups/batches?	• 5S • Visual management • Standard work • Pull systems
Motion	Any excess movement of the employee	• Searching for anything (e.g., information, supplies, equipment, patients) • Hand-carrying paperwork to another area	• Poor physical layout • Poor system/process design	• How does the current layout impede the process flow? • Can walking be reduced by repositioning equipment, people, and/or supplies?	• 5S • Physical layout • Visual management • Standard work
Extra processing	Extra or unnecessary steps performed that do not add value to the process	• Ordering more tests than the diagnosis warrants • Entering repetitive/duplicative information	• Complex or multiple forms • Ineffective policies and procedures	• Is there more information available than what needs to be processed?	• VSM • Visual management • Workload balancing • Standard work

Table A.13 Lean engagement communication plan.

Event/item	Timing	Key messages/ objectives	Delivery mechanism	Deliverables	Completed by	Recipients	Date	Comments
Kickoff	Before start of project	Review: lean approach, communication plan, kaizen event expectations (participation/ engagement of *all* staff, leadership support), set target kaizen event dates	Meeting	• Process owners assigned • Communication plan approved (dates and times set for meetings) • Agreement on number of kaizen participants and their time commitment	Lean leaders	VP/ department management	12/29	Establish clear expectations; identify sponsor/ process owner and keep them fully engaged start to finish; review communication plan and decide how it will roll out
All-staff presentation	Before start of VOC	Purpose of project, what to expect, who the lean leaders are and what they will be doing (our DMAIC process)	Announcement at staff meeting, distribute and post team profile, hand out kaizen idea card		VP with lean leaders	All staff	1/5	Share the vision, why are we doing this?
Lean information	Start of project	What is lean, what is a kaizen event, what to expect	Handouts	• High-level overview	Lean leaders	All staff	1/5	
Weekly management update	Weekly (from start to kaizen)	Status update on project (DMAIC deliverables)	Management meetings, phone call, e-mail	• Review project status • Discuss issues, barriers, concerns • Approve charter	Lean leader/ team leader	VP/ department management	1/5 to 2/2	Engage department, identify and address barriers, keep progress moving forward
Staff meeting presentation	2 weeks before kaizen	What is a kaizen event; date, time, location, what to expect	Communication handout, team profile	• Collect idea cards	VP/dept. leader/lean leaders	All staff	1/20	Communicate what will happen and how they can contribute

KAIZEN

		Decision on recommendation changes	Presentation/ discussion		Lean leaders	VP/ department management	
Kaizen action plan	End of kaizen			• Decision on recommendations • Staff education/ communication plan	Lean leaders	VP/ department management	2/2
Improvements/ changes communication	1 week after kaizen	Kaizen outcomes (action plan, next steps)	Short update at staff meeting, action plan handout		VP/dept. leader/ lean leaders/ kaizen team	All staff	
Action plan update	Week 2 and 4	Control phase update, issues or barriers discussion	Management meeting		Team leader for lean team	VP/ department management	2/9
Project results	5–8 weeks after kaizen	Project outcomes	Staff meeting		Team leader for lean team	All staff	2/16 to 2/27
Report out forms	6–8 weeks after kaizen	Results: A3 report, presented by VP (kickoff), lean leaders, and representatives of kaizen team	Management update; operations meeting	• Kaizen A3 report	Lean master/ lean team	Management	3/9
Report out forms	6–8 weeks after kaizen (after MU presenta- tion)	Results: A3 report, recognition of kaizen team and lean leaders	Intranet homepage	• Intranet posting/ article	Lean master/ director of commu- nications dept.	Management	3/30

Ensure we are on track to complete deliverables

Solicit thoughts, experiences with new changes

Communicate success, lessons learned

Communicate success, lessons learned

LEAN OPPORTUNITY GUIDE

Description: Table A.14 generalizes lean opportunities based on processes and performance metrics. The guide facilitates opportunity identification.

When to use it: Before project initiation to identify appropriate project selection

Table A.14 Lean opportunity guide.

\multicolumn{3}{c}{General improvement opportunities}		
Staffing	Workflow Workflow balancing	Time management Productivity
Physical organization/ inventory management	Ordering processes/par levels Space allocation	Visual management Physical layout/organization
\multicolumn{3}{c}{Examples of lean project metrics}		
Turnaround time Cycle/processing time	Throughput time (lead time) Customer, patient, employee satisfaction	Quality output Cost savings/avoidance

\multicolumn{3}{c}{Examples of department/function-specific improvement opportunities}		
Business services	Timeliness and accuracy of results/reports Transactional throughput	Request turnaround time
Emergency departments	Length of stay Door to triage Door to physician	Door to disposition Door to discharge Admission order to transfer from ED
Diagnostic and ancillary departments	Patient transportation Patient registration Order to result	Request to completion Exam/procedure/testing scheduling Work assignments
Nursing and clinical units	Bed availability Bed empty to fill turnaround time	Patient flow Workload balance
Physician practice	Exam room utilization Access/scheduling	Patient flow Workload balance
Supply chain	Par levels Product standardization Space allocation/organization	Inventory locations Distribution process
Surgical services	Decontamination and sterilization processes Instrument availability Case assembly Operating room utilization	First case on-time start Scheduling process Operating room turnover Patient flow

VOC WASTE QUESTIONNAIRE

Description: VOC interviews can include questions from the "Define Phase" section in Chapter 8: (1) What is working? (2) What is not working? (3) What frustrates you at work? (4) If you could change one or two things, what would you change and why? Or facilitators can take a targeted approach to determine specific DOWNTIME waste problems. The tool assists in facilitating discussion around waste and potential solutions (Figure A.14).

When to use it: During VOC interviews

Required? Optional, but strongly recommended in operational areas

Name B. LaFell

Job title Office Manager

Improving Physician Office Patient Flow through Lean:

How can we improve throughput and eliminate waste?

How can we improve patient throughput?	Improve coordination of staff. Enhance communication across disciplines (MAs, RNs, physicians, administrative staff).	
What frustrates you? What doesn't work well?	No visual cues to identify who is needed, where. Patients are unhappy because process is slow and inefficient. Employees don't know who is supposed to do what or how long tasks should take.	
What would you do differently?	Cross-train administrative and MA team to facilitate front-end flow. Improve visuals and communication throughout.	
Type of waste	**Please describe an example of this waste in your work environment**	**Please describe your ideas about what we can do to reduce or eliminate it**
Defects Rework, errors, incomplete or incorrect information	Patient charts missing demographic or insurance information.	Require some verification process to ensure all needed information is obtained.
Overproduction Producing more than what is currently needed (too much or too soon)	Chart prep (paper) process occurs at end of day in advance of following workday. Sometimes prepare a lot more than actual patient volume.	Prepare supplies as needed rather than in advance.
Waiting Delays, waiting for anything (people, paper, equipment, or information)	Patients wait for a long time in the waiting room and in the exam rooms.	Not sure; this is why we need help!

Figure A.14 VOC waste questionnaire example.

Appendix C
Measure Folder

PROCESS VALUE ANALYSIS

Description: Chapter 3 explains use of the process value analysis tool (Figure A.15).

Required? Yes (if applicable)

Figure A.15 Process value analysis Excel screenshot example.

WORKFLOW VALUE ANALYSIS

Description: Chapter 3 describes how to use the workflow value analysis tool (Figure A.16).

Required? No

Figure A.16 Workflow value analysis Excel screenshot example

Appendix D
Analyze Folder

5S AUDIT TOOL

Description: Chapter 4 outlines use of the 5S audit tool (Figure A.17).

Required? No

Figure A.17 5S Audit tool Excel screenshot example.

SWIMLANE TEMPLATE

Description: Chapter 3 summarizes swimlane mapping techniques. The Microsoft Excel-based template makes it easy to document various flows by position (Figure A.18).

Required? No

Figure A.18 Swimlane Excel screenshot example.

Appendix E
Improve Folder

RIE PRESENTATION

Description: The RIE presentation drives the RIE agenda. There are placeholders throughout the slideshow for project documents (i.e., project charter, high-level process map and SIPOC, data analysis, and VOC summary). The presentation also includes the five-step kaizen problem-solving process. Each step has slides for the associated tools. Facilitators can modify the presentation to include only the tools they select to use.

When to use it: During the RIE, the presentation contains content for the current state review as well as instructions for using the various problem-solving tools.

Required? Yes

RIE FACILITATOR EVALUATION FORM

Description: Distribute evaluations to RIE participants at the conclusion of the event (Figure A.19). Participants complete the form, hand it in, and then adjourn. Facilitators review the evaluations as part of a debrief. Ideally, the team conducts a self-evaluation using the same form before reviewing participant feedback.

When to use it: At the conclusion of the RIE

Required? No, but strongly encouraged

**Rapid Improvement Event
Facilitator Evaluation**

Event title: _____ **Date:** _____

In order to assess and improve the effectiveness of the facilitators, please provide open and honest feedback on the event you attended.

Thank you for your participation!

Facilitator's ability to:	Poor 1	Satisfactory 2	Good 3	Excellent 4
Lead the event				
Clearly explain objectives, teach content, and describe next step				
Listen and communicate with the team				
Manage time				
Motivate and engage participants				

The event:	Strongly disagree 1	Disagree 2	Agree 3	Strongly agree 4
Included the right people				
Achieved the objectives				
Was worth my time and efforts				

What two aspects of the event were most valuable for you?

-
-

What two suggestions could you offer to improve future events?

-
-

Figure A.19 RIE facilitator evaluation form.

Appendix F
Control Folder

KAIZEN A3 REPORT

Description: The "Control" section in Appendix A explains kaizen A3 reports. Figures A.20 and A.21 demonstrate how to document improvement projects.

Required? Yes

CONTROL PHASE ACTION PLAN

Description: The control phase action plan is a Microsoft Excel–based tool (Figure A.22). The contents derive from the action plan worksheet and approved recommendations. Each action item has its own row (indicated by a number in column B). "What" refers to the action item. Columns F–M detail the update meetings during the control phase team meetings. Specific dates can replace generic ones. "Comments/details" in column N stores the "how/why," "resources," and "expected outcome" from the action plan worksheet.

The control phase action plan serves as the agenda for the team meetings. The team reviews every action item. The person responsible (column D, "Who") provides an update. Update summaries are documented in the row with the corresponding meeting date. "Status" is indicated by "not started," "in progress," or "complete." Stoplight colors provide visual management for action item progress.

Figure A.23 shows an example of the control phase action plan in use. The first item, "Utilize visual cues (exam room flags)," was completed after week 3. Progress was made during weeks 1 and 2. Rows 9–12 include verbatim updates from the individual responsible for completing the assigned task. These updates are critical pieces of information that enable the project lead to track progress over time and reduce the likelihood of participants being unprepared since everything is appropriately documented.

The second action item in Figure A.23 demonstrates another effective way to use the tool. From a quick glance, it is clear that nothing has been initially accomplished, as indicated by two consecutive updates in red. The verbatim updates in rows 19 and 20 tell a story of inaction (i.e., "no update"). Action items that are slowly developing or have not started require energy to shift inertia. At a high level, this tool enables effective identification of vulnerable or underperforming areas. As the action plan list grows to 8–15 or more items, the stoplight indicators supply a quick visual cue for areas of focus and concern.

268 *Appendix F*

Standardizing Phlebotomy Work Baskets
Carrie L.; Glenn D.; Roseann P.; Beth-Ann S.; Scott G.

Background
The 5S lean team conducted organizational audits of work areas throghout the Center City campus. Opportunities were identified, evaluated, and prioritized based on resource requirements, scope, timeline, and need. Phlebotomy work baskets were selected for the first 5S area of focus given their clinical importance and inventory management struggles.

Problem statement
Variation in phlebotomy cart and baskets leads to oversupplying and risks expiration. Current inventory management issues and internal audits for expired supplies indicate an opportunity for standardization and improvement.

Project objective
Through the 5S approach (sort, store, shine, standardize, sustain), we will remove all unused, outdated, or unnecessary equipment and standardize the cart/basket layout.

Kaizen team
Dominique S., Damien F., Stephen M., Damond B., Hans A., Carrie L., Glenn D. Roseann P., Beth-Ann S., Scott G., Dennis D.

Sort
The group was divided into two teams to sort the baskets and determine what supplies were necessary and in what quantity.

Store
The two teams decided on locations for the supplies within the baskets.

Shine
The two teams shined and cleaned the baskets. Excess inventory was removed from each basket.

Standardize

Sustain
Build awareness on why the change was needed. Benefits include baskets that are interchangeable, visually organized, and quicker to stock at the end of the shift; less waste of expired tubes and supplies; and better control of inventory.

Next steps: Solicit additional input from phlebotomists, standardize all carts/baskets.

Figure A.20 Kaizen A3 report example: Phlebotomy 5S event.

Improving Decision Making During Rapid Responses
Brian G., Michael L., Kathleen P., Linda S.

Background

The purpose of the rapid response team (RRT) system is to improve patient care by providing prompt recognition, early advanced assessment, enhanced communication with physicians, and appropriate intervention to patients with perceived changes in or deterioration of their condition. The RRT comprises staff nurse, RRT physician, surgeon, anesthesiologist, ICU nurse, respiratory therapist, and primary team physician.

Problem statement

There is a lack of standardization and lack of consistency of workflow during the rapid response process. There is a lot of potential for duplication of work along with excessive staff at patient bedside during the process. Without a standardized workflow there is also the potential to miss key processes and/or equipment.

Project/proposal objective

The project objective is to standardize workflow during a rapid response and facilitate efficient and accurate decision making. Implementation of a standardized process will improve the time rapid response was initiated to patient disposition along with notification of RRT to attending physician. This process will be implemented at the Center City campus initially and then will eventually be implemented across campuses.

High-level process map (SIPOC)

The group was divided into two teams to sort the baskets and determine what supplies were necessary and in what quantity.

Suppliers	Inputs	Process	Outputs	Customer (CTQ)
Patient at point of IRF	Patient requires immediate attention	Clinical decline detected	Unit RN activates page for RRT	Clinical decline detection timely and accurate
Unit nurse	Unit RN activates page for RRT	RRT called	RRT paged	Appropriate team identified for IRF
Page operator	RRT paged	RRT arrives	Management of patient initiated by RRT	Identify specific intervals for evaluation
RRT	Management of patient initiated by RRT	Patient assessed	RRT evaluates patient/identifies issue	Consistent resources
RRT, lab, radiology	RRT evaluates/identifies issue(s)	Etiology or organ system identified	Treatment plan developed and ordered	Standardize info
RRT, pulmonary, pharmacy	Treatment plan developed and ordered	Treatment initiated	Team assesses response to treatment	Rx evaluation timely and accurate
RRT, ICU staff, bed manager	Team assesses response to treatment	Disposition identified	Patient arrives at appropriate clinical setting	Documentation from RRT

The high-level process map SIPOC illustrates the current rapid response process with multiple suppliers and duplication of processes.

Analyze qualitative data

The fishbone diagram depicts the four major areas that are affected due to lack of standardization.

Countermeasures

- Implement RRT checklist to guide the rapid response process including time-specific checkpoints
- Implement availability of medical record at bedside via workplace on wheels, physical chart
- Assess crowd control at bedside
- Conduct brainstorming session with key players
- Revise current debriefing process to include questionnaire

Results

Metrics to be monitored:
- Time rapid response was initiated to patient disposition
- Notification of RRT to attending physician
- % RRT with completed RRT checklist
- Qualitative data from debriefing questionnaire

Next Steps

- Finalize RRT checklist along with debriefing questionnaire—December 30, 2013
- Educate RRT on process—January 2–15, 2014
- Promote awareness of new process on multidisciplinary level—January 2–15, 2014
- Initiate RRT checklist, at City Center campus—January 15, 2014
- Monitor progress and communicate findings—January 15–February 15, 2014
- Refine process based on findings—February 15–18, 2014
- Implement across campuses—March 1, 2014

Figure A.21 Kaizen A3 report example: Rapid responses.

270 Appendix F

Figure A.22 Control phase action plan screenshot.

Figure A.23 Control phase action plan screenshot example.

When to use it: The action plan worksheet transfers to this tool. The control phase action plan is updated weekly and disseminated to the project team.

Required? Yes

CONTROL PHASE ACTION PLAN—GANTT TEMPLATE

Description: The Gantt chart is a project management tool used to outline project deliverables (Jacobs and Chase 2008). The tool is a horizontal bar graph depicting the sequence and duration of project tasks (Figure A.24). Column B lists tasks, and columns C–F, respectively, list the responsible party, status, and start and end dates. Columns H–N contain the appropriate time intervals for the project (i.e., days, weeks, months). To create the graph, calculate the duration to complete individual tasks as start date minus end date. The blue bar represents the task duration, beginning on the start date and concluding at the defined end date. Simply enter

"1" in the cells that make up the task duration (they will automatically turn dark blue). Gantt charts provide a high-level project timeline and communication visual. The bars defining task duration enable quick identification of proper sequences (i.e., run in parallel versus progressively) as well as the rate-limiting steps that need to be closely monitored. In other words, if a particular task is delayed, will the entire project be negatively affected?

When to use it: Accompanying the control phase action plan, the Gantt chart is an effective communication tool for senior leaders regarding the project status and timeline.

Required? Optional, but strongly recommended

#	Task	Responsible Party	Status	Start Date	End Date	2-Feb	9-Feb	16-Feb	23-Feb	2-Mar	9-Mar
1	Utilize visual cues (exam room flags)	R. Gronkowski	Complete	2/2/15	2/20/15						
2	Define roles and responsibilities through Swimlane Mapping	M. Hoomanawanui R. Ninkovich	Complete	2/2/15	2/18/15						
3	Survey patients on process change- solicit input on other suggestions for improvement	R. Ninkovich	Complete	2/9/15	2/23/15						
4	Do check-out upon sign-in	D. Revis	Complete	2/2/15	3/9/15						
5	Post performance dashboard on weekly basis, review at huddles	S. Vollmer D. Revis	Complete	2/9/15	2/23/15						
6	Start "Employee of the Month" award program for staff member creating/ implementing positive change	R. Gronkowski	In Progress	2/16/15	3/2/15						
7	Post changes as a result of patient feedback in the waiting room so patients can see improvements are	S. Vollmer D. Revis	Complete	2/16/15	3/2/15						
8	Implement new Information System to track financial and operational metrics	S.A. Moose & G.L. Lohman	Complete	2/2/15	3/2/15						
9	Implement financial incentives for staff based on performance to target	S.A. Moose & G.L. Lohman	Complete	2/9/15	3/2/15						

Figure A.24 Gantt chart screenshot example.

References

Advisory Board. 2020a. "Cheat sheet: Strategies to optimize PPE and equipment." https://www.advisory.com/daily-briefing/resources/primers/cheat-sheet-strategies-to-optimize-ppe.

Advisory Board. 2020b. "'Do Your Planning Now': EvergreenHealth CNO's Stark Warning to American Hospitals." https://www.advisory.com/daily-briefing/2020/04/01/evergreen.

Advisory Board. 2020c. "Your COVID-19 Checklist to Expand Capacity." https://www.advisory.com/daily-briefing/resources/primers/your-covid-19-checklist-to-expand-capacity

Aij, K. H., F. E. Simons, G. A. Widdershoven, and M. Visse. 2013. "Experiences of Leaders in the Implementation of Lean in a Teaching Hospital--Barriers and Facilitators in Clinical Practices: A Qualitative Study." *BMJ Open* 3(10), e003605-2013-003605. doi:10.1136/bmjopen-2013-003605.

Al, M., T. Feenstra, and W. Brouwer. 2005. "Corrigendum to 'Decision Makers Views on Health Care Objectives and Budget Constraints: Results from a Pilot Study." *Health Policy*. 74:109–11.

Andersen, H., K. A. Rovik, and T. Ingebrigtsen. 2014. "Lean Thinking in Hospitals: Is There a Cure for the Absence of Evidence? A Systematic Review of Reviews." *BMJ Open* 4(1), e003873-2013-003873. doi:10.1136/bmjopen-2013-003873.

Armstrong, S., E. Fox, and W. Chapman. 2013. "To Meet Health Care's Triple Aim, Lean Management Must Be Applied Across the Value Stream: Comment on 'Management Practices and the Quality of Care in Cardiac Units." *JAMA Internal Medicine*, 1-2. doi:10.1001/jamainternmed.2013.4080.

Aronson, S., and K. Gelatt. 2006. *"Lean" Models at Health Care Institutions.* (Original Inquiry Brief). Washington, DC: The Advisory Board Company.

ASQ. 2013. "Systematically Improving Operating Room Patient Flow through Value Stream Mapping and Kaizen Events" (October).

Ballé, M., and A. Régnier. 2007. "Lean as a Learning System in a Hospital Ward." *Leadership Health Services* 20:33–41.

Bass, I. 2007. *Six Sigma Statistics with Excel and Minitab.* New York: McGraw-Hill.

Berwick, D. M., T. W. Nolan, and J. Whittington. 2008. "The Triple Aim: Care, Health, and Cost." *Health Affairs* (Project Hope) 27(3), 759-769. doi:10.1377/hlthaff.27.3.759; 10.1377/hlthaff.27.3.759.

Bicheno, J., and M. Holweg. 2008. *The Lean Toolbox,* 4th edition. Buckingham, MK: Picsie Books.

Bradley, E. H., L. A. Curry, E. S. Spatz, J. Herrin, E. J. Cherlin, J, P. Curtis, . . . H. M. Krumholz. 2012. "Hospital Strategies for Reducing Risk: Standardized Mortality Rates in Acute Myocardial Infarction." *Annals of Internal Medicine* 156(9): 618-626. doi:10.1059/0003-4819-156-9-201205010-00003; 10.1059/0003-4819-156-9-201205010-00003.

Bradley, E. H., J. Herrin, Y. Wang, B. A. Barton, T. R. Webster, J. A. Mattera,... H. M. Krumholz. 2006. "Strategies for Reducing the Door-to-Balloon Time in Acute Myocardial Infarction." *The New England Journal of Medicine* 355(22): 2308-2320. doi:10.1056/NEJMsa063117.

Breakthrough Management Group International. n.d. Lean master training materials. https://www.bmgi.com/.

Brennan, T. A., A. Gawande, E. Thomas, and D. Studdert. 2005. "Accidental Deaths, Saved Lives, and Improved Quality." *The New England Journal of Medicine* 353(13), 1405-1409. doi:10.1056/NEJMsb051157.

Cavallo, J., D. Donoho, and H. Forman. 2020. "Hospital Capacity and Operations in the Coronavirus Disease 2019 (COVID-19) Pandemic—Planning for the nth Patient." *Journal of the American Medical Association.* https://jamanetwork.com/channels/health-forum/fullarticle/2763353.

Centers for Disease Control and Prevention. 2020a. "Comprehensive Hospital Preparedness Checklist for Coronavirus Disease 2019 (COVID-19)." https://www.cdc.gov/coronavirus/2019-ncov/hcp/hcp-hospital-checklist.html.

Centers for Disease Control and Prevention. 2020b. "Coronavirus Disease 2019 (COVID-19)." https://www.cdc.gov/coronavirus/2019-ncov/hcp/steps-to-prepare.html?CDC_AA_refVal=https%3A%2F%2Fwww.cdc.gov%2Fcoronavirus%2F2019-ncov%2Fhealthcare-facilities%2Fsteps-to-prepare.html.

Centers for Disease Control and Prevention. 2020c. "Get Your Clinic Ready for Coronavirus Disease 2019 (COVID-19)." CDC.gov/COVID19.

Chalice, R. 2007. *Improving Healthcare Using Toyota Lean Production Methods,* 2nd edition. Milwaukee: ASQ Quality Press.

Chan, H., S. Lo, L. Lee, W. Lo, W. Yu, Y. Wu, et al. 2014. "Lean Techniques for the Improvement of Patients' Flow in Emergency Department." *World Journal of Emergency Medicine* 5(1): 24-28. doi:10.5847/wjem.j.1920-8642.2014.01.004.

Chopra, V., E. Toner, et al. 2020. "How Should U.S. Hospitals Prepare for Coronavirus Disease 2019 (COVID-10)?" *Annals of Internal Medicine*. doi: 10.7326/M20-0907.

Classen, D. C., R. Resar, F. Griffin, F. Federico, T. Frankel, N. Kimmel, . . . B. C. James. 2011. "'Global Trigger Tool' Shows That Adverse Events in Hospitals May be Ten Times Greater than Previously Measured." *Health Affairs* (Project Hope) 30(4): 581-589. doi:10.1377/hlthaff.2011.0190; 10.1377/hlthaff.2011.0190.

Curry, L. A., E. Spatz, E. Cherlin, J. W. Thompson, D. Berg, H. H. Ting, . . . E. H. Bradley. 2011. "What Distinguishes Top-Performing Hospitals in Acute Myocardial Infarction Mortality Rates? A Qualitative Study." *Annals of Internal Medicine* 154(6): 384-390. doi:10.1059/0003-4819-154-6-201103150-00003; 10.1059/0003-4819-154-6-201103150-00003.

de Souza, L., and M. Pidd. 2011. "Exploring the Barriers to Lean Health Care Implementation." *Public Money Management* 31:59–66.

de Souza, L. 2009. "Trends and Approaches in Lean Healthcare." *Leadership in Health Services* 22(2): 121-139.

Delisle, D. R., and V. Freiberg. 2014. "Everything is 5S: A Simple Yet Powerful Lean Improvement Approach Applied in a Pre-admission Testing Center." *The Quality Management Journal* 21(4): 10-22.

Delisle, D. R. and K. Jaffe. 2015. Let it flow: improving perioperative patient flow using lean improvement strategies. *Six Sigma Forum Magazine*. 14(2).

Delisle, D. R. 2013. "Systematically Improving Operating Room Patient Flow through Value Stream Mapping and kaizen events. American Society for Quality: Making the Case for Quality." (October).

Deloitte. 2020. "COVID-19 Response Capabilities: Rapidly Combating COVID-19 with Resilience." https://www2.deloitte.com/content/dam/Deloitte/us/Documents/life-sciences-health-care/us-lshc-covid-19-response-capabilities-final.pdf.

Dentzer, S. 2011. "Still Crossing the Quality Chasm--or Suspended Over It?" *Health Affairs* (Project Hope) 30(4): 554-555. doi:10.1377/hlthaff.2011.0287; 10.1377/hlthaff.2011.0287.

Dye, C. F., and A. N. Garman. 2015. *Exceptional Leadership: 16 Crucial Competencies for Healthcare Executives.* Chicago: Health Administration Press.

Farrokhi, F. R., M. Gunther, B. Williams, and C. C. Blackmore. 2013. "Application of Lean Methodology for Improved Quality and Efficiency in Operating Room Instrument Availability." *Journal for Healthcare Quality.* doi:10.1111/jhq.12053.

Gawande, A. 2009. *The Checklist Manifesto: How to Get Things Right.* New York: Picador.

General Electric Company. 2006. Change Acceleration Process (CAP) Workshop. Fairfield: General Electric Company.

Going Lean in Health Care. 2005. Cambridge, MA: Institute for Healthcare Improvement.

Graban, M., and J. Swartz. 2012. *Healthcare Kaizen: Engaging Front-Line Staff in Sustainable Continuous Improvements.* Boca Raton, FL: CRC Press.

Graban, M. 2012. *Lean Hospitals,* 2nd edition. Boca Raton, FL: CRC Press.

Graban, M., and A. Prachand. 2010. "Hospitalists: Lean Leaders for Hospitals." *Journal of Hospital Medicine* 5(6): 317-319. doi:10.1002/jhm.813.

Grout, J. 2007. *Mistake-Proofing the Design of Health Care Processes.* Rome, GA: Agency for Healthcare Research and Quality.

Heath, C. 2010. *Switch: How to Change Things When Change is Hard.* New York: Crown Publishing Group.

Hina-Syeda, H., C. Kimbrough, W. Murdoch, and T. Markova. 2013. "Improving Immunization Rates Using Lean Six Sigma Processes: Alliance of Independent Academic Medical Centers National Initiative III Project." *The Ochsner Journal* 13(3): 310-318.

Hrebiniak, L. 2013. *Making Strategy Work: Leading Effective Execution and Change,* 2nd edition. Upper Saddle River, NJ: FT Press.

Imai, M. 1997. *Gemba Kaizen.* New York: McGraw-Hill.

Jacobs, F., and R. Chase. 2008. *Operations and Supply Management: The Core.* New York: McGraw-Hill.

Jimmerson, C. 2010. *Value Stream Mapping for Healthcare Made Easy.* New York: Taylor & Francis Group, LLC.

Jimmerson, C., D. Weber, and D. K. Sobek. 2005. "Reducing Waste and Errors: Piloting Lean Principles at Intermountain Healthcare." *Joint Commission Journal on Quality and Patient Safety/Joint Commission Resources* 31(5): 249-257.

Joint Commission on the Accreditation of Healthcare Organizations. 2006. *Doing More with Less: Lean Thinking and Patient Safety in Health Care.* Oakbrook, IL: Joint Commission Resources.

Jones, D., and A. Mitchell. 2006. *Lean Thinking for the NHS.* London: NHS Confederation.

Kaplan, G. S., S. H. Patterson, J. M. Ching, and C. C. Blackmore. 2014. "Why Lean Doesn't Work for Everyone." *BMJ Quality & Safety* 23(12): 970-973. doi:10.1136/bmjqs-2014-003248.

Kenney, C. 2011. *Transforming Health Care: Virginia Mason Medical Center's Pursuit of the Perfect Patient Experience.* New York: Productivity Press.

Kohn, L., M. Donaldson, and Committee on Quality of Health Care in America, Institute of Medicine. 2000. *To Err is Human: Building a Safer Health System.* Washington, DC: The National Academies Press.

Kotter, J. 1995. "Leading Change: Why Transformation Efforts Fail." *Harvard Business Review* 73(2): 59-67.

Kotter, J. 1996. *Leading Change.* Boston: Harvard Business School Press.

Kotter, J. 2001. "What Leaders Really Do." *Harvard Business Review* 79(11).

Kotter, J., and D. Cohen. 2002. *The Heart of Change: Real-Life Stories of How People Change Their Organizations.* Boston: Harvard Business Review Press.

Langley, G., R. Moen, K. Nolan, T. Nolan, et al. 2009. *The Improvement Guide: A Practical Approach to Enhancing Organizational Performance,* 2nd edition. San Francisco: Jossey-Bass.

Lawal, A. K., T. Rotter, L. Kinsman, N. Sari, L. Harrison, C. Jeffery, et al. 2014. "Lean Management in Health Care: Definition, Concepts, Methodology and Effects Reported (Systematic Review Protocol)." *Systematic Reviews* 3, 103-4053-3-103. doi:10.1186/2046-4053-3-103.

Leading Change: Implementing Improvements in the Health Care Organization. 2011. Washington, DC: The Advisory Board Company.

Lean Enterprise Institute. n.d. "Principles of Lean." Retrieved from http://www.lean.org/WhatsLean/Principles.cfm

Leape, L. L., and D. M. Berwick. 2005. "Five Years After to Err is Human: What Have We Learned?" *JAMA: The Journal of the American Medical Association* 293(19): 2384-2390. doi:10.1001/jama.293.19.2384.

Lighter, D. 2013. *Basics of Health Care Performance Improvement: A Lean Six Sigma Approach.* Burlington, MA: Jones & Barltlett Learning.

Liker, J. 2004. *The Toyota Way: 14 Management Principles from the World's Greatest Manufacturer.* Madison, WI: McGraw Hill.

Liker, J., and D. Meier. 2006. *The Toyota Way Fieldbook: A Practical Guide for Implementing Toyota's 4 Ps.* New York: McGraw-Hill.

Maister, D. 1985. "The Psychology of Waiting Lines." Retrieved from http://www.columbia.edu/~ww2040/4615S13/Psychology_of_Waiting_Lines.pdf

Mann, D. 2010. Creating a Lean Culture, 2nd edition. New York: Taylor and Francis Group, LLC.

Martens, L., G. Goode, J. F. Wold, L. Beck, G. Martin, C. Perings, et al. 2014. "Structured Syncope Care Pathways Based on Lean Six Sigma Methodology Optimizes Resource Use with Shorter Time to Diagnosis and Increased Diagnostic Yield." *PloS One* 9(6), e100208. doi:10.1371/journal.pone.0100208.

Martin, L., C. Neumann, J. Mountford, M. Bisognano, and T. Nolan. 2009. Increasing Efficiency and Enhancing Value in Health Care: Ways to Achieve Savings in Operating Costs Per Year. IHI Innovation Series white paper. Cambridge, Massachusetts: Institute for Healthcare Improvement.

Mason, D., and C. Friese. 2020. "Protecting Health Care Workers Against COVID-19 and Being Prepared for Future Pandemics." *Journal of the American Medical Association.* https://jamanetwork.com/channels/health-forum/fullarticle/2763478.

Mauer, R. 2002. *Why Don't You Want What I Want? How to Win Support for Your Ideas Without Hard Sell, Manipulation, or Power Plays.* Austin, TX: Bard Press.

Mazur, L., J. McCreery, and L. Rothenberg. 2010. Facilitating Lean Learning and Behaviors in Hospitals During the Early Stages of Lean Implementation. *Engineering Management Journal* 24:11–22.

McChesney, C., S. Covey, and J. Huling. 2012. *The 4 Disciplines of Execution.* New York: Free Press.

McConnell, K., R. C. Lindrooth, D. R. Wholey, T. M. Maddox, and N. Bloom. 2013. "Management Practices and the Quality of Care in Cardiac Units." *JAMA Internal Medicine,* 1-9. doi:10.1001/jamainternmed.2013.3577.

Meyer, H. 2010. "Life in the 'Lean' Lane: Performance Improvement at Denver Health." *Health Affairs* 29(11): 2054-2060. doi:10.1377/hlthaff.2010.0810.

Nakajima, S. 1988. *Introduction to TPM.* Cambridge, MA: Productivity Press.

National Incident Management System. n.d. Retrieved April 23, 2020, from https://www.fema.gov/national-incident-management-system.

Neufeld, N. J., E. H. Hoyer, P. Cabahug, M. Gonzalez-Fernandez, M. Mehta, N. C. Walker, R. S. Mayer, et al. 2013. "A Lean Six Sigma Quality Improvement Project to Increase Discharge Paperwork Completeness for Admission to a Comprehensive Integrated Inpatient Rehabilitation Program." *American Journal of Medical Quality: The Official Journal of the American College of Medical Quality,* doi:10.1177/1062860612470486.

Niemeijer, G. C., A. Trip, L. J. de Jong, K. W. Wendt, and R. J. Does. 2012. "Impact of 5 Years of Lean Six Sigma in a University Medical Center." *Quality Management in Health Care* 21(4): 262-268. doi:10.1097/QMH.0b013e31826e74b7.

Øvretveit, J. 2005. "Leading Improvement." *Journal of Health Organization Management.* 19:413–30.

Overview of Lean Six Sigma. 2011. Lean and Six Sigma International Board. Retrieved from http://image.slidesharecdn.com/01-overviewofleansixsigma-121114045047-phpapp01/95/01-overview-of-lean-six-sigma-25-638.jpg?cb=1352890536.

Palmer, Brien. 2004. *Making change work.* Milwaukee, WI: ASQ Press.

Pande, P., and L. Holpp. 2002. *What is Six Sigma?* New York: McGraw-Hill.

Project Management Institute. 2008. *A Guide to the Project Management Body of Knowledge,* 4th edition. Newtown Square, PA: Project Management Institute, Inc.

Rother, M. 2010. *Toyota Kata: Managing People for Improvement, Adaptiveness, and Superior Results.* New York: McGraw-Hill.

Rycroft-Malone, J., A. Kitson, G. Harvey, et al. 2002. Ingredients for Change: Revisiting a Conceptual Framework. *Quality Safety Health Care* 11:174–80.

Shojania, K. G., and J. M. Grimshaw. 2005. "Evidence-Based Quality Improvement: The State of the Science." *Health Affairs* (Project Hope) 24(1): 138-150. doi:10.1377/hlthaff.24.1.138.

Shortell, S. M., and S. J. Singer. 2008. "Improving Patient Safety by Taking Systems Seriously." *JAMA: The Journal of the American Medical Association* 299(4): 445-447. doi:10.1001/jama.299.4.445; 10.1001/jama.299.4.445.

Shortell, S. M., T. G. Rundall, and J. Hsu. 2007. "Improving Patient Care by Linking Evidence-Based Medicine and Evidence-Based Management." *JAMA: The Journal of the American Medical Association* 298(6): 673-676. doi:10.1001/jama.298.6.673.

Shortell, S. 1998. Assessing the Implementation and Impact of Clinical Quality Improvement Efforts: Abstract, Executive Summary and Final Report. Agency for Health Care Policy and Research.

Silverstein, D., P. Samuel, and N. Decarlo. 2009. *The Innovator's Toolkit: 50+ Techniques for Predictable and Sustainable Organic Growth.* Hoboken, NJ: John Wiley & Sons, Inc.

Slobbe, L., J. Smit, J. Groen, et al. 2011. Cost of Illness in the Netherlands 2007: Trends in Healthcare Expenditure 1999–2010. The National Institute for Public Health and the Environment website.

Smith, B. 2003. *Lean and Six Sigma: A One-Two Punch.* Milwaukee: ASQ Quality Press.

Snee, R., and R. Hoerl. 2003. *Leading Six Sigma: A Step-by-Step Guide Based on Experience with GE and Other Six Sigma Companies.* Upper Saddle River, NJ: FT Press.

Sobek, D., and A. Smalley. 2008. *Understanding A3 Thinking: A Critical Component of Toyota's PDCA Management System.* Boca Raton, FL: Productivity Press.

Spear, S. J. 2005. "Fixing Health Care from the Inside, Today." *Harvard Business Review* 83(9): 78-91, 158.

Studer, Q. 2009. *Straight A leadership: Alignment, Action, Accountability.* Gulf Breeze, FL: Fire Starter Publishing.

Swensen, S. J., J. A. Dilling, C. M. Harper, Jr, and J. H. Noseworthy. 2012. "The Mayo Clinic Value Creation System." *American Journal of Medical Quality: The Official Journal of the American College of Medical Quality* 27(1): 58-65. doi:10.1177/1062860611410966.

Tague, N. 2005. *The Quality Toolbox,* 2nd edition. Milwaukee: Quality Press.

Takahashi, Y., and T. Osada. 1990. *TPM Total Productive Maintenance.* Tokyo, Japan. Asian Productivity Organization.

Tapping, D., S. Kozlowski, L. Archbold, and T. Sperl. 2009. *Value Stream Management for Lean Healthcare.* Chealsea, MI: MCS Media, Inc.

Teich, S. T., and F. F. Faddoul. 2013. "Lean Management: The Journey from Toyota to Healthcare." *Rambam Maimonides Medical Journal* 4(2), e0007. doi:10.5041/RMMJ.10107.

The Advisory Board Company. 2011. *Leading Change: Implementing Improvements in the Health Care Organization.* Washington, DC: The Advisory Board Company.

Toussaint, J., and R. Gerard. 2010. *On the Mend.* Cambridge, MA: Lean Enterprise Institute.

Tuckman, B. 1965. Development Sequence in Small Groups. *Psychological Bulletin* 63 (6)384-399.imai.

Tyrrell, R., and R. Lazerow, et al. 2020. "Coronavirus Scenario Planning: 12 Situations Hospital Leaders Should Prepare For." Washington, DC: Advisory Board. https://www.advisory.com/research/health-care-advisory-board/resources/2020/coronavirus-scenario-planning

Ulvnes, R. 2015. "From Management to Leadership Using Tight-Loose-Tight." Linkedin. https://www.linkedin.com/pulse/tight-loose-better-management-mantra-rune-ulvnes/

U.S. Department of Health & Human Services. 2020. COVID-19 Healthcare Planning Checklist. https://www.phe.gov/emergency/events/COVID19/Documents/COVID-19%20Healthcare%20Planning%20Checklist.pdf.

Vermeulen, M. J., T. A. Stukel, A. Guttmann, B. H. Rowe, M. Zwarenstein, B. Golden, et al. 2014. "Evaluation of an Emergency Department Lean Process Improvement Program to Reduce Length of Stay." *Annals of Emergency Medicine* 64(5): 427-438. doi:10.1016/j.annemergmed.2014.06.007.

Wachter, R. M. 2004. "The End of the Beginning: Patient Safety Five Years after 'To Err is Human'." *Health Affairs* (Project Hope), Suppl Web Exclusives, W4-534-45. doi:10.1377/hlthaff.w4.534.

Womack, J. 2011. *Gemba Walks.* Cambridge, MA: Lean Enterprise Institute, Inc.

Womack, J. P., and D. T. Jones. 2005. "Lean Consumption." *Harvard Business Review,* 83(3): 58-68, 148.

Womack, J., and D. Jones. 1996. *Lean Thinking.* New York: Free Press.

Wysocki, B. 2004. "To Fix Health Care, Hospitals Take Tips from Factory Floor." *The Wall Street Journal.*

Zidel, T. 2012. Lean Done Right. Chicago, IL: Health Administration Press. http://www.rivm.nl/dsresource?objectid=rivmp:61294&type=org&disposition=inline&ns_nc=1

Index

Note: Page numbers followed by *f* or *t* refer to figures or tables, respectively.

A

A3 reports, 154, *155f*
action plans, 175–178, *176f*, *177t*, 247, *248t*
action plan worksheets, 176, *177t*
activation teams, 209
Affordable Care Act, xx
Akao, Yoji, 6
Alice in Wonderland (quotation), 5
analyze phase checklists, 148–150, *149f*
analyze tools and templates
    5S audit tool, 263, *263f*
    swimlane template, 264, *264f*
anxiety, wait time and, 87
assembly line, origins of, 86
aviation checklists, 101

B

barriers to change, 194–195
baseline data, 240
batching vs. single-piece flow, 110–111
Berger, Thomas, 119
Blanchard, Ken, 85
Breakthrough Management Group
    International, xxiv

C

case studies
    clinical lab workflow, 27–30
    GI office flow, 90–93
    inpatient admission from ER, 124–125
    office visit evaluation, 90–93
    OR performance dashboards, 134
    OR/SPCC VSM event, 59–61
    pandemic preparedness, 203–224
    patient flow, 18, 75–78
    patient flow through SPU, 156–159
    patient transportation, 109
    pharmacy batching, 112
    pharmacy inventory, 114–116
    pre-admission testing, 75–82
    rapid changeover, 96–97
change, hardwired, 196–197
change, micro- and macro-level, 184, *184t*
change, resistance to, 185, 189, 190–191, *190f*, 194–195
change leadership
    central elements of, 192
    chapter challenge, 200–201
    key stakeholder groups, 192
    lean management, 184–187
    lessons from Jefferson Health, 197–200
    overview, 183–184, *183f*, *184t*
    strategic approach to, 188–197, *188f*
change management, 3
changeover, rapid, 95–97
change readiness, 145, *145f*, 210
change readiness profile, 189, 237
chapter challenge questions
    change leadership, 200–201
    flow principle, 102
    lean DMAIC model, 159–160
    lean fundamentals, 83
    lean improvement projects, 159–160
    lean thinking, 9
    pandemic preparedness case study, 204–224
    perfection principle, 134–135
    pull principle, 117
    rapid improvements, 180–181
    value definition, 31
    value stream mapping, 61–62
checklists, 101
communication, 185, 222

communication plans, 144, 193, 207, 233
consensus voting, 169–170
continuous flow. *See* flow principle
continuous improvement, xxiii, 4, 98–101
control phase
    action plans, 177, *177t*, 250, 267, 268–*270f*, 270–271, *271f*
    checklists, 152–156, *153f*
    Gant templates, 270–271, *271f*
    kaizen A3 reports, 267, *268f*, *269f*
    lean improvement projects, 152–156
cooking analogy, 99
Covey, Stephen, 1
COVID-19 case study. *See* pandemic preparedness case study
crisis response teams, 208
critical steps to quality (CTQ), 233
current state evaluation, 222
current state maps, 34–40, *34f, 35f, 36f, 37f, 38f,* 64–65, *66f*
current state VSM, 40, 240, *241f*
customer demand, flow and, 88–97
customer value definition, 14–17, *15f, 16t, 17t, 18f*
cycle time, VSM and, 40, 43

D

data analysis results, 243
data collection and analysis, 51–55, *52f, 54f, 55f,* 218
data collection plans, 211–212, *211t*
da Vinci, Leonardo, 103
defects, as waste, 22
define phase checklists, 143–146, *143f*
define tools and templates
    downtime matrix, 253, *254t*
    lean engagement communication plans, 253, *256t*
    lean opportunity guide, 258, *258t*
    VOC waste questionnaire, 259, *259f*
Delisle, D.R., xix, xxiii
    Everything is 5S, 75
    "Let It Flow," 156
Deming, W. Edwards, 51–52
direct issue-to-solution brainstorming, 171, *172f*
disaster planning, 208
discipline, for change, 186–187
divergent activities, 165, 170
DMAIC checklist (case study)
    analyze phase, 218–220, *218f*
    control phase, 223–224, *223f*
    define phase, 205–210, *206f*
    improve phase, 220–223, *221t, 222f*
    measure phase, 210–218, *210f, 211t,* 216–*217t*
    overview, 204, *205f*
DMAIC checklist (lean model), 140–141, *142f*
DMAIC framework, 3
dot voting, 169, *169f*
DOWNTIME matrix, 253
DOWNTIME wastes, 19–24, *19f, 20t, 25f, 28f,* 55–59, *56f, 58f*

E

electronic information, 5S and, 68–69
elevator speech, vision and, 193
email, triage system for, 68–69
emergency operations plan, 222
employee buy-in, for change, 185, 188–189, 194–195
employee empowerment, 187
employee flow, 86
entropy, law of, 64
environmental scan, 144
equipment flow, 86
error-proof processes, 125–129, *126f, 128f*
escalator analogy, 110, 111
Everything is 5S (Delisle and Freiberg), 75
evidence-based leadership, 6
external communication, 207
extra processing, as waste, 23

F

facilitation guidelines, RIE and, 162–163
facilitator's role, RIE and, 178–180, *179t*
facilitator team, 143
feedback, essential nature of, 195, *196t*
financial analysis, 218
financial impact, 224
firefighting mentality, 14, 15
first-pass yield, VSM and, 43, 58
fishbone diagrams, 166, *166f,* 244, *245f*
5-8-4 concept, 199–200, *200f*
5S framework
    audit tool, 66, *67f,* 68, *68f, 69f, 70f,* 263, *263f*
    email and electronic information, 68–69
    overview, 64–66, *65t, 66f, 66t*
    pre-admission testing case study, 75–82, *76f, 77f, 78t, 79f, 80f, 81f, 82f*
    process example, *66f*

flow principle
    case study: rapid changeover, 96–97
    case study: workload balance, 90–93, *91f, 92f, 93f*
    chapter challenge, 102
    checklists and, 101
    customer demand and, 88–89, *88f, 89f, 90f*
    healthcare types and, 86
    overview, 85–88, *85f*
    process balancing and, 89–90, *90f, 91f, 92f, 93f*, 94–95
    rapid changeover, 95–97
    standard work and, 98–101, *98f, 100t, 101f*
    wait times and, 86–88
FMEA, 219–220
Ford, Henry, Sr., 11
Ford River Rogue Plant, 86
formal results presentation, 156
Franklin, Ben, 203
free-for-all brainstorming, 166
Freiberg, V.
    Everything is 5S, 75
future state VSM, 40, 247, *249t*

G

Gantt template, 270–271, *271f*
gemba walks, 51–52, 185–186
Goethe, 137
group dynamics, 178–180, *179t*
guiding coalition, 191–192

H

hardwired change, 196–197
healthcare, lean thinking in, xx, 1
hidden leaders, 191–192
high-level process maps, 233
high-level process map SIPOC, 233–236
high-level project plans, 229
Hoshin Kanri cascade, 6, *7f*
huddles, 186
human resources, lean and, 4

I

improvement events, 146
improvement kata, 138–139, *139f*
improvement philosophy, 6
improve phase checklist, 150–151, *151f*

improve tools and templates
    RIE facilitator evaluation form, 265, *266f*
    RIE presentation, 265
incident activation, 217
in-control/out-of-control template, 167–168, *168f*, 195
incremental improvement, 4
inertia, change and, 194–195
information flow, 86
in-process wait time, 87
internal communication, 207
internal/external customers, 15
inventory, as waste, 23
inventory management
    case study: pharmacy inventory, 114–116
    kanban example, 113–114, *114f*
    overview, 112–113
    par levels, 113–114
    pull principle, 112–114. *113f*
    pull system creation, 104–110

J

Jaffe, K.
    "Let It Flow," 156
Jefferson, Thomas, 33
Jefferson Health. *See also* Thomas Jefferson University
    inpatient admission case study, 124–125
    Lamina tree, 174, *175f*
    lean DMAIC checklist and, 141
    lessons from lean leaders, 197–199
    OR case study, 134, 156–159
    patient flow and SPU, 156–159
just-in-time production, 104

K

kaizen A3 report, 250, *251f*, 267
kaizen lean improvement projects, 137–140, *140f*
kaizen problem-solving process, 163–178
    action plans, 175–178, *176f, 177t*
    issues and barriers, brainstorming, 164–166, *165f, 166f*
    issues and barriers, filtering and prioritizing, 167–170, *167f, 168f, 169f*
    overview, 163–164, *164f*
    solutions, brainstorming, 170–172, *171f, 172f*
    solutions, filtering and prioritizing, 172–175, *173f, 174f, 175f*

kanban cards, 113–114, *114f*
kata, 138–139
key performance indicators, 6
key themes/risks, 212
kickoff meetings, 143–144, 206–207
Kotter, John
    "Leading Change," 188
KPI analysis, 224

L

lagging metrics, 6
Lamina, Caroline, 174, *175f*
Lamina tree tool, 174–175, *174f, 175f*
law of entropy, 64
layout, work area, 69–72, *69f, 70f, 71f, 72f*
leadership, evidence-based, 6
leadership, lean and, 4
leadership vs. management, 188
leader standard work, 185–186
"Leading Change" (Kotter), 188
leading metrics, 6
lead time, VSM and, 40, 43
lean, five principles of, 7
lean DMAIC model
    analyze phase, 148–150
    case study: patient flow and
        SPU, 156–159
    chapter challenge, 159–160
    control phase, 152–156
    define phase, 143–146
    formal results presentation, 156
    improve phase, 150–152
    measure phase, 146–148
    overview, 140–142, *141f, 142f*
lean engagement communication plan, 253
lean framework, xxiv
lean fundamentals, 63–84
    5S and electronic information, 68–69
    5S audit tool, 66, *67f, 68f*
    5S overview, 64–66, *65t, 66f*
    case study: patient flow, 75–82
    chapter challenge, 83
    layout, 69–71, *69f, 70f, 71f, 72f, 73f*
    overview, 63–64, *63f, 64t*
    visual management, 72–74, *74f*
lean improvement projects, 137–160
    analyze phase, 148–150
    case study: patient flow, 156–159
    chapter challenge, 159–160
    control phase, 152–156
    define phase, 143–146
    DMAIC model, 140–143

    improve phase, 150–152
    measure phase, 146–148
    overview, 137
lean management, 184–187
lean opportunity guide, 258
lean process roadmap, xxv, 7, *8t*
lean project opportunity guide, 7, *8t*
lean thinking
    chapter challenge, 9
    in healthcare, xx, 3
    lean process roadmap, 7, *8t*
    overview, 1, 3–4, *5f*, 6, *7f*
    performance improvement
        methodologies, 1, *2t*, 3
lessons learned, 146, 197–199, 250
"Let It Flow" (Delisle and Jaffe), 156
lowhanging fruit, 174–175, *174f, 175f*

M

Maister, D., 86–88
management, lean approach to, 4
management teams, 208–209
management vs. leadership, 188
Mann, David, 63
martial arts analogy, 3
measure phase, 146–148
measure tools and templates
    checklists, 147-148, *147f*
    process value analysis, 261, *261f*
    workflow value analysis, 262, *262f*
more of/less of chart, 192, *193f*
motion, as waste, 23

N

next case checklist, *97f*
nonutilized skill/intellect, as waste, 22

O

occupied wait time, 86
overproduction, as waste, 22

P

pandemic preparedness case study
    chapter challenge, 224–225
    DMAIC checklist, 204–224 (*See also*
        DMAIC checklist case study)
    overview, 203–204
parking lot, in RIE, 163
patient flow, 24–25, *25f, 26f*, 39, 86

INDEX   285

payoff matrix, 173–174, *174f*, 245, 247
PDCA model, 138, *138f*
perfection principle, 119–135
    case study: inpatient admission from ER, 124–125
    case study: OR performance dashboard, 134
    chapter challenge, 134–135
    error-proof processes, 125–129, *126f, 128f*
    overview, 119
    performance dashboards, 130–133, *131t, 132f, 133f, 133t*
    root causes, 119–125, *120f, 121f, 122f, 123f, 124f*
    sustaining improvements, 129–133, *129f, 130t*
performance dashboards, 130–133, *131t, 132f, 133f, 133t*
performance excellence framework, xxiv, xxv, 6, 7
performance improvement methodologies, 1, *2t*, 3
pit crew analogy, 95
planning teams, 208
pre-admission testing case study, 75–82, *76f, 77f, 78t, 79f, 80f, 81f, 82f*
previous events review, 211
process and workflow analyses, 212
process balancing, 90–94, *91f, 92f, 93f*
process flow, 4, *5f*, 35–38
process mapping steps, 40
process maps, 11, *12f*, 13–14, *14f, 35f, 36f, 37f*, 209–210
process map structure, *12f*
process scoping, *13f*
process value analysis, 52–56, *54f, 55f, 56f*
process value analysis results, 238, *238f*
process value analysis tool, 261, *261f*
project charters, 145, 229, 230–233*f*
project management, lean and, 3
project metrics, 6
"The Psychology of Waiting Lines" (Maister, 1985), 86–88
pull principle, 103–117
    batching vs. single-piece flow, 110–111, *110f, 111f*
    case study: patient transportation, 109
    case study: pharmacy batching, 112
    chapter challenge, 117
    inventory management, 112–114, *113f*
    kanban cards, 113–114
    overview, 103–104
pull systems, 106–108

purpose, process, people framework, 4, *5f*, 6, *7f*
push systems, 105–106

Q

questions, asking the right, 4

R

RACI chart, 242–243, *244t*
rapid changeover, 95–97
rapid improvement event portfolio
    action plans and recommendations, 247, *248t, 249t*
    baseline data for key metric(s), 240
    change readiness profile, 237, *237f*
    communications plan, 233
    control phase action plan, 250
    current state VSM, 240, *241f, 241t*
    data analysis results, 243
    fishbone diagram, 244, *245f*
    future state VSM, 247, *249f*
    high-level process map, 233, *236f, 236t*
    high-level process map SIPOC, 233, 236
    high-level project plan, 229, *230t*
    high-level SIPOC, *236t*
    kaizen A3 report, 250, *251f*
    lessons learned, 250
    payoff matrix, 245, *247f*
    process value analysis results, 238, *239f*
    project charter, 229, *232f*
    RACI chart, 242–243, *244t*
    RIE agenda, 244, *246t*
    stakeholder analysis, 242, *243t*
    system and process profile, 237, *238f*
    value of customer summary, 240
    voice of customer more of/less of, 240, *242t*
    waste diagnostic, 233, *235t*
    waste observations, 233, *235t*
    workflow value analysis results, 238, *239f*
rapid improvement events (RIE)
    chapter challenge, 180–181
    facilitation guidelines, 162–163
    facilitator's role, 178–180, *179t*
    ground rules, 163
    kaizen problem-solving process, 137, 163–178, *164f, 165f, 166f, 167f, 169f, 171f, 172f, 173f, 174f, 175f*
    overview, 161–162
    parking lot, 163
    roles and responsibilities, 162

recipes analogy, 99
recommendations, *249t*
reflective questions, 152
resistance to change, 185, 189, 190–191, *190f*, 194–195
response plan, 222
response team status updates, 223
reverse engineering, 171–172, *172f*
RIE agenda, 244, *246t*
RIE facilitator evaluation form, 265
RIE presentation, 265
roles and responsibilities, 187, *187f*, 206
root causes, 119–125, *120f, 121f, 122f, 123f, 124f*
run chart, post-improvement, *154f*

S

Saban, Nick, 183
scenario planning, 208
scope determination, 11–14, *12f, 13f, 14f*, 99
Shewhart, Walter A., 138
short-term wins, 195–196, *196t*
silent brainstorming, 165
single-person process, 101
single-piece flow vs. batching, 110–111
SIPOC diagrams, 11–14, 12*f, 13f, 14f*
solution development, 170–172, *171f, 172f*
spaghetti diagrams, 69, *70f*
Spear, Steven, 161
Spear's four rules, 170
sponsors, 206–207
staff flow, 86
staffing resource strategy, 213–214
staff training and deployment, 219
stakeholder analysis, 218, 242
stakeholder debrief, 224
standard work, 98–101, *98f, 100t, 101f*, 185–186
Studer, Quint, 6
supplies flow, 86
supply chain assessment, 212
surge plans, 214–215, *216–217t*
sustainability, 101, 129–133, *129f, 130t*, 195
SVP batch process, 112
swimlane maps, 48, *49f, 50f, 51f*
swimlane template, 264
system creation, 104–109
systems and process profile, 145, *146f*, 210, 237, *238f*

T

Takt time, 88–94, *88f, 89f, 91f, 92f, 93f*
Thomas Jefferson University, xix, xxiii. *See also* Jefferson Health
threat vs. opportunity matrix, 190–191, *190f*
tight-loose-tight model, 196–197
Toyota Kata (Rother, 2010), 138
transition state, 183, 185, 195, *196t*
triage system, for email, 68–69

U

unexplained waits, 87–88
urgency for change, 190–191, *190f*

V

VA, NVA, NVA-R activity, 15–18, *16t, 17t, 18f*, 24–25, *25f, 26f*, 64, *66f*, 85–88
value-adding ratio, 40, 43
value analysis, *28f*
value definition, 11–30
    case study: clinical lab workflow, 27–30, *27–30f*
    case study: patient flow, 18, *18f*
    firefighting mentality, 14, 15
    internal/external customers, 15
    process maps, 11, *12f*, 13–14, *14f*
    scope determination, 11–14, *12f, 13f, 14f*
    SIPOC diagrams, 11–14, *12f, 13f, 14f*
    through customer eyes, 14–17, *15f, 16t, 17t, 18f*
    VA, NVA, NVA-R activity, 15–18, *16t, 17t, 18f*
    waste identification, 19, *19f*, 20–21*t*, 22–26, *24f, 25f, 26f*
value stream mapping, 33–62
    calculations, 43
    case study: OR/SPCC VSM event, 59–61, *59f, 60f, 61f*
    case study: patient flow, 55–58, *56f, 57f*
    chapter challenge questions, 61–62
    current state map, 34–39, *34f, 35f, 36f, 37f, 38f*
    data collection and analysis, 51–55, *52f, 54f, 55f*

example: physician office, 35, *35f, 36f, 37f*, 38, *38f*
first-pass yield (FPY), 38, *38f*, 39
gemba for, 51–52
key terms, 40
process evaluation phase, 58
rework, 38
steps for building VSM, 40–48
swimlane maps, 48, *49f, 50f, 51f*
tips for, 47
VSM process maps, 39–51, *41f, 42f, 44f, 45f, 46f, 47f*
workflow value analysis, 56–57, *57f, 58f*
vision, leadership change and, 192–194
visual management, 72–74, *74f*
VOC interviews, 144, 209
VOC waste questionnaire, 259
voice of customer more of/less of, 240, *242t*
voice of customer summary, 240, *241f*

W

waiting, as waste, 22
wait time, core principles of, 86–88
wait time, VSM and, 43
waste, flow and, 85–88
waste, standard work and, 98
waste diagnostic tool, 23, *24f*, 233
waste identification, 19, *19f*, 20–21*t*, 22–26, *24f, 25f, 26f*
waste observations, 233
waste walk, 209
waste walk questions, 144
weight loss analogy, 6, 186
Womack, James, 4
work area layout, 69–71, *69f, 70f, 71f, 72f, 73f*
workflow value analysis, 56–57, *57f, 58f*, 238, *239f*
workflow value analysis tool, 262, *262f*
workload balance process, 90–94, *91f, 92f, 93f, 94f*

About the Author

Dr. Dennis R. Delisle is a transformational healthcare professional and nationally recognized lean and change leadership expert. He has a passion for operational excellence and team-based leadership. Dennis currently serves as the executive director for The Ohio State University Wexner Medical Center's flagship University Hospital. Prior to this role, Dennis was the vice president of operations for Jefferson Health in the South Philadelphia market. He is the author of *Executing Lean Improvements* and *Transformation and Your New EHR*. Through the Thomas Jefferson University College of Population Health, Dennis founded and oversees the master of science degree program in operational excellence, one of the first of its kind in the nation.

Dennis holds certifications as a Lean Master, Six Sigma Black Belt, Change Agent, and Project Management Professional (PMP). He was also trained as a Baldrige Examiner through Pennsylvania's performance excellence program. Dennis is a Fellow of the American College of Healthcare Executives. He completed his bachelor of science in biology from Syracuse University, master of health services administration from The George Washington University, and doctor of science in health systems management from Tulane University.

NOTES

NOTES

NOTES

NOTES

NOTES